Classics in Film and Fiction

Film/Fiction

The Film/Fiction series addresses the developing interface between English and Media studies, in particular the cross-fertilisation of methods and debates applied to analyses of literature, film and popular culture. Not only will this series capitalise upon growing links between departments of English and Media, it will also debate the consequences of the blurring of such disciplinary boundaries.

Editors
Deborah Cartmell – I.Q. Hunter – Heidi Kaye – Imelda Whelehan

Advisory Editor
Tim O'Sullivan

Pulping Fictions: Consuming Culture Across the Literature/ Media Divide (1996)

Trash Aesthetics: Popular Culture and its Audience (1997)

Sisterhoods: Across the Literature/Media Divide (1998)

Alien Identities: Exploring Differences in Film and Fiction (1999)

Anyone interested in proposing contributions to Film/Fiction should contact the editors at the Departments of English and Media Studies, School of Humanities, De Montfort University, Leicester, LE1 9BH, UK.

Film/Fiction volume 5

Classics in Film and Fiction

Edited by
**Deborah Cartmell, I.Q. Hunter, Heidi Kaye
and Imelda Whelehan**

Pluto  Press

LONDON • STERLING, VIRGINIA

First published 2000 by Pluto Press
345 Archway Road, London N6 5AA
and 22883 Quicksilver Drive,
Sterling, VA 20166–2012, USA

British Library Cataloguing in Publication Data
A catalogue record for this book is available from the British
Library

ISBN 0 7453 1593 3 hbk

Library of Congress Cataloging in Publication Data
Classics in film and fiction / edited by Deborah Cartmell ... [et al.].
        p. cm.— (Film/fiction ; v. 5)
     Includes bibliographical references.
     ISBN 0–7453–1593–3 (hbk)
      1. Film adaptations—History and criticisms. 2. Motion
pictures and literature. 3. Canon (Literature) I. Cartmell,
Deborah. II. Series.

PN1997.85 .C56 2000
791.43'6—dc21
                                                                00–020428

Designed and produced for Pluto Press by
Chase Production Services, Chadlington OX7 3LN
Typeset from disk by Stanford DTP Services, Northampton
Printed in the EU by TJ International, Padstow

Contents

Notes on Contributors

Stuart Burrows is a PhD candidate in the English Department at Princeton University. Born in Bromley, Kent, he earned his BA from the University of Southampton and an MA from Northeastern University in Boston, MA. A regular reviewer of fiction in the *New Statesman*, Burrows is currently completing his dissertation, which examines the influence of photography on the writing of Henry James, William Faulkner, Zora Neale Hurston and James Agee.

Deborah Cartmell is Principal Lecturer in the Department of English, De Montfort University. She has published on Shakespeare and film adaptations, Renaissance poetry and Afro-American literature. Her most recent books include *Adaptations* (Routledge, 1999: edited with I. Whelehan) and *Interpreting Shakespeare on Screen* (Macmillan, 2000).

Martin Halliwell is Lecturer in English and American Studies at Leicester University. He has published articles on modern American and European literature and is the author of *Romantic Science and the Experience of Self: Transatlantic Crosscurrents from William James to Oliver Sacks* (Ashgate 1999). He is currently working on a book on *Modernism and Morality* for Macmillan.

Lesley Higgins is an Associate Professor of English at York University (Toronto), whose research and teaching interests include modernism, gender studies and textual studies. Her essays can be found in the *Southern Review, Gender in Joyce* and *Victorian Studies*. She has also published numerous essays on Gerard Manley Hopkins and Walter Pater. With Marie-Christine Leps she has produced articles for *College literature and Rethinking Marxism*, and they are developing a project concerning *Forms of Governance in Twentieth-Century Writing: The Critical Fictions of Foucault, Woolf, Auster, Ondaatje.*

Lisa Hopkins is a Senior Lecturer in English at Sheffield Hallam University. Her publications include *John Ford's Political Theatre* (MUP, 1994) and *The Shakespearean Marriage: Merry Wives and Heavy Husbands* (Macmillan, 1998). She is currently completing the Macmillan literary life of Marlowe.

I.Q. Hunter is Senior Lecturer in Media Studies at De Montfort University, Leicester. He is joint editor of Routledge's British Popular Cinema series, for which he edited *British Science Fiction Cinema* (1999), and co-editor of the film/fiction series. He is currently writing a book on Hammer's science fiction and fantasy films.

Heidi Kaye was a Senior Lecturer in English and Women's Studies at De Montfort University. She is a co-editor of the Film/Fiction series and has forthcoming articles on Jane Austen and cinema, the *X Files*, Gothic film and *Star Trek – Deep Space Nine*. She is now a software training consultant and writes freeform role-playing games in her spare time.

Marie-Christine Leps is Associate Professor of English and Social and Political Thought at York University (Toronto) and specialises in literary theory and cultural critique. She is the author of *Apprehending the Criminal: The Production of Deviance in Nineteenth-Century Discourse*, and essays concerning the information age. With Lesley Higgins she has produced articles for *College literature* and *Rethinking Marxism*, and they are developing a project concerning *Forms of Governance in Twentieth-Century Writing: The Critical Fictions of Foucault, Woolf, Auster, Ondaatje.*

Paul M. Malone is an Assistant Professor in the Department of Germanic and Slavic Languages and Literatures at the University of Waterloo, Ontario, Canada. His doctoral dissertation dealt with four stage adaptations of Kafka's novel *The Trial*. In addition to teaching in German language, literature, culture and film, he researches in theatre and film history, the impact of computer technology on performance, and literary translation of theatre.

Sara Martin teaches English Literature at the Universitat Autònoma de Barcelona and the Universitat Oberta de Catalunya, Spain. She has published articles on film and literature, gender studies, contemporary British fiction, popular fiction and cultural studies.

Nick Peim teaches in the School of Education at the University of Birmingham. He is author of *Critical Theory and the English Teacher* (Routledge, 1993) – an attempt to take on the institutionalised practices of English. His research interests include the cultural politics of education, language and education, gender and education, the history of the emergence and development of state education and media education.

Sergio Rizzo teaches courses in American literature and popular culture at the University of Houston-Downtown. Currently he is working on Hollywood's representation of Bill Clinton and the American Presidency

Deborah Ross is a Professor of English at Hawaii Pacific University, where she has taught since 1985. She is the author of a book-length study of women and fiction, entitled *The Excellence of Falsehood: Romance, Realism, and Women's Contribution to the Novel* (1991). Her recent research interests include female narratives in popular culture, including television soap operas as well as Disney movies.

Paul Wells is Professor and Head of the Media Academic Section at the University of Teesside. He has written widely on various aspects of popular culture, specialising in Animation and Comedy. His latest publication is *The Horror Genre: Belezebub to Blair Witch* (Wallflower Press) and a further book, *Animating America* (Edinburgh University Press), is due out shortly.

Imelda Whelehan is Principal Lecturer in English and Women's Studies at De Montfort University, Leicester. She is author of *Modern Feminist Thought* (Edinburgh University Press, 1995), joint editor of *Adaptations* (Routledge, 1999) and co-editor of the film/fiction series. Her feminist critique of anti-feminism in contemporary culture, *Overloaded*, will be published by The Women's Press in 2000.

Kay Young is an Assistant Professor of English at the University of California, Santa Barbara. She has recently completed a manuscript on how novels and films create states of intimacy and happiness, entitled *Ordinary Pleasures*. She has written on the nature of team comedy, the musical comedy of Stephen Sondheim and the philosophical works of Søren Kierkegaard. She is currently at work on a series of essays on the interrelation between aesthetics and cognition.

Introduction: Classics Across the Film/Literature Divide

Heidi Kaye and Imelda Whelehan

No one ever reads a classic novel, according to Italo Calvino. Everyone says that they are *re-reading* a classic, the assumption being that a well read person has already encountered the classics at least once.[1] David Lodge invented the parlour game 'Humiliation' in his campus novel *Changing Places* (1975) in which academics compete by admitting *not* to have read a classic text which they 'ought' to know, scoring points for each colleague who *has* read it.[2] Classics have snob value because they are inherently elitist; an intellectual coterie confers value on certain works and judges an individual's value on familiarity with such 'high' cultural artefacts, thereby allowing her or him to enter the elite. Schools inculcate a canon of works considered to be of literary merit along with a set of aesthetic and ideological criteria by which to validate such works as canonical.

Critical theory in the past thirty years or so has put under question such criteria and such canonisation, and yet educational policy continues to reinforce such values. Newspapers report scare stories about Shakespeare being replaced by soap operas in our schools and universities, despite all the arguments in favour of the value of Cultural Studies engaged in by academics. It is difficult enough to define a 'classic' in literature, let alone find agreement about what a classic in a newer, more 'popular' medium such as film might be. The contributors to this collection of the Film/Fiction series attempt in various ways to tackle this question, as well as to interrogate the value of such labels as 'classic' and 'popular' when dealing with film and fiction. What happens when a classic text is adapted for a new

1

commercial medium and how contemporary concerns interact with literary history will also be investigated.

Since the beginnings of cinema, adaptations of classic fiction have been prominent. The Oscars awarded each year for best adapted and best original screenplay indicate that film relies on both forms for its source material. It has been observed that approximately three-quarters of the awards for Best Picture go to adaptations.[3] Adaptations of 'classic' works have traditionally been seen as high-prestige enterprises for film-makers.

David Bordwell, Janet Staiger and Kristin Thompson's 'classic' work of cinematic scholarship, *The Classical Hollywood Cinema* (1985), however, does not define 'classic' film in terms of aesthetic status and cultural prestige. Rather, they discuss narrative form, character types and mode of production in terms of stylistic norms which define the 'typical' work of the studio system between 1917 and 1960. Although they look at 'notions of decorum, proportion, formal harmony, respect for tradition, mimesis, self-effacing craftsmanship, and cool control of the perceiver's response – canons which critics in any medium usually call "classical"', they do not grant privilege to individual masterpieces which either shape or challenge conventions, 'not to the aberrant film that breaks or tests the rules but to the quietly conformist film that tries simply to follow them'.[4] In this sense, their 'classical cinema' does not hold any cultural capital, being standardised or middlebrow rather than high culture.

In Pierre Bourdieu's terms, 'cultural capital' signifies the status and authority accruing to familiarity with what is considered to be superior aesthetic taste in 'scholastic' or 'legitimate' culture. Bourdieu's *Distinction* (1979) links taste distinctions with socioeconomic class, education and value, arguing that high cultural tastes privilege aspects such as the audience's contemplative distance from the work and the artist's formal experimentation. 'Classical' cultural investments, those acquired largely through education, are described as 'safer' since they are legitimated by the dominant class.[5] Thus, Henry Jenkins argues, 'Aesthetics is a discourse of power, claimed as the exclusive property of dominant classes as a club to use against the "debased" tastes and preferences of the lower orders.'[6] This is why in Lodge's sense there is 'humiliation' in admitting to ignorance of the artefacts associated with knowledge and power.

As Bourdieu's analysis implies, both classroom and social class seem implied in our use of the term 'classic'. Academic education instils canons which embody the dominant culture's values. Andrew Ross affirms that 'The intellectual's training in discrimination is an indispensable resource in such a process. For this is where the intellectual's accredited power of discrimination reinforces the power to subordinate even as it presents itself in the form of an objective critique of taste.'[7] Just as the academic study of English was originally modelled on Classics in order both to give the subject authority and to train 'the lower orders' – women and the working class – in the values of the dominant culture,[8] so a belief in 'classics' superior to other works reproduces that hierarchical society and its power.

Defining a classic is therefore difficult once one recognises that it is not a question of a 'pure' approach to aesthetics but rather a highly politicised issue. What occurs in adapting a classic for another medium opens up a whole range of new, and equally difficult, issues. Style, intention, financing, stars, context (to name a few), all may be considered as influencing the interpretation of an adaptation. Brian McFarlane derides the overwhelming focus on the question of 'fidelity', implying the superiority of the originary text, which has dominated criticism of adaptations. Instead he distinguishes between 'what may be *transferred* from one narrative medium to another and what necessarily requires *adaptation proper* ... by which other novelistic elements must find quite different equivalences in the film medium'.[9] In this way, McFarlane attempts to allow for the analysis of other elements of inter-textuality involved in a film's production as well as in its narrative form.

Calvino, despite his own postmodern aesthetic, believed in the notion of classics as 'benchmarks' of quality first encountered at school which helped an individual to construct a canon of classics which spoke to her or him more personally.[10] But he argued for the importance of the contemporary context in interpreting a text's significance: 'In order to read the classics, you have to establish where exactly you are reading them "from", otherwise both the reader and the text tend to drift in a timeless haze.'[11] Adaptations of classics can reveal as much about the concerns of their own time as they can about those of the original text.

The first chapter in this collection reviews recent moral panics about the substance of what might be studied under 'English' in secondary schools in order to unpick the assumptions beneath such concerns. As Nick Peim observes, the rise of media and cultural studies invites cross-fertilisation with the textual strategies adopted in literary studies, and yet English resolutely continues to insist that Literature, rather than literature is its proper object. His comparison of *Blade Runner*, a popularly acknowledged film 'classic' of its genre, and Gide's *Symphonie Pastorale* – at best an uncertain classic by Peim's own admission, yet packaged ostentatiously as a 'modern classic' in its Penguin incarnation – yields wide possibilities for exploration beyond that normally endorsed by literary textual practices fostered by most British state schools. Further, Peim offers metaphorical parallels between the tensions surrounding identity in both texts, and continued attempts to situate boundaries between English and the 'replicant' threats of media and cultural studies. As Peim reflects, to examine the status of the classic achieved by some fictional and filmic texts is to begin to interrogate the multifarious perspectives and text/critic/audience/commercial dynamics which inform the means by which such status is achieved. The classic in the context of education offers more than a rescue from cultural 'humiliation'; it shores itself up against the perceived chaos and 'dumbing down' effects of intertextuality and determines our attitudes and approaches to the text in ways that are denied popular film narratives. Educational English governs modes of access to its discursive framework in unashamedly class-determined ways and by its end-directed structure – where examinations become the measure of literary skills – carrying with them, as Peim observes, 'significant social consequences'.

In the realm of adaptations of classic literary texts the invisible rules of the game assume textual 'fidelity' (despite the obstacles to this outlined by Brian McFarlane) and expect it as part of the adaptation's 'duty' that it serve the cause of the originary text, or more properly the mainstream cultural appropriation of its preferred meaning. Nowhere are the rules of the game more evident than in screen adaptations of Shakespeare where, as Deborah Cartmell has noted, the study of such adaptations 'is firmly placed within the literary canon'.[12] As Sara Martin's chapter illustrates, such canonisation of the role of Shakespearean adaptation also facilitates collective high cultural condemnation of those who do not exercise the appropriate kind of respect for the plays, or rather for the idea of the Bard preserved behind these preferred readings. As Martin demonstrates, Fred Wilcox and Peter Greenaway are two such Shakespeare desecrators from this perspective; indeed she asserts that Wilcox's *Forbidden Planet*, at present, is denied 'classic' status as part of the canon of preferred Shakespeare adaptations (although arguably it is a seminal SF film), while Greenaway dramatises his challenge to the authority of the Shakespearean 'original' where his position as *auteur* intentionally challenges Shakespeare's perceived unrivalled authority.

Just as Olivier and Branagh might be seen to be the 'classic' Shakespeare adapters, so the appearance of a new film version may latterly confer classic status on its elder sibling upon which it may derive some of its shape. This is the case with Franco Zeffirelli's and Robert Young's 1995 and 1997 versions of *Jane Eyre* which, Lisa Hopkins asserts, owe much to Robert Stevenson's 1943 version, starring Joan Fontaine and Orson Welles, and yet are both committed to creating new readings. In Zeffirelli's case this means reshaping some of the novel's concerns; but in Young's this all too often results in anachronism where periodicity is faithfully maintained and language and displays of emotions 'updated'. These versions, mindful of the power of Stevenson's film as the classic adaptation, also demonstrate their location in the competitive world of costume drama where their versions are vying for attention among a rash of high-quality classic adaptations.

Three recent adaptations of Henry James novels – *The Portrait of a Lady*, *The Wings of the Dove* and *The American* – as Martin Halliwell observes, do qualify for the costume drama epithet in terms of fidelity to period but he goes on to demonstrate how this term would not do justice to their appeal, not least because of their transatlantic scope in reflecting James's concern with representing the effects of clashes between cultures. Halliwell's adoption of the term 'transcultural aesthetic' attempts to convey how these adaptations of James's novels depict the effects of that clash. While James's place as a classic writer is largely due to the anglicising criticism of F.R. Leavis, Halliwell shows how these adaptations pick up on James's concerns 'by destabilisation of national identity and ... by interrogating the status of characters who are uncertain and, at times, paralysed in the face of historical change'. In this way texts are brought to bear on current issues without losing a sense of the original's influence, and in fact display through their own dynamics the constraints of heritage film.

Sergio Rizzo explores the apparent 'failure' of Roland Joffe's *The Scarlet Letter* against the 'success' of Nicholas Hytner's *The Crucible,* in their efforts to represent history in the process of adapting each author's view of the Puritan past. Their will to revisit the 'historical' elements of these classic texts clashes with their desire to 'update' the psychological and emotional subtexts (particularly channelled through the female leads) which become anachronistic. Rizzo looks at the films via a 'birth of the actor' approach, at the contrasting career trajectories of the two female stars: Demi Moore's 'descent' into the popular and lowbrow, and Winona Ryder's association with the highbrow – which also entrench perceived distinctions in their personalities. Moore is represented as the tough, brash one, and Ryder as the childlike self-effacing one. Neither, he suggests, are able to convey an act of female resistance in these representations of female hysteria and therefore transcend the heavy-handedness of the adaptations' interpretations.

Lesley Higgins and Marie Christine Leps, in their chapter on two recent adaptations of Virginia Woolf's novels, show how the term 'classic', suffocating in its universalising intentions, can only reflect the artistic and cultural prejudices of its time. Marleen Gorris and Sally Potter in their adaptations of *Mrs Dalloway* and *Orlando* respectively, recognise what McFarlane would term the needs of adaptation proper, in a sense responding to Woolf's own speculations on the future of film. Unlike the most popular 'costume drama' adaptations of nineteenth-century realist texts, these reflections on Woolf's own concept of subjectivity do not allow a reconstruction of the past which is not self-consciously reflexive of the film-makers' present and the films' concerns with the fabric of the film medium through which the literary text is 'translated'.

Stuart Burrows's chapter on Luchino Visconti's *Death in Venice* shows how the ascription of the term 'classic' to a piece of literature often refers to a preferred interpretation of the text which, if later put into question by an oppositional reading or indeed an adaptation, is a means by which the later interpretation is rejected. This Burrows argues is the fate of Visconti's adaptation, which as a self-conscious re-reading of the text, rather than an attempt at transcription, could equally be seen to preserve the pertinency of the novella's classic status. Its ability, as cinema, to implicate the audience in the gaze intensifies the power of the visual which must by definition yield differing interpretative possibilities to those of the fictional text.

In her discussion of two quite disparate classics, Joyce's *Ulysses* and Hitchcock's *Rear Window*, Kay Young notes the irony of how the movie immobilises its protagonist, whereas in the 'Lotus-eaters' episode of *Ulysses* Leopold Bloom is described as constantly in motion. As Young observes, *Ulysses* as the classic modernist text with its homage to classic literature, signalled by positing a narrational relationship to *The Odyssey,* simultaneously 'declassifies' itself as a novel in its exploration of that most 'cinematic' feature of motion, where the streets of Dublin become the other main 'character'. Joyce narrates the directions Bloom takes rather than the qualities of his movement or the consciousness of the character. In *Rear Window*, Stewart is the 'watcher at the window', as Henry James describes the fictional narrator, watching the courtyard at the rear of his apartment as if it were a movie, using a series of lenses – from the naked eye to binoculars, to zoom lens. In fact he only produces 'stills' which he must decipher in order to prove a murder has taken place.

Paul Malone's account of Orson Welles's and David Jones's adaptations of Kafka's *The Trial* (1963 and 1993) reflects on the problems of adapting a 'classic' text where the mythological identity of its author, and indeed the adjective that comes to connote the perceived atmosphere of his work – Kafkaesque – predominate. Kafka, himself adopted and posthumously 'adapted' for classic status by Max Brod, has become arguably a product of critical over-determination or, as Milan Kundera put it, 'Kafkology', offers distinct challenges to the film adapter who is looking for a new kind of textual fidelity. As Malone shows, Welles and Jones opt for directly opposing strategies – Welles's dreamlike expressionism is supplanted, clearly in answer to Welles as much as an attempt to revisit the text, by studied naturalism, down to the film's location in Prague. Just as Demi Moore and Winona Ryder bring the effects of their screen/offscreen personae to the parts they play in *The Scarlet Letter* and *The Crucible,* so Malone shows how Anthony Perkins's role as Norman Bates in *Psycho* determines to some extent the psychological dimensions of his role in the Welles's film; whereas Kyle MacLachlan's presence reminds us of his work with David Lynch playing characters confronting bizarre mysteries in disarmingly normal circumstances. Here again we see powerful evidence of how a film's intertexuality begins the interpretative process of the 'classic' text and how questions of fidelity are set against the need to interpret in order to present.

Truman Capote's *In Cold Blood* takes as its object a series of 'true' events, a docu-drama style, creating what is popularly believed to be one of the classic postwar American novels. The novel itself raised crucial questions about moral and ethical responsibility on the part of the author, and Capote's investigative methods overlaid by his own creative imperatives were criticised. As Paul Wells shows in his chapter, the 1967 film adaptation, in its commitment to realism, returns us to some of the debates which surround the novel, such as when dramatisation of murder becomes exploitative of the victims, casting off any sense of moral obligation in art. In a sense the casting of a reporter within the film inserts Capote's authorial function within the adaptation itself. Richard Brooks's attempt to shoot the film in authentic locations leads to the victims' household being used as the set for the re-enactment of the murders – itself arguably far more exploitative than Capote's fictional arrangement of the 'facts'. If Capote's novel and Brooks's adaptation anticipate the 'killer culture' of the 1980s and 90s, the 1996 television adaptation is produced at the tail end of a raft of serial killer fictions and films, and real life tragedies. As Wells indicates, this latest version offers comfort and even nostalgia in the figuring of good against evil.

It is a rare classic adaptation that sets out to make millions, but when the adapter is the Disney Corporation such a goal is integral to the whole process. As Deborah Ross outlines in her chapter on the animated version of *Alice in Wonderland*, the Disney *oeuvre* is currently packaged on videos as if they were precious keepsakes that a child will take through to adulthood. First released in 1951, its longevity makes *Alice* a clear contender for Disney classic status with an uncontested place within the Disney collection; it also forms part of a subset of Disney offerings which use as their inspiration folktales or children's classics and produce from this source a narrative that insists upon its own wholesomeness. Disney's claim that these texts are 'gifts of imagination' is contested by Ross who shows how Carroll's radical investment in the power of wonder frees Alice's imagination from the constraints of her assumed social and gendered position in realist terms, whereas Disney's leaps into imagination are abruptly forestalled with the Tulgey Wood sequence of the cartoon where Alice decides to flee back to reality and into passivity and books with no pictures.

The essays in this volume explore what 'classic' status might mean in fiction and film, demonstrating it to be an historically mutable term, connected to commercial considerations, class-determined modalities of taste and necessarily situated in the boundaries between 'high' and 'low' culture. Harriet Hawkins speculates that if *King Kong* were to replace *King Lear* on the syllabus, we would still have similar debates about which version of the text was most 'authentic', or would question why another comparable film was not being studied, again giving 'rise to grumbles about the "canon"'.[13] In her assertion that all categorisation leads to the elevation of some texts above others she adds that 'even bad film buffs find certain bad films more gloriously awful than others',[14] suggesting that the will to create canons brings with it a whole new batch of 'classics'. Indeed it is argued here that the film adaptation can usurp the appellation 'classic' from its literary source, as in the case of Visconti's *Death in Venice*. Yet, as this collection shows, the new 'classics' and new approaches to old 'classics', offer the potential to fuse high and low cultural trends with far-ranging interpretative possibilities.

Notes

1. Italo Calvino, 'Why Read the Classics?' in *Why Read the Classics?*, trans. Martin McLaughlin (London: Jonathan Cape, 1999), p. 3.
2. David Lodge, *Changing Places* (London: Penguin, 1975), p. 96.
3. See R. Giddings, K. Selby and C. Wensley (eds), *Screening the Novel: The Theory and Practice of Literary Dramatization* (Basingstoke: Macmillan, 1990), p. 4.
4. David Bordwell, Janet Staiger and Kristin Thompson, *The Classical Hollywood Cinema* (London: Routledge, 1988 [1985]), pp. 4, 10.
5. Pierre Bourdieu, *Distinction: A Social Critique of the Judgement of Taste*, trans. Richard Nice (London: Routledge and Kegan Paul, 1986, orig. pub. 1979).
6. Henry Jenkins, 'Historical Poetics' in Joanne Hollows and Mark Jancovich (eds), *Approaches to Popular Film* (Manchester: Manchester University Press, 1995), p. 111.
7. Andrew Ross, *No Respect: Intellectuals and Popular Culture* (London: Routledge, 1989), p. 61.
8. For an account of the rise of academic English, see Terry Eagleton, *Literary Theory: An Introduction* (Minneapolis, University of Minnesota Press, 1983), Ch. 1, Chris Baldick, *The Social Mission of English Criticism 1848–1932* (Oxford: Basil Blackwell, 1983), Ch. 1, and Brian Doyle, *English and Englishness* (London: Routledge, 1989), Ch. 3.

Further Reading

Donaldson, Peter, 'Shakespeare in the Age of Post-Mechanical Reproduction: Sexual and Electronic Magic in *Prospero's Books'* in Lynda E. Boose and Richard Burt (eds), *Shakespeare: The Movie* (London and New York: Routledge, 1997).

Doyle, Brian, *English and Englishness* (London: Routledge, 1989).

Ellis, William, 'The Spatial Structure of Streets' in Standford Anderson (ed.), *On Streets*, (Cambridge: M.I.T. Press, 1986).

Foucault, Michel, 'What is an Author' in David Lodge (ed.), *Modern Criticism and Theory* (London: Longman, 1988).

Genette, Gerard, *Narrative Discourse*, trans. Jane E. Lewin (Ithaca: Cornell University Press, 1985).

Giddings, Robert, Keith Selby and Chris Wensley (eds), *Screening the Novel: The Theory and Practice of Literary Dramatization* (Basingstoke: Macmillan, 1990).

Gillen, Francis, 'From Novel to Film: Harold Pinter's Adaptation of *The Trial'* in Katherine H. Burkman and John L. Kundert-Gibbs (eds), *Pinter at Sixty* (Bloomington: Indiana University Press, 1993).

Hawkins, Harriet, *Classics and Trash* (Hemel Hempstead: Harvester Wheatsheaf, 1990).

Higson, Andrew, 'The Heritage Film and British Cinema' in Andrew Higson (ed.), *Dissolving Views: Key Writings on British Cinema* (London: Cassell, 1996).

Hollows, Joanne and Mark Jancovich (eds), *Approaches to Popular Film* (Manchester: Manchester University Press, 1995).

James, Henry, 'The Art of Fiction' in Roger Gard (ed.), *The Critical Muse: Selected Literary Criticism* (Harmondsworth: Penguin, 1987).

Jarman, Derek, *Dancing Ledge* (1984; rpt. London: Quartet, 1991).

Kermode, Frank, *The Classic: Literary Images of Permanence and Change*, 2nd edn (Cambridge, MA: Harvard University Press, 1983).

Kundera, Milan, 'In Saint Garta's Shadow: Rescuing Kafka from the Kafkologists', trans. Barbara Wright, *Times Literary Supplement*, 24 May 1991.

Lanier, Douglas, 'Drowning the Book: *Prospero's Books* and Textual Shakespeare' in Robert Shaughnessey (ed.), *Shakespeare on Film* (London: Macmillan Press, 1998).

Leavis, F.R., *The Great Tradition* (Harmondsworth: Penguin, 1993).

McFarlane, Brian, *Novel to Film: An Introduction to the Theory of Adaptation* (Oxford: Clarendon Press, 1996).

Peim, Nick, *Critical Theory and the English Teacher* (London: Routledge, 1993).

Ross, Andrew, *No Respect: Intellectuals and Popular Culture* (London: Routledge, 1989).

Schickel, R., *The Disney Version* (New York: Simon and Schuster, 1968).

Shaughnessy, Nicola, 'Is S/he or isn't S/he?: Screening *Orlando*' in Deborah Cartmell, I.Q. Hunter, Heidi Kaye, Imelda Whelehan (eds), *Pulping Fictions: Consuming Culture Across the Literature/ Media Divide* (London: Pluto Press, 1996).

Sinyard, Neil, *Filming Literature: The Art of Screen Adaptation* (New York: St. Martin's Press, 1986).

Smoodin, Eric (ed.), *Disney Discourse: Producing the Magic Kingdom* (New York: Routledge, 1994).

Twitchell, James B., *Carnival Culture: The Trashing of Taste in America* (New York: Columbia University Press, 1992).

Vaget, Hans Rudolph, 'Film and Literature. The Case of *Death in Venice*: Luchino Visconti and Thomas Mann', *The German Quarterly*, LIV No. 2 (March 1980).

Wagner, Geoffrey, *The Novel and the Cinema* (Madison: Farleigh Dickinson University Press, 1975).

Woods, Alan, *Being Naked Playing Dead: The Art of Peter Greenaway* (Manchester: Manchester University Press, 1996).

1

'If Only You Could See What I've Seen with Your Eyes': *Blade Runner* and *La Symphonie Pastorale*

Nick Peim

By what strange logic of subject practice might texts of such disparate identities as *Romeo and Juliet* and *Home and Away* be brought together within the same pedagogic frame? Or *Hamlet* and *Terminator 2* (Cameron, 1991)? Or *Great Expectations* and *Dawson's Creek*? Of course, the list of possible disparate pairings could go on forever, and the popular press has frequently, in recent times, been scandalised by the improper incursion of popular culture into the domain of literary study – giving rise to a series of implausible textual pairings, usually cast in the form of eternal oppositions. So, Chuck Berry or Chaucer, Marvell or Madonna is the common cry that tends to represent these cultural icons as belonging forever to different worlds, times and social spaces. How can the texts of popular culture represent serious occasions for study? What might such textual material be doing in an educational context anyhow? Popular representations of these questions present the conclusions as foregone, but within the domain of the subject the tensions to which they may give rise are critical in relation to subject structure and practice.

How much academic English remains concerned with textual exegesis raises important issues for the subject's identity, orientation and constitution. An exploration of the relations between English and its textual field may highlight some residual but important questions about the cultural politics of the subject, its premises and its characteristic practices. Is English delimited by a specific textual field? How is that field determined? Or is English concerned more with modes of reading and interpretation, with the field of meaning in a more open, unbounded sense? How do the texts and reading practices of English stand in relation to their spheres of operation – their institutional contexts – and the conditions, therefore, of their significance? This chapter will offer an exploration of textual identities from the perspective of the specific institutional habitus of English teaching in the secondary school – where questions about textual identities within the textual field have a sharp political inflection.[1]

The relations between English teaching and textuality remain problematical in the light of contemporary theories of meaning and culture. What are the relations, *now*, between English, cultural studies, media studies and sociolinguistics? In these problematic questions the very integrity of the subject is at stake. English in schools – defined by national curricula in many cases – is caught between traditionalist and liberal subject models vaguely organised through the slippage of 'Literature' into 'literature'. While the textual field may expand the range of literature, the problem of the popular remains. Within English there remains an impossible duality – between literature and everything else. There remains a vestigial but powerful Leavisite mistrust of the unorganised textual realms that exist beyond the pale of literature. At the same time, a residual investment in the cultural authority of Literature is evident. Texts like the film *Blade Runner* (Scott, 1982) – given the status of the classic within the realms of the popular and taking on cult status – and André Gide's novel *La Symphonie Pastorale* (Gide, 1919) – an uncertain classic packaged though as classic literature – tactically provide a useful transgression of borders. Exploring the idea of the classic offers an occasion for revisiting the canonical/popular opposition and for rethinking mass educational practices in the field of textuality. Setting a classic work of fiction against an instance of the classic popular is a tactical device for exploring textual status and for indicating the institutional nature of all such statuses. Such a paired reading forms a rare but illustrative example of a pedagogical practice constructed on alternative lines to the present order of things in secondary school English teaching. Here I am proposing such a tactical reading of two texts, constructing parallels by reading through certain categories before exploring some of the issues relating to the constitution of contemporary English teaching. The two texts have been yoked arbitrarily together and will act as metaphors – or 'pretexts' – for an exploration of the construction of identity – including the construction of textual identities within institutionalised practices of the subject English in the field of education, textuality and culture. Political questions about reading, institutions and literacy inevitably follow. The specialist forms of literacy cultivated and sustained in the governmental practices of state schooling – which powerfully determine subject identities – will be exposed to a critique that suggests alternative practices. Constructing parities between disparate texts is designed to demand an anti-essentialist approach to textual practices in education.

Both texts I have chosen to address probe the sources of identity and express a sombre concern with filiation. Looming out of the chaotic urban environment that is twenty-first-century Los Angeles in *Blade Runner* is the hypermodern Tyrell corporation, which has managed to produce living human identity from the implanted bits and pieces of garnered memories. In this gloomy world of uncertain identity a replication test might expose the inauthenticity of your memories and confer upon you the deadly status of replicant. In a doomed attempt to ensure a clear distinction between human and constructed human, replicants are outlawed on earth, allowed only to inhabit off-world colonies. Somewhere in all this is the question of how identity gets constructed, how we know – or don't know – what we are. A group of replicants returns to earth in search of answers to questions about their own longevity: 'How long have I got'. As with all replicants, they are endowed with specific and often superhuman characteristics. The film noir style narrative is structured around the figure of Deckard, a hard-bitten 'blade runner' (replicant killer) with the Los Angeles police who is sickened by the work but who can not evade the call. Ironically, Deckard 'falls for' the vulnerable Rachel – a replicant; 'It doesn't know what it is', Deckard accuses Tyrell, Rachel's 'maker'. 'But then again who does?'

is the response that reverberates through the film, echoing with the glib realisation that a postmodern, apocalyptic future problematises identity and accentuates being. Deckard responds to Rachel as the outward form of femininity, a 'literal' simulation, but soon realises that there is no difference anyway, that being and identity in any case are the functions of a field of determination. In the meantime, Deckard pursues his day job which involves killing (replicant) women. He confronts the super-masculine Roy who has led the returned group of replicants and who seeks vengeance for the 'retired' (murdered) women. Before the confrontation with Deckard, Roy manages to meet and kill his creator, the author (father) of himself and his angst over longevity. In the ensuing fight to the death Deckard is doomed until Roy, for no apparent reason, decides to grant him his life at the moment when Roy himself realises that he is about to become the victim of his own inbuilt obsolescence. Maybe Roy simply needs an audience for his poignant dying panegyric on the wonders of life and on its brevity – 'like tears in rain'. As Roy's soul departs his body, symbolised by the dove he releases as his body finally seizes up, Deckard is left with a crushed hand and the realisation that he *must* find Rachel, his necessary other, replicant or not. At the end, one version has Deckard flying into the distance with Rachel with the voice-over reminding us of the hard fact that we are all on short-term contracts anyhow and we had better make the most of the time we have. In another, alternative ending – the (more authentic?) director's cut – there is no reassuring voice-over and Deckard is left wondering whether he is himself a replicant. Maybe, in the end – and as *La Symphonie Pastorale* might encourage us to think – we are all replicants of one kind or another.

In contrast to the darkly futuristic domain of *Blade Runner*, *La Symphonie Pastorale* is located in the apparent daylight of nineteenth-century France. In the utterly different – but equally fictional – context of a small Jura village, the apparently honest pastor finds a blind girl who has been kept as an untutored wild child. The tone is as sombre as the location is bright. The text soon enacts displaced blindness as a central though inexplicit metaphor as the novel trudges through soft snow, inaccessible routes and ambiguous domestic relations. The all-seeing Pastor, like Tyrell, fatally constructs the blind, abandoned girl in his own image. She falls in love with what she thinks she sees in the pastor, her creator, in effect. Replication is central to *La Symphonie Pastorale* as it is to *Blade Runner*. The pastor who has brought the child/adolescent into his home to the growing consternation of his family – especially his wife – lavishes attention on the girl and her education. Her blindness and her lack of socialisation mean that he must mediate her perception of all things. He lessons her in language and beyond, ultimately into the realms of classical music, represented as the highest expression of the human spirit – hence the novel's titular reference to Beethoven's 'pastoral' symphony. The girl becomes his creation and the means through which he rediscovers the freshness, beauty and innocence of the world. The innocence is corrupted, however, by the nature of his love for her. As he realises his son has fallen for his beloved Gertrude, he becomes engrossed in his own passion, sexually consummating their relationship (represented in the novel by ellipses, '…', as in *Blade Runner* with a fade-out) while sending his son into exile. In the course of time, the girl is sent for treatment and her sight is miraculously restored. She is now able to see the world for herself. Registering its hitherto unimaginable beauty she is also struck by the unhappiness she has caused in the pastor's household, and seeing her own misperception of things decides to end her own life. The pastor, who narrates the story, is left to ponder the consequences of his attempt to construct what she should be and see in the world. In a grim reversal of the beginning of the novel, Gertrude's sight has enabled the pastor to see his own tragic alienation for the first time: 'If only you could see what I've seen with your eyes', as Roy the superpotent replicant puts it in *Blade Runner*.

These brief synopses might suggest points for comparison between these two texts of different identities from different textual orders. A number of possibilities come to mind. A thematic approach might see comparisons between the idea of replication, between the figure of Tyrell and the pastor, for example. This approach might explore the issue of identity – what is it that makes us what we are and how do we construct a sense of ourselves out of fragmentary experience, memory and reflected identity? What is meant by paternity, by inheritance and what are the limits these things impose on identity? What are contemporary discourses on identity, genetics, cultural inheritance, the technologies of social reproduction and cybernetics? The film is replete with references to the relations between the human and the technological; the novel with the human technology of cultural replication. Another obvious thematic strand would focus on gender difference and the projection and representation of both femininity and masculinity. Other approaches might be more formalistic, offering mechanisms for the identification and exploration of textual characteristics. The texts might be explored as narratives – analysed through the cultural, symbolic, semic, proiaretic and hermeneutic codes. Textual relations might also be considered in terms of how already existing textual knowledge enables the codes and conventions of certain types of narrative fictions to be activated, an invitation to explore the phenomenon of intertextuality. Questions about where that textual knowledge comes from can also be explored. Interpretations and perspectives could also be investigated, including intertextual networks, cultural pressures and the general phenomenology of texts (and textual relations).

Exploring the relations between what is in texts and what is outside texts can also provide pedagogic material that reaches beyond the specificities of the text in question to touch on general questions of textuality. Time and place, for example, apparently consistent features, can be seen as the effects of certain textual strategies and are replicated through the tactical deployment of certain signs. Using these two texts as starting points it is quite possible to imagine (and to realise) a practice of the teaching of textuality that is theoretically informed, that takes an anthropological view of texts and textuality, that teaches 'reading' in an expansive sense of 'reading the world', that is informed by semiotics, 'narratology' and that also takes into account the antiformalist tendencies of much recent media and cultural theory. In any case, both *Blade Runner* and *La Symphonie Pastorale* seem to encourage the idea that identity is not something given once and for all. It is mobile, partial, capable of dissolution and reinvention and is constructed from the bits and pieces of self-awareness and the perceptions of others. Any of the approaches suggested here proposes possibilities for textual engagement that go far beyond the still predominant practices of personal response and textual meaning that continue to organise textual practices in school curricula. The idea of replication might serve as a metaphor for the continuation of *literary* textual practices in state school systems. As in *Blade Runner*, it turns out to be impossible to restrict replicated identities to their intended limits. Just as Roy turns on Tyrell and murders the mind that conceived of him, so cultural studies, media studies and other offshoots threaten to undo the integrity of English.

My descriptions of *Blade Runner* and *La Symphonie Pastorale* may suggest a narrative 'core'. Of course, no such core exists – except as another encoding. The meaning of *Blade Runner* and *La Symphonie Pastorale* cannot be contained within textual practices that dwell exclusively on specific textual features, or on particular types of 'natural' response – as is the case with English in schools in its approach to literature and textual material. Properties of texts cannot be analysed or understood independently of textual orders. Classic status is one category of textual identity among a potential host of different taxonomies. The issue of status and identity is itself a potentially significant, if not officially valorised, approach to textuality. A probing of classic status might be a useful starting point for proposing an alternative pedagogy to mainstream subject practices, and might also provide an occasion for exploring the cultural politics of English teaching. Broaching the question 'How is it that *Blade Runner* enjoys the status of a classic?' may give rise to a rich vein of thought on the foundations of textual identities. Classic status might be determined by the film's critical reputation, by the interest it generates among certain segments of an audience, by the extent to which it gets referred to in all the related discourses that cluster around the reception and reproduction of film texts and which become an established orientation towards the text. In the case of *Blade Runner*, classic status was perhaps confirmed by the release of the 'director's cut' – indicating an interest in versions reserved for classic texts and conferring on the film the distinction of authorship that also tends to characterise the literary classic. Practices of reproduction, re-editing and re-release ensure that film texts get reaffirmed in their classic status. Tracking back through the history of film a pantheon of classics might be identified of very different genres and identities, but which have been established through a range of discourses and practices of reception, reproduction and circulation that sustain classic status. This process works independently of any specific qualities or characteristics of the text itself. At least since Derrida, all such ascriptions of intrinsic quality have been under erasure, more a matter of ascriptions of classic status than properties in common.

But then again, *La Symphonie Pastorale* also enjoys a kind of classic status, conferred by the reputation of authorship of a specific kind. That is certainly how it is purveyed in its Penguin incarnation, where the novel comes packaged as a 'Modern Classic'. The cover – showing a detail from 'Monastery in the Snow' by K.F. Lessing from the Wallraf Richartz Museum, Cologne – signifies the great tradition of western European representational art with grand seriousness. *La Symphonie Pastorale* is classical by association. The inside cover refers to the stature of the author, who, in spite of his 'irregular and lonely upbringing', 'became devoted to literature'. Other possible references to Gide's sexuality, which may confer on his status as classic author a rather different inflection, are not raised. It is the 'distinguished' author-figure that is supported by reference to literary devotion. While *La Symphonie Pastorale* may appear as a rather 'obscure' literary text, it might be said to enjoy a more secure classic status than *Blade Runner*, belonging, as it does, to the arena of literature where a more deeply institutionalised set of ideas, practices and knowledge might confirm it within a textual pantheon. The status of literature has resonances in the public sphere of culture, distinction and 'taste'. Literature is also associated with certain powerful institutional educational practices – and in the context of state schooling such questions resonate beyond philosophical, phenomenological issues and interesting abstract questions about identity and meaning.

Such questions themselves suggest a whole strand of textual pedagogies in secondary schooling that might productively displace the more narrow concerns with the literary that dominate English in that context.

Phenomenological questions might begin with simple descriptions of subject/object relations and complicate these with the introduction of the concepts of positionality, perspective and aspect. How are we positioned in relation to this object? What do we understand to be the nature of the 'object'? What cultural knowledge must there be to give shape to the object in question and what are the specificities of this knowledge and its associated practices within our own cultural context? In the case of *Blade Runner*, clearly, it would be necessary to examine what kind of 'object' is a narrative fiction film – giving rise potentially to a further series of questions that might encourage a revision of the idea of the text as 'object'. We might further explore the very idea of themes – self-announcing 'aspects' or determined by the position of the subject or spectator? What kinds of themes might arise from an exploration of the film as a textual experience and how might these themes be ordered, prioritised? Within the realms of English teaching, this line of enquiry might be usefully taken into more conventional components of the subject. *Blade Runner*, approached from this angle, might lead into an examination of the way Shakespeare gets read and the way that certain approaches and persistent themes get defined in examination questions, in teaching practices and in various literatures on Shakespeare.

From *Blade Runner* to Shakespeare is an easy enough transition, narrative fiction providing a point of linkage. Equally, any of the themes briefly sketched above for *Blade Runner* might also be seen as categories through which Shakespeare might be read. Similarly, the institutionally sustained habit of reading Shakespeare might just as easily slip into reading contemporary popular narratives; the parallels can always be found, between *Othello* and *The Cosby Show*, *Hamlet* and *Terminator 2*. The concept of intertextuality proposes just such mobility of textual relations. One thing may lead to another through an utterly non-linear logic of connectivity. So *Blade Runner*'s 'themes' – urban social chaos, the power and frailty of the body, gender differences and the foundations of identity – provide occasions for slippage from one text to another, from one textual domain to another, from popular/cult film fictions to the realms of classic literature. But they also might meander through an unbounded plethora of texts and textual forms – news narratives, MTV video films, conversational narratives, jokes and so on. Conversely, intertextuality might also be a means for seeing how texts get located within different domains, how these might give rise to different attitudes, orientations and practices in relation to different types and orders of text. After all, textual fields and domains are not unbounded and are more or less carefully guarded by the discourses and institutional practices that define their limits. *La Symphonie Pastorale* belongs in some important social, institutionalised sense within the domain of serious fiction, perhaps within the domain of the classic novel – in terms of its 'demeanour', its construction, its style and its packaging. Exercises of transposition provide useful teaching techniques for exploring narrative components and for defining specific elements of textual genres. The genre of narrative fiction is generally associated with a certain type of classic status – the nineteenth-century classic realist novel exemplified in the works of Eliot, Turgenev, Tolstoy and James, for example. Where does the novel stand in relation to the still powerful order of literature? Is its place in that domain secure? We can imagine transpositions of form – into more populist forms and genres – that would reduce the gravitas of its comportment while retaining central features of its narrative logic. Imagining rewriting *La Symphonie Pastorale* as a supermarket bestseller highlights some of the issues that this line of enquiry into textual identities could generate. Again, we might then return to the question: how do we understand the constituent elements of the object? Is *La Symphonie Pastorale* what it is according to its narrative logic, its textual comportment, or might it be more to do with its packaging and its reception? By exploring the relations between these aspects of textual identity, pedagogy seeks to highlight reading as social practice and raises questions about the specific practices that supervene in the context of education. The text as an essential object-in-itself dissolves and becomes a pretext for the exploration of intertextual relations, textual domains and the determinations of meaning. This form of practice opens up the textual field so that its limits become much more problematic and the favoured textual focuses of English become increasingly arbitrary.

The anti-formalistic tendencies of contemporary linguistic, textual and cultural theory all point towards the realisation that classic status confers a certain set of behaviours and orientations towards the text in question – for example in references to authorship, in the practice of quotation, in the sense of textual longevity and attribution of special distinction. The aura of classic status can be identified as belonging to a set of practices likely to attach to texts that might claim quite different modes of being classic. Classic status is always already overburdened with institutional determinations. Certain modes of engagement with certain types of text – literary texts, for example – are much more attuned to the cultural habitus of some social groups than others and enjoy higher status in the public sphere. As a consequence, the practices of literature in schooling, while they may operate within a discourse of access, *actually* work towards (cultural/social) exclusion. Literature as a cultural practice cannot realise the liberal, inclusive aim it may aspire to. In national curricula in English there is a definite tension between the desire to represent the subject as liberal and open to all and the desire to key into discourses of cultural heritage and to give credence to the distinctness of the specifically literary experience. *Blade Runner* and *La Symphonie Pastorale* are bound up with these issues, just as are *Hamlet* and *Terminator 2*, Madonna and Marvell, and any of the other characteristic oppositions that appear to scandalise public consciousness from time to time with the outrageous inclusion of unashamedly popular material in tertiary education courses.

It is, then, in quite significantly different and arguable senses that both *Blade Runner* and *La Symphonie Pastorale* can lay claim to classic status. The attribution of a common status to such disparate elements of the textual world raises

questions about determinations and orders of texts. Wittgenstein's anti-essentialist account of meaning – 'Don't ask for
the meaning; look at the use!' – seems to propose an anthropological view of textuality, emphasising 'language games'
and the relations between specific language practices and
forms of life.[2] On this view to understand the grammar of the
word 'classic' is to identify the 'forms of life' – or social
practices – that give rise to and embed expressions of classic
identity. So it is possible to imagine an examination of the
inflections of the term 'classic' that might explore modes of
cultural distinction employed in the language games of
classical music and art which might slip from the realms of
high culture to the popular. Anyone familiar with the
language game of football commentary will be familiar with
the deployment of the term 'classic' in reference to a goal ('a
classic free kick from Beckham'), a defensive formation ('a
classic flat back four') or an entire game ('a classic FA Cup
semi-final') as a 'text' replayed from time to time for its
'classic' footballing qualities. In the realm of cultural studies
the term 'classic' might be deployed to refer to textual
material distinguished not so much by its assumed inherent
qualities as identified by its enjoyment of a certain status
among a certain group of people and serving as a common
point of reference.

The tactical advantage of such an anthropological approach
to meaning is that it can enable the exploration of textual
material across diverse fields of social practice. On this view
classic status comes in many shapes and sizes and may serve
quite different functions. Of course, textuality is not an
entirely open field and this is very sharply the case within
education practices that determine textual categories and that
define texts as object for study. Foucault's approach retains a
sense of differentiated practices relating to forms of life, but
brings a more critical edge to bear upon the familiar categories
that still determine much educational textual practice. In
Wittgenstein's case, language practices are simply 'there',
embedded in forms of life. For Foucault, discourses *produce*
the objects of which they speak within historically shifting
regimes of truth.[3] Such regimes inhabit institutions and are
involved in the determination of subjectivities. English in

education is a case in point. The meaning, weight and effects of the term 'classic' are clearly different in the context of the educational practices of English teaching than in the more loosely institutionalised practices of film-going and film-watching, football commentary or MTV.

In a classic statement on authorship, Foucault questions the *unities* of familiar discourses on text and language and meaning, interrogating the singular identity of the 'work' and displacing the very idea of authorship with the notion of the 'author-function', an effect of the organisation and policing of discourse which emerged towards the end of the eighteenth century. Foucault links the 'author-function' with 'the juridical and institutional system that encompasses, determines, and articulates the universe of discourses'.[4] Foucault's argument might be applied more generally to the various unities of English teaching: 'As soon as one questions that unity it loses its self-evidence; it indicates itself, constructs itself, only on the basis of a complex field of discourse.'[5]

Poststructuralism in general deals with linguistic/textual issues that demand a sustained rethinking of the English curriculum and its relations to language and culture. Derrida's reworking of signification, textuality and writing/speech proposes a more mobile and decentred theory of language and meaning than any imagined by English teaching.[6] Foucault emphasises the provisional nature of meanings, their essential relationship with specific social practices. His thesis of a shift in the nature and scope of government also has serious implications for the normative practices of education, and is particularly interesting in relation to the personalist elements of English.[7] At the level of subjectivity Lacanian theory emphasises positionality and the symbolic order (reworked by Althusser as 'interpellation'), rendering the central idea of writing/speaking/responding as self-expression entirely problematic and inverting the established, commonsense assumptions of liberal and traditional models of English about language, meaning and the individual.[8]

The emphasis that the practices of English teaching *still* gives to single texts and authors, personal responses, creative writing, with its necessary exclusions of alternative forms of expression and cultural experiences, becomes questionable – especially in relation to the normative judgements made by examinations that have significant social consequences. English cannot, within the theoretical framework outlined above, claim to speak univocally to disparate social groups with an evenly distributed cultural orientation. If textual meanings are (at least partly) dependent on the positioning of subjects, and if the identity, status and even the *being* of texts are already dependent on a textual field rather than being intrinsic, this poses questions for the subject as a social practice in the field where culture and education most glaringly meet. For a brief period in its recent history, English (in tertiary education, at least) seemed to be on the verge of momentous changes, at the edge of its own dissolution. *Rereading English* (1982) and *Rewriting English* (1985) appeared in fairly rapid succession, threatening to dislodge the very foundations of the subject and exposing its institutionalised complicity with the politics of cultural surveillance.[9] English in tertiary education may seem to have incorporated theory and critique but remains contradictory in its relations with textual identities and practices. The issue of cultural surveillance is clearly more evident in the much more limited textual practices of English in school, but these are not entirely unrelated to subject affiliations of English graduates who are trained to cultivate a subject orientation through degree courses.

There is some significant relation between conceptions of Literature that are evidently central to English in state schooling – where the 'juridical' system at work in English teaching is most visible – as well as to English in tertiary education, where ideas like 'author' and 'period' are still deployed to give mythical unity and depth to the subject, even where they may coexist with theoretical components that challenge these very categories. Foucault, like Derrida, identifies the necessarily polysemic character of texts, but puts characteristic and necessary emphasis on the whole historically specific 'juridical', 'institutional' character of the discourses of authorship and literature. English in tertiary education now tends to incorporate the critique of the very categories that still must define its distinct identity.

The accumulated impact of sociology, sociolinguistics, cultural and 'literary' theory provide a theoretical nexus that enables a critical rethinking of the school as socio/cultural milieu, indicating the cultural biases of the curriculum and of the very language of schooling. English, the liberal tradition of English teaching would have it, has historically been thought of as the space on the school curriculum for creativity, for empowerment, for self-realisation and for the free exploration of self and world through literature – a powerfully embracing form of education, always reaching beyond itself.[10] In the light of theory, English now seems pre-eminently to be that segment of the curriculum concerned with naturalising normative forms of language assessment, and with promoting a normative view of *significant* cultural experience – especially in the way it divides off certain cultural objects, icons and reading practices from popular culture.[11]

In its efforts to liberally embrace all possibilities, English has at times borrowed from and allied itself with adjacent subject areas such as media studies or cultural studies; however, this association is far from unproblematic. Key studies argue against the reductive idea of popular culture as simply hegemonic material imposed on an uncritical, passively consuming public.[12] The questioning of the category of literature implicit in the history and deconstruction of textual identities suggests that the realm of literature, even its more generous, liberal formulation, is a 'cultural arbitrary' imposed on the curriculum and is the symptomatic trace of a lingering Leavisism in English.[13] Bourdieu explores extensively how fields of cultural production generate and sustain class cultural differences.[14] Literature seems an increasingly inappropriate basis for an educational arena claiming to operate in the name of equality, access and social mobility.

The impact of the poststructuralist unsettling of textual integrity, the increasingly strong claims made on behalf of the popular, the decentring of the idea of culture implied in discourses of the postmodern influenced English towards an awkward self-consciousness that necessitated a shift in the grounds for engaging with literature.[15] The clustering of English with cultural studies, women's studies and media studies has encouraged flexible approaches to textual orders, identities, meanings and the positions from which they might be engaged. Like some powerful and dangerous replicant, born from its own reflexive impulses and which has developed its own intelligence of the world, cultural studies threatened to displace English by undermining the very foundations of its superiority.

The state of English and questions about its identity and orientation are significant in terms of the cultural politics of education. The *social* role of western-style education systems has been shifting in terms of public rhetoric – with emphasis being given to both centralised curriculum control and measurable performance or 'performativity'.[16] Considerable emphasis has recently been given to education as a force in maintaining national competitiveness in global markets. At the same time, education provides the necessary function of sustaining the idea of the social sphere as essentially merito-cratic. The professional identity of English teachers is sustained in training, induction and in the centralised deter-mination of established knowledge.[17] The textual field in educational practices of English is configured around literature as a critically defining category. The discourses of literature 'produce the objects of which they speak'.[18]

One pedagogic tactic that might be deployed in order to explore this arbitrary and culturally loaded division of the textual field is to see what happens when texts of disparate identity and status are set side by side. There might be interesting implications for the elevated status of classic English literature if Marvell's 'To His Coy Mistress', for example, gets set against some 'classic' Madonna videos, especially if we conduct the comparison through the category of gender. *Hamlet* set against *Terminator 2* might similarly be found questionable in terms of how it puts gender difference into play or in terms of how it confronts issues around masculinity and fatherhood. A kind of English teaching that might explore the effects of putting *Blade Runner* alongside *La Symphonie Pastorale* is eminently conceivable. Explorations of elements of narrative, genres, codes and conventions of the different communications media, of different semiotic systems and effects, for instance, are all perfectly plausible in the context of secondary state schooling. It seems also that this kind of textual pedagogy offers one way of addressing the problematic issue of 'habitus' and the cultural politics of schooling. It certainly avoids the arbitrary privilege ascribed to the category of literature in a variety of national contexts where English remains a central component of school curricula that are increasingly subject to surveillance. English has long been a key pressure point in state education, a symbolic focus through which arguments about the nature and purposes of state schooling have been conducted.

According to Ian Hunter, English teaching was always itself a mechanism of governmentality. It was the ideal vehicle for the human technology developed in nineteenth-century elementary schools – the end point of which was to produce the self-governing, self-regulating individual. In its most liberal form – involving the apparently open invitation to consider textual responses – the classic English 'reading' lesson enacted the problematisation of the self and self-consciousness. The significance of this governmental view is that it includes power in its description of professional practice and thus avoids the liberationist fallacy that school English could be a vehicle for the self-realisation of democratic populations.[19] Liberal pedagogies that are now fairly deeply embedded in certain regular pedagogic practices are actually powerful methods for masking the governmental function of the school – the more liberal, the more governmental. There is no escaping the governmental power that is activated in the English lesson, however. The human technology of pastoral surveillance that the modern school deploys, though, might be put to work to produce a variety of effects – to cultivate the intransitive practices of personal response, for example, or, on the other hand, to supervise training in anti-sexist or anti-racist reading practices. But this governmental power is also always inflected with cultural authority – in the case of English with the determination of the textual field. English in schools has been formally and informally defined to exclude spaces for cultural studies work on an expanded textual field, sustaining traditionalist notions of classic status associated with literature (hence the persistence of Shakespeare) – universality, centrality and intrinsic moral and aesthetic value.

Powerful institutional and historical determinants cannot be dismantled by discourses that claim to liberate English from the traditionalist and liberal models that ensure a dubious function of social selection based on class/cultural differences. It is possible, however, to rethink the premises and scope of the subject in relation to textuality – and to construct a practice, within given institutional and historical determinants, that is also aware of those determinants. The pairing of *Blade Runner* and *La Symphonie Pastorale* offers an instance of a textual practice that seeks to make central to itself the exploration of textual identities and the consciousness of their institutional determinations. In the context of English in secondary state schooling, questions about the identity and proper orientation of the subject have very significant social and cultural effects in terms of public definitions of literacy and the determination of social destinies. To reconsider the idea of the classic through an anti-essentialist approach to textual material may be to offer an opening into an alternative and 'knowing' approach to texts, readers and textual practices. In turn, any attempt to consider the cultural dimension of English in education will need to cultivate an awareness of dominant, historical practices of the subject English as ensconced in teacher consciousness, habitual pedagogies, exam practices, publications and institutions. Classic status is simply one point of entry for such a self-conscious, historically and culturally informed practice.

Notes

1. The term 'habitus' is borrowed from Pierre Bourdieu and Jean-Claude Passeron, *Reproduction in Education, Society and Culture* (London: Sage, 1977), a classic statement of the cultural milieu of education and its discriminatory social and political effects. English-speaking nations now tend to have similar educational structures. National curricula are common in one form or another to the UK (England and Wales, strictly speaking), Australia, New Zealand, Canada and the US. South Africa is on the way to developing a national curriculum.

2. Ludwig Wittgenstein, *Philosophical Investigations* (Oxford: Basil Blackwell, 1968), p. 43.
3. Michel Foucault, *The Archaeology of Knowledge* (London: Tavistock, 1977), pp. 48–9.
4. Foucault, 'What is an Author' in David Lodge (ed.), *Modern Criticism and Theory* (London: Longman, 1988), p. 202.
5. 'The Order of Discourse' in Robert Young (ed.), *Untying the Text* (London: Routledge and Kegan Paul, 1981), pp. 48–78.
6. See Jacques Derrida, *Of Grammatology* (London: The Johns Hopkins University Press, 1976), *Writing and Difference* (London: Routledge and Kegan Paul, 1978), *Margins of Philosophy* (Brighton: Harvester, 1982) and *Positions* (London: Athlone, 1987).
7. Foucault, *Archaeology of Knowledge*, *Discipline and Punish* (London: Allen Lane, 1977), *Technologies of the Self* (London: Tavistock, 1988).
8. See Jacques Lacan, *Ecrits: A Selection* (London: Tavistock, 1977), *The Four Fundamental Concepts of Psychoanalysis* (Harmondsworth: Penguin, 1979), Rosalind Coward and John Ellis, *Language and Materialism* (London: Routledge and Kegan Paul, 1977), Jacqueline Rose, *Sexuality in the Field of Vision* (London: Verso, 1986), Juliet Mitchell, *Women: The Longest Revolution* (London: Virago, 1984) and Bice Benvenuto and Roger Kennedy, *The Works of Jacques Lacan* (London: Free Association Books, 1986).
9. Peter Widdowson (ed.), *Rereading English* (London: Methuen, 1982); Janet Batsleer, Tony Davies, Rebecca O'Rourke and Chris Weedon (eds), *Rewriting English* (London: Methuen, 1985).
10. The classic statement of liberal English teaching is John Dixon's *Growth Through English* (Oxford: Oxford University Press, 1967).
11. A more lengthy elaboration of this position is available in Nick Peim, *Critical Theory and the English Teacher* (London: Routledge, 1993).
12. John Tomlinson's survey of positions and general thesis in *Cultural Imperialism* (1991) indicates a more interesting and more complex sense of the interactions between

media and media users. Ien Ang's various accounts of rethinking the audience, including her 'classic' study, *Watching Dallas* (London: Methuen, 1985), epitomise a movement away from a monolithic view of popular culture; see also *Desperately Seeking the Audience* (London: Routledge, 1991) and *Living Room Wars* (London: Routledge, 1996). See also John Fiske, *Understanding Popular Culture* (London: Unwin Hyman, 1989) and *Reading the Popular* (London: Unwin Hyman, 1989).

13. For a synoptic account of the development of English teaching, see Margaret Mathieson, *The Preachers of Culture* (London: Allen and Unwin, 1975).

14. See Bourdieu, *Distinction* (London: Routledge and Kegan Paul, 1986) and *The Field of Cultural Production* (Cambridge: Polity Press, 1993).

15. See Antony Easthope, *British Post-Structuralism* (London: Routledge, 1988).

16. Jean-François Lyotard, *The Postmodern Condition* (Manchester: Manchester University Press, 1986), subtitled 'A Report into the Condition of Knowledge' – itself a classic – defines some tendencies that are currently visible in education policy in western-style nation states.

17. See Roy Lowe's argument in *Schooling and Social Change* (London: Routledge, 1997), pp. 164–71.

18. Foucault, *Archaeology of Knowledge*, pp. 48–9.

19. See Ian Hunter, *Culture and Government* (London: Macmillan, 1988).

2

Classic Shakespeare for All: *Forbidden Planet* and *Prospero's Books*, Two Screen Adaptations of *The Tempest*

Sara Martin

Fred McLeod Wilcox's science-fiction film *Forbidden Planet* (1956) and Peter Greenaway's art-house film *Prospero's Books* (1991) might seem to have practically nothing in common. Both are, however, original and successful adaptations of Shakespeare's *The Tempest* and, by virtue of their daring choice of filmic language, valuable commentaries on the impact of Shakespeare's textual and theatrical legacy on cinema. *Forbidden Planet* and *Prospero's Books* resist the authority of the text and its sacralised literary aura by forcing Shakespeare's words to compete against the elaborate visualisation and innovative production design dominating the screen. *Forbidden Planet* is an intertextual adaptation that radically rewrites its original literary source for the popular medium of the 1950s science-fiction film. Never intended to be a canonical film version of Shakespeare – he is not even credited in the titles – *Forbidden Planet* lacks the cultural self-consciousness of other adaptations of Shakespeare's plays. The director and his collaborators at MGM studios felt free to use *The Tempest* to suit their own commercial and creative needs in a way that recalls how Shakespeare appropriated other materials for the plot of his plays. In contrast, Greenaway's film incorporates *The Tempest* into the personal artistic world of the director, who stamps this version of the Bard's text with his own unmistakable *auteur* signature. The film is an eccentric adaptation for a minority of filmgoers that questions the scholars' stifling respect for the literary text by flaunting practically all of Shakespeare's original words in an excessive, carnivalesque rendering of the play. Wilcox's and Greenaway's films use the Bard as a dynamic influence on the new media of cinema rather than as a static literary icon that must be worshipped from a distance.

In terms of their visual appeal, *Forbidden Planet* and *Prospero's Books* appear to be masterpieces of postmodern kitsch. James B. Twitchell distinguishes three categories of the vulgar: schlock, kitsch and camp. 'Schlock', he writes, 'is truly unpretentious, kitsch has pretensions towards taste and camp is just good fun'.[1] Postmodern kitsch mixes kitsch itself and camp: it does have artistic pretensions but it is self-conscious about them; it uses, therefore, a measure of camp to poke fun at those pretensions. The result, when postmodern kitsch is successful, as is the case of *Forbidden Planet* and *Prospero's Books,* is a highly pleasing aesthetic category which hovers right on the verge of the tasteless but which is fascinating in its bravura mix of the vulgar and the refined. Technicolor settings dominate *Forbidden Planet* as the naked, ordinary bodies of material spirits dominate *Prospero's Books*, placing each intended audience in slightly displaced positions. As a popular science-fiction film, *Forbidden Planet* seems to focus excessively on the static appeal of its settings; as an art-house film, *Prospero's Books* relies immoderately on its technological visual innovations and its dynamic special effects. Each film's visual gimmicks ultimately modify our perception of Shakespeare's text.

The discourse of monstrosity in these films is crucial to their visualisation of *The Tempest. Forbidden Planet* contradicts the idea of the monster as the alien Other, the feared invader, and embarrasses paranoiac audiences by making them face the idea that the worst monster lies within us. The film also stresses the Foucauldian argument that the highest civilisation accumulates enough power to shape the ultimate horror. The hidden menace lurking in our minds is portrayed by the film's Caliban, an invisible monster literally made of power coming from the Prospero-character's subconscious and the atomic generators controlling the planet's entropic system. Ariel appears in contrast as the charming robot Robby, epitomising the dream of controlled technology. *Prospero's*

Books shows greater interest in the contradictions surrounding our notions of beauty and ugliness, the vulgar and the sublime. The film taunts the viewer with the mixture of the low and the high: the 'preposterous costumes of Alonso's royal party', which 'convey their enervated civilisation' are displayed next to the shocking view of the hidden mysteries and miseries of human and animal anatomy.[2] With its beautiful yet obscene dancing Caliban, the film also challenges its viewers to rethink the notion of Otherness in order to move away from the simple-minded identification of ugliness with monstrosity.

Forbidden Planet clearly ranks lower than *Prospero's Books* among the adaptations of *The Tempest*. This does not mean, though, that *Prospero's Books* is unanimously regarded as a suitably canonical adaptation of Shakespeare. Film versions that use Shakespeare in alternative ways have begun to be accepted and even acclaimed only in recent years. 'Though it has been presented repeatedly on film throughout the twentieth century', Vaughan and Vaughan wrote not so long ago in reference to *The Tempest*, 'no director of Olivier's or Branagh's stature has attempted a popular cinematic version. Instead, *Tempest* films are roughly divided between low-budget television presentations and more expensive adaptations that abandon Shakespeare's text altogether.'[3] 'Popular' means here, clearly, didactic; the list of capable Shakespearean directors is reduced to just two – Olivier and Branagh, the ones generally endorsed by the Shakespearean academic industry. As John Collick notes, Shakespearean adaptations are evaluated depending on the proficiency of the adapter/director in the articulation of the 'truths of the text' understood as poetical truths but also as narrative fidelity.[4] The film adaptations that deviate from the text are often discounted as failures or, what is worse, as disloyalties to the Shakespearean canon. 'Films which don't appear to reinforce the supremacy of the poetry or the values it supposedly embodies', Collick adds, 'are ignored, suppressed or re-appropriated'.[5]

This was the case of Derek Jarman's daring version of *The Tempest* (1979), a significant instance of the difficulties that the absurd sacralisation of the classics imposes – or may have imposed until recently – on alternative film interpretations of canonical literary texts. In his autobiographical book *Dancing Ledge*, Jarman describes the process that led him to the making of the film.[6] Jarman's work was determined by a few essential notions. Budget limitations (the film cost only £150,000 to make) made him embrace the idea of setting the action in a rather artificial English country mansion rather than a tropical island; his would be an 'island of the mind'.[7] The sexual tension between the virginal Miranda and Ferdinand was displaced in the film towards Caliban and Ariel. The casting of punk star Toyah Wilcox as Miranda and the poet Heathcote Williams as the first young, healthy Prospero was original enough. But the film relied rather on the interplay between Caliban as 'the "old queen" figure who masquerades as the heterosexual lustful for Miranda'[8] and Ariel as a 'feminised gay male'.[9] The spirits were duly performed by pre-Jean Paul Gaultier gay sailors and Ferdinand appeared as a matinee idol.

This sexual playfulness had much to do with Jarman's main notion, namely, that the stage productions and screen adaptations of *The Tempest* had all missed Shakespeare's sense of fun – a point Wilcox and Greenaway would arguably agree with. *The Tempest*, Jarman insisted, is a masque – a view Greenaway also sustains.[10] As such, it must be fun to perform and to watch. Jarman's idea of fun included, however, much more than the eccentric visualisation of the play or the questioning of its heterosexual politics, extending to the rearranging and opening up of the text, a sin scrupulous critics were not ready to forgive. Basically, Jarman assumed he was free to take the greatest possible freedom with Shakespeare's play but failed to take into account the impact that negative reviews might have on his novel approach. Cinema audiences in Britain responded well to Jarman's challenge – at least the small audience that felt addressed by Jarman's film. *The Tempest* was originally released at the Edinburgh Film Festival to high acclaim, but flopped in the US. A furious attack mounted by Vincent Canby, the *New York Times* critic, destroyed not only the film's chances in America but also Jarman's chances to get funding for new projects in the midst of his most fruitful years. Canby, as was to be expected, objected to the freedom Jarman had indulged in regarding the text. 'In such a fragmented culture', Jarman writes in reference to Canby's US, 'messing with Will Shakespeare is not allowed. The Anglo-Saxon tradition has to be defended; and putting my scissors in was like an axe-blow to the last redwood'.[11] Possibly no such thing would have happened if Jarman had chosen to call his film by another name, as Greenaway did, thus diverting anxieties about its faithfulness to Shakespeare. Today, though, Jarman's version – just released on video – may find the open-minded audiences that it lacked twenty years ago. It seems to have already found a warm critical response that values the emotions elicited by performance over literariness. 'Jarman's movie', Harris and Jackson write 'though often bizarre, engages the feelings; it is genuinely moving and the emotions it arouses are essentially those aroused by Shakespeare's play'.[12]

Knowing Shakespeare's *The Tempest* is not a prerequisite to enjoying *Forbidden Planet*; nor does the film overtly intend to recruit new readers for *The Tempest*. Wilcox's film is rooted, rather, in the tradition of popular science-fiction films, novels, pulps and comics. In the encyclopaedic survey *Science Fiction*, Phil Hardy describes *Forbidden Planet* as 'one of the most charming works in the Science Fiction genre', adding with some perplexity that it 'is nothing less than an updated version of Shakespeare's *The Tempest*'.[13] Hardy's use of the word 'updated' is equivocal for it suggests that Shakespeare's plays are dated and can only interest contemporary popular audiences after radical revamping. He also notes that 'the film is clearly mounted as a juvenile offering',[14] mainly because of the magnetic presence of Robby the Robot and Wilcox's reputation as the director of the sentimental *Lassie Come Home* (1943). Hardy's praise is thus undermined by his own patronising references to the adolescent public the film may have originally targeted; in fact, a 1950 review noted, the film was meant to charm adult audiences although 'the kiddies will be there too'.[15] Prejudice against younger audiences has negatively affected *Forbidden Planet*, but the wrong assumption that it is a B series product – one among the many monster films produced in the 1950s – had damaged its reputation even more. Actually, *Forbidden Planet* was conceived as a high-budget film aiming at making science fiction respectable.[16] The choice of *The Tempest* as its source suggests that producers may have pinned their hopes on the idea that a classic source – even if unacknowledged – would guarantee a certain respectability for the film; the appealing production design was expected to do the rest.

The Forbidden Planet of the title is Altair-4, home to the lost survivors of a mission sent to explore it. In the final decade of the twenty-first century, the United Planets, presumably a confederation of the Earth and all its colonies, run a complex colonial system. The colonial discourse is implicit here as in most science fiction and, arguably, *The Tempest,* but it is left aside in favour of self-consciously Freudian – perhaps, properly, Jungian – motifs. Dr Morbius, the only survivor of the expedition, has entered into a dangerous alliance with the extinct Krel civilisation, the original inhabitants of the planet, that leads him to abuse the power of technology. He keeps, in addition, a questionable hold on his daughter Altaira, born on the planet.

There are some basic similarities with Shakespeare's *The Tempest*: Morbius and Altaira clearly recall Prospero and Miranda; Robby, their servant robot, and the monster of the id that attacks the visitors are versions of Ariel and Caliban, respectively. Prospero's magic is the technology of the Krels, akin to Shakespeare's invisible spirits; Prospero's books become the Krels' brain enhancer that Morbius uses as link to their civilisation. But the visitors arrive in Altair with very different intentions and motivations. Morbius's exile is initially an accident, but his solitude on Altair-4 becomes a cherished loneliness as his fondness for his daughter grows. Far from attracting his visitors, he does the utmost to repel them, including indirectly murdering some of them, whereas Shakespeare lets all his characters survive. Unlike the courtiers shipwrecked on Prospero's island, the spaceship crew is out on a mission to visit Altair-4; they are only confused as to what is attacking them, but not as to their situation. Captain Adams recalls Ferdinand and Ostrow is close to Gonzalo in wisdom, but little more. The spaceship's cook is a mixture of

Stephano and Trinculo, yet, beyond this, the similarities with the royal party that lands on Prospero's island are very few.

This is because *Forbidden Planet* ignores the plot of treason to focus instead on the issue of monstrosity. The film was released just a month after *Invasion of the Body Snatchers* (Don Siegel, 1956) in the midst of a decade marked by the Cold War and fears of secret invasions. Yet, it was different from other monster films of the period because it was 'a handsome and colourful epic in which the enemy *was* our minds and souls'.[17] Morbius's tragedy derives from Prospero's magic world and also from the technophobic world of Mary Shelley's *Frankenstein*, which, according to Brian Aldiss, is the novel that originated science fiction.[18] It is also the first to present science and technology as a source of danger rather than progress. Its theme was, therefore, appropriate to the Cold War, a period ambiguously split between the celebration of one's own (American) technology and the intense mistrust of the Other's (Soviet) science.

Mary Shelley's creature is a mixture of Ariel and Caliban – he is Ariel when, still unseen, he helps the family whose shack he has occupied; he is Caliban when he kills Frankenstein's brother and bride. Shelley portrayed Prospero not as an old magician but as a young scientist who cannot control the power that Prospero wields so masterfully. Shelley's Ariel-Caliban rebels against Frankenstein, begging not for freedom but for responsible parenthood; possibly, like Prospero, Frankenstein is a harsh master and a callous father. In *Forbidden Planet* Morbius is a new Frankenstein capable of creating a pleasant metallic monster – Robby – but incapable of controlling the dark side of his personality, the monstrous id of his unconscious. In this he differs from Prospero: while Prospero acknowledges Caliban, whom he calls his 'thing of darkness', the positions of master and slave are clearly demarcated in their relationship; Morbius, in contrast, projects a murderous Jungian shadow, which being part of his subconscious is out of his control. This id monster is directly associated with the misuse of technology and with Morbius's 'dangerous' desire to know.

The alien Krel technology enables Morbius to outdo his limited human capacities, turning him from philologist – a lover of books like Prospero – to creator, like Frankenstein. Mary Shelley's creature is split again in two: a new Ariel, this Robby who clearly precedes the charming C3P0 and R2D2 of *Star Wars* (George Lucas, 1977) and a new Caliban which is pure rage, pure energy. Even though the Freudian reading is clearly spelled out for the audience by Captain Adams when he forces Morbius to let Miranda-Altaira go and then die before destroying the planet,[19] there are more relevant elements in the film, above all the fear of nuclear annihilation and the concept that even the best civilisation will eventually self-destruct like the Krel. The film 'correctly notes that it takes energy to create the monster',[20] energy coming from a technology based on the use of nuclear power. The 9200 nuclear reactors of Altair do not act alone; they shape the hatred in Morbius's mind, and the Foucauldian message of the film is that an excess of power – in both the literal and figurative senses – in the hands of a single man leads to disaster. Since Morbius is a civilised gentleman, his derangement (Morbius becoming morbid) is potentially that of any man faced with the same Shellyan temptation to explore forbidden knowledge.

Morbius epitomises the idea that every man is an island; his monster of the id is not, despite the easy Freudian reading, a creature born of forbidden desire for his daughter but an entity born out of bereavement and misanthropy. The monster, which killed the survivors of the previous mission soon after Altaira's birth, may well have been unleashed by Morbius's grief at the death of his wife, who, like Prospero's wife, died in childbirth. Morbius tolerates nothing but himself, and for him Robby and Altaira are no more than extensions of himself; his intolerance is the origin of his Caliban. In this, *Forbidden Planet* follows Mary Shelley's path again, as Frankenstein's hatred is what elicits his monster's latent violence. But the shadow of Robert Louis Stevenson also looms large: Frankenstein creates the intolerable, the child of his science; Dr Jekyll discovers the intolerable in himself; Dr Morbius projects the intolerable in himself onto an aberrant creation that emerges from the sum total of his subconscious and the Krels' technology. No trace of compassion for Caliban can be found here, for how could there be any compassion for the monster of the id? There is some left, though, for Morbius after his fall when he finally acknowledges that this thing of Miltonic darkness visible – for the monster is invisible energy – is his. Morbius is lost and so the Krels' warning that the highest civilisation leads to the worst destruction is enacted in this cautionary tale.

Steinbrunner and Goldblatt claim that *Forbidden Planet* marked a main turning point in the history of science fiction. They maintain that 'the cinematic science fiction and fantasy screen was not to widen its horizons again until *2001* (1968), more than a decade later',[21] with yet another technophobic tale of monstrous creation and another Krel-like superior civilisation. Still, *Forbidden Planet* does not enjoy the same respectable artistic status as *2001*. The first reviewers were rather blind to the film's merits. At the time of its release, Parish and Pitts remark, 'some reviewers took the project to be a comedy dressed in sci-fi trappings'; they quote the *New York Times* reviewer who saw in the film 'some of the most amusing creatures conceived since the Keystone Cops',[22] though it is not clear whether he meant Robby or Altaira. *Forbidden Planet* is indeed amusing at points, but then so are Shakespeare's plays. Steinbrunner and Goldblatt come possibly closer to the main reason for the film's disappointing the high hopes that MGM studios had put in it:

> Quite a few reviewers were unsettled by a monster from so Freudian a source, evidently preferring – one could read between lines – a more substantial and traditional adversary. As a result of this reception, MGM scrapped whatever intellectual appeal its advertising was reaching for and concentrated instead on Robby the robot carrying off Altaira in his arms. *Forbidden Planet* drew sizeable audiences, but perhaps not the audiences it deserved.[23]

'Not the audiences it deserved' is an ambiguous phrase. It seems to mean 'not enough filmgoers, considering it was a good film' but it could also mean 'not the right kind of audiences'. Implicit here is Phil Hardy's observation that *Forbidden Planet* was geared at young, emotional audiences, hence it must be automatically inferior to adult, intellectual (science fiction) films such as Stanley Kubrick's *2001*. There is no doubt that *Forbidden Planet* has juvenile charm, with its love of strong colours, easygoing sexuality, and manly heroic space captains, but no less so than *The Tempest* with its young Miranda and Ferdinand, its magic island and its spirits and monsters. Appreciation of Wilcox's film is obviously handicapped by prejudices against its genre and its target audience – possibly also because it dares not credit Shakespeare at all. But it is clear that *Forbidden Planet* finds in Shakespeare much that is relevant to the time when it was made, dramatising fears of post-WWII American and, by extension, Western culture. This is the unfairness of colonial exploitation, not even the fear of the Other which most invasion films dramatised, but a deeper fear that we all recognise: the fear that Caliban is both us and the technology that surrounds us.

Forbidden Planet is often not regarded as an adaptation of *The Tempest* because it focuses on reworking aspects of Shakespeare's plot and neglecting his actual words. *Prospero's Books*, as the title implies, claims a higher degree of allegiance to Shakespeare's text. But, apart from shifting the dark qualities of monstrosity away from Caliban onto Prospero, both films also share an ambiguous approach to technology. 'The cinema', Douglas Lanier writes, 'has more readily taken up the challenge of textual authority than has the theatre'.[24] *Forbidden Planet* radically denies the authority of the text by literally dis-crediting Shakespeare, whose work is used to spell a technophobic message only tangentially related to his play. *Forbidden Planet* denounces technoscience while simultaneously parading before the viewers the attractions of film technology. Greenaway seems also interested in challenging through technology the authority of the Shakespearean text. In his case, though, his choice is to make Shakespearean textuality and his own filmic text compete against each other, 'remaining faithful (or, perhaps more accurately, "faithful") to the play's received text.'[25] Less concerned by technophobia than by the dissociation between high art and high technology, Greenaway sets out to prove that Prospero is a double for Greenaway himself 'as the digital cinema artist as much as for Shakespeare the playwright'.[26] The art-house film, *Prospero's Books* suggests, should ideally accumulate all the visual and technological innovations of art, literature and the stage since Shakespeare's time. The different uses of special effects become thus the bridge linking popular and art-house adaptations of *The Tempest*.

Prospero's Books was Greenaway's first literary adaptation and his first commission. John Gielgud – an illustrious, experienced stage Prospero[27] – chose Greenaway to direct a film version devised for his own playing of Prospero as a 'master manipulator' and 'prime originator' of plot and characters.[28] *Prospero's Books* was to be Gielgud's own farewell to Shakespeare, if not to acting altogether.[29] Technology played the second key role in the making of *Prospero's Books*. A substantial part of the funding came from Japanese business partners interested in publicising high definition television. Although released in cinemas, Greenaway's film was originally made for this system, which employs more dots and lines than conventional television to broadcast a sharper image. The Japanese television company NKH allowed Greenaway the free use of their futuristic technological resources during postproduction in exchange for publicity. This allowed him to create richly textured scenes that would otherwise have cost more than the whole film.[30] Greenaway also used infographics developed by the Paris company Mikros Image, creators of the Graphic Paintbox. The film's many three-layered scenes, used mainly to show Prospero's beautiful books, flood the spectator's brain with simultaneous overlapping images. Greenaway, Adam Barker writes, 'is wary of the film being seen as a "technological freak", but believes he has only scratched the surface of the technical possibilities.'[31] *Prospero's Books* is, thus, a Shakespearean adaptation but also a showcase for a mixture of cutting-edge European and Japanese technologies.[32] Special effects unusually serve high culture in an effort to lend respectability to the new technologies of television, though, as the names Gielgud, Shakespeare and Greenaway suggest, the target audience is certainly not that of popular primetime television.

Greenaway once declared that he is mainly interested in allegory rather than in three-dimensional characters or human psychology.[33] But Shakespeare's *The Tempest*, sometimes interpreted as an allegory of the artist's farewell to art and the power of the imagination, does not satisfy him. This might be the source of his personal challenge to Shakespeare's authority and textuality. In Greenaway's view, throwing away knowledge, as Prospero does when he destroys his books, makes no sense.[34] Instead, Greenaway has Caliban retrieve the last book that Prospero throws away – Shakespeare's *First Folio*. This gesture is read by Paul Washington as Greenaway's failure to protect the coherence of the postcolonial reading of *The Tempest* from the director's own challenge to Shakespeare's authority.[35] Actually, Greenaway questions the now popular postcolonial reading by completely ignoring it; it is much more tempting to see Caliban's retrieving of the Book as an opening up of Shakespeare's texts to other possible audiences through new versions or adaptations.[36] Greenaway's adaptation uses Shakespearean allegory to explain how the imagination works and, above all, how authors relate to their own work. This reflection is couched in daring film aesthetics clearly inspired both by Greenaway's passion for sixteenth- and seventeenth-century painting – especially Dutch – but also by the Elizabethan and Jacobean masques. Greenaway pays as much homage to Inigo Jones, the celebrated masque designer, as to late twentieth-century technology.

The Tempest is often read as Shakespeare's farewell to the stage. In this sentimental view of the play Prospero is Shakespeare's alter ego, whose magic signifies the power of the playwright to produce the illusion of life on the stage. Mariacristina Cavecchi suggests that Greenaway's artificial and mannerist rendering of *The Tempest* 'constitutes a cinematic equivalent to Shakespeare's theatrical illusionism'.[37] This is why in Greenaway's film 'there is a deliberate amalgamation or confusion between Shakespeare, Gielgud and Prospero'.[38] The mechanics of theatrical performance clearly concern Greenaway, but *Prospero's Books* is more than filmed theatre responding to the challenge of technology. This is made clear by Greenaway's main contribution to *The Tempest*: there are 24 books in Prospero's library, the number of frames per second of film.[39] The books, conspicuous signs of Greenaway's erudite and playful cinematic universe, often interrupt the flow of Shakespeare's original text, arresting the 'performance' of the play. Shakespeare's *play* becomes the excuse for Greenaway to *play* a game in which the text is both a physical object photographed for the film and the structure sustaining Greenaway's display of visual artistry.

The ubiquitous Prospero ambiguously mirrors Greenaway's interest in authority – his own and Shakespeare's. It has been frequently noted how the analogies between Prospero's role and that of the playwright force a double vision on the play. Paul A. Cantor observes that from the second scene onwards, '*The Tempest* develops a consistent double perspective for the audience. We see events as the characters think they are unfolding, and we see events as Prospero is ordering them.'[40] Barker and Hulme have suggested that 'what is staged here in *The Tempest* is Prospero's anxious determination to keep the sub-plot of his play in its place'.[41] This anxiety runs parallel to Greenaway's resolution to keep the diverging literary and visual elements of his *Tempest* under control. Like Gielgud's Prospero, Greenaway manipulates his filmic text in full view of the spectator; the awareness of the manipulation is used to prevent the spectator from engaging in the emotional identification with the characters that would be habitual in a straightforward adaptation of Shakespeare. Instead, Greenaway forces the spectator to acknowledge simultaneously Shakespeare's authority – kept practically intact in Prospero's words – and his own as film director. Greenaway uses technology perhaps not so much to resist Shakespeare's authority as to establish his own, rejecting the view that an adaptation is a work necessarily subordinated to its source.

The discourse on monstrosity features less prominently in *Prospero's Books* than in *Forbidden Planet*. It is actually just one aspect of a wider discourse on the body inscribed within the film's excessive visualisation. The flamboyant clothes of the civilised courtiers and the majestic Prospero sharply contrast with a panoply of naked bodies, the spirits of the island played by dozens of actors of all ages and physical types.[42] As

Ann Griere notes – one of the few reviewers to overcome their embarrassment at so much nudity – this is not erotic nudity but 'la nudité naturelle de la Renaissance'.[43] Greenaway condemns the automatic linking of nudity with eroticism and sex in contemporary culture and has often claimed to be interested as a painter in the representation of human variety. Within this framework, monstrosity would not be radical Otherness but just a particular position within the immense range of variation on the human body.

Greenaway nonetheless invests much more creativity in imagining the monster Caliban than in the angelic Ariel. In consonance with the variety of human bodies and the overlapping of images on the screen, Ariel is played by four blond, curly-haired actors, whose ages range from seven to about twenty-five and who represent the sum total of the four elements: air, water, earth, fire. Attractive as this multiple Ariel is, Caliban, played by the Scottish dancer and choreographer Michael Clark, is much more challenging, a beautiful dancing satyr, fully human except for the tiny horns sprouting from his head. His naked, supple, elegant yet obscene Caliban never ceases touching the ground as he dances, an aspect that underlines his links to matter in sharp contrast with the airy Ariel. Dance – inspired both by Inigo Jones's masques and by contemporary dance – is an essential element in the film. But whereas other actors dance to music, Clark's innovative Caliban dances to Shakespeare's words, 'adding his sinuous movements to Shakespeare's vivid language'.[44]

Caliban springs from a collaboration between Clark and Greenaway that stresses Clark's authorship as a choreographer and his reputation as an unconventional dancer opposed to traditional ballet training. Greenaway and Clark saw Caliban as the embodiment of both good and bad, the ugly and the sublime. The deformed monster of more traditional productions was eschewed in favour of a view of monstrosity as essential ambiguity rather than Otherness. Clark declared that:

> It has been hard to resist the usual interpretations, but I see him as very much a water-based creature, and I have tried to bring the human elements out. A lot of the initiation for

the movement has come from the pelvis – dance is at root a sexual thing despite everyone's shocked denials – and I think this is appropriate for Caliban's sense of the source of his power, and his hunger for Miranda.[45]

Paradoxically, Clark's water-based Caliban is sensual but narcissistic, hardly showing his desire for Miranda. This dancing Caliban is, ironically, not quite a monster but 'the most beautiful creature in the film: beauty as the beast'.[46] The conventionally pretty Miranda cannot compete in sexual appeal with the beast. He is the only focus of genuine emotion in an otherwise emotionless film.

Greenaway's version elicited mixed opinions from the reviewers. Nathaniel Bird concluded that 'this film is indeed Shakespeare's play', which, of course, it cannot be, despite closely following the Bard's words.[47] Jonathan Romney describes Greenaway's 'ostentatious erudition' as kitsch, 'but then it is quite knowingly so'.[48] Actually, the film's refined imagery troubled most reviewers: some criticised Greenaway's bad taste,[49] others his claustrophobic visualisation of Prospero's magic island. Generally, reviewers and audiences alike complained about Greenaway's abuse of technology. The film is a veritable orgy of multilayered images, too intricate even for the experimental art-house film spectator to capture at once in a single viewing. This multiplicity of visual signs may finally leave the spectator exhausted and frustrated. Audiences more interested in Shakespeare than in Greenaway may feel antagonised by his display of artistic narcissism. Greenaway fans may well ignore Shakespeare to focus on the director's habitual visual games. But, as Douglas Lanier argues, ultimately Greenaway's challenge to Shakespeare's textuality fails. 'In the end', Lanier writes, 'Greenaway's film is itself destined to become a cinematic "text", to be "read" according to interpretative protocols of close reading and with many of the same assumptions about "textual" monumentality.'[50]

Jonathan Romney considered *Prospero's Books* 'only indirectly a "version" of *The Tempest* ... a variation in the musical sense, an annotated commentary'.[51] This opinion agrees well with the view sustained in performance criticism that the play's text is a score or blueprint for stage performance. This notion that each different stage production is an interpretation rather than a copy of the playwright's text should be exported to screen adaptations of the 'classics'. Being fixed by photography once and for all, the film production does not allow the variability of actual live performance. *Forbidden Planet* and *Prospero's Books* should be, thus, regarded as free variations on a particular score composed by Shakespeare and, possibly, his stage collaborators.

Cinema also provides an important reference to reconsider Shakespeare's position as an author. Shakespeare's plays were themselves adaptations of miscellaneous sources. They were not written with the Romantic idea of original authorship in mind, but rather in the same way that contemporary scripts for television and cinema are written. Respect for his authorship was not, simply, part of Shakespeare's frame of mind as an author; similarly, screen writers have only recently started demanding that their authorship be acknowledged. Unlike his adapters, Shakespeare was unencumbered by the weight of the textuality and authorship of his sources and would possibly find it quite difficult to understand the restrictive politics of Shakespearean film adaptations (as indicated by Jarman). Given the existence of different screenplays for *Forbidden Planet* and *Prospero's Books, The Tempest* should perhaps be regarded as the ur-(screen)play from which both films descend rather than the fixed textual object to which they pay homage.

Forbidden Planet and *Prospero's Books* are intertextual critical readings of *The Tempest* rather than mere textual copies. They question and subvert not so much Shakespeare's own authorship as the artificial dominance of the text over the image and performance. Wilcox and his MGM studio team chose to make the Bard an anonymous source, as invisible to their popular film audience as Shakespeare's own sources must have been for his theatre audience. Greenaway prefers, instead, to consider and vindicate his own authorship as a film-maker in competition with and at the expense of a source that would be recognised by his art-house audience. In both films the freedom of interpretation and visualisation is channelled through the use of innovative cinematic language. Special effects and lush production design play a decisive role in the effort to free the films from 'the constraints of bookishness' that beset Shakespearean cinema.[52] Despite the cultural distance between them and the different reasons that they were made, both films suggest that screen adaptation should be understood as a critical reading expressed through the plastic beauty of the film screen rather than as a 'truthful' reading in search of the poetry of the written word.

Notes

1. James B. Twitchell, *Carnival Culture: The Trashing of Taste in America* (New York: Columbia University Press, 1992), p. 54.
2. Douglas Lanier, 'Drowning the Book: *Prospero's Books* and Textual Shakespeare' in Robert Shaughnessey (ed.), *Shakespeare on Film* (London: Macmillan Press, 1998), p. 186.
3. Alden T. Vaughan and Virginia Mason Vaughan, *Shakespeare's Caliban: A Cultural History* (Cambridge: Cambridge University Press, 1991), p. 200.
4. John Collick, *Shakespeare, Cinema and Society* (Manchester and New York: Manchester University Press, 1989), p. 4.
5. Ibid., p. 4.
6. Derek Jarman, *Dancing Ledge* (1984; rpt. London: Quartet, 1991), pp. 182–206.
7. Ibid., p. 186.
8. Ibid., p. 116.
9. Ibid., p. 116.
10. Lanier insists, though, that 'Jarman interrogates content, Greenaway form' ('Drowning', p. 182) in their recuperation of Shakespearean theatricals and the masque.
11. Jarman, *Dancing Ledge*, p. 206.
12. Diana Harris and MacDonald Jackson, 'Stormy Weather: Derek Jarman's *The Tempest*', *Literature/Film Quarterly*, Vol. 25, No. 2 (1997), pp. 90–8, p. 97. They ignore the troubled reception of Jarman's film.
13. Phil Hardy (ed.), *Science Fiction: The Aurum Film Encyclopedia* (1984; rpt. London: Aurum Press, 1985), p. 157.

14. Ibid., p. 157.
15. In *Variety Film Review*, Vol. 9: 1954–1958 (New York and London: Garland Publishing Inc., 1983). Review date: 13 March 1956.
16. Chris Steinbrunner and Burt Goldblatt, '*Forbidden Planet*' in *Cinema of the Fantastic* (New York: Saturday Review Press, 1972), p. 270.
17. Ibid., p. 270.
18. Brian Aldiss, *Billion Year Spree* (London: Corgi, 1973).
19. Commentators read the film as a tale of a father's most improper sexual attachment to his daughter, yet Morbius does not seem to restrict Altaira's relaxed dress code or her behaviour at all. In fact, it is Captain Adams who forces her to dress more modestly and to restrict her childish sensuality only to himself.
20. Leroy W. Dubeck, Suzanne E. Moschier and Judith E. Boss, *Fantastic Voyages: Learning Science through Science Fiction Films* (New York: American Institute of Physics, 1994), p. 24.
21. Steinbrunner and Goldblatt, '*Forbidden Planet*', p. 271.
22. James Robert Parish and Michael R. Pitts, *The Great Science Fiction Pictures* (Metuchen, N.J.: Scarecrow Press, 1977), p. 137.
23. Steinbrunner and Goldblatt, '*Forbidden Planet*', p. 280.
24. Lanier, 'Drowning', p. 178.
25. Ibid., p. 181.
26. Peter Donaldson, 'Shakespeare in the Age of Post-Mechanical Reproduction: Sexual and Electronic Magic in *Prospero's Books*' in Lynda E. Boose and Richard Burt (eds), *Shakespeare: The Movie* (London and New York: Routledge, 1997), p. 171.
27. Gielgud had played the role four times: in 1930, at the Old Vic, directed by Harcourt Williams (he was only 26 at the time, thus anticipating Jarman's young Prospero); in 1940, again at the Old Vic directed by George Devine; in Peter Brook's 1957 production at Stratford-upon-Avon and, finally, in Peter Hall's *Tempest* at the National Theatre in 1974 when he inspired Jarman to make his version. Further information about the making of *Prospero's Books* is provided by Peter Greenaway,

Prospero's Books: A Film of Shakespeare's The Tempest (London: Chatto & Windus, 1991) and his *Prospero's Subjects* (London: Chatto & Windus, 1992), a journal written on the set.

28. Allarts Productions, '*Prospero's Books*', promotional leaflet, (1991).

29. Fortunately, Gielgud is still active, having recently played roles in Shakespearean films *Hamlet* (1996) and *Looking for Richard* (1997).

30. Jorge Gorostiza, '*Prospero's Books*: Venticuatro Libros', *Peter Greenaway* (Madrid: Cátedra: 1995), p. 178.

31. Adam Barker, 'A Tale of Two Magicians: An Interview with Peter Greenaway', *Sight and Sound* (May 1991), p. 28.

32. In Spain, for instance, the film was first seen in 1992 within a festival of new technologies for the screen staged by the Science Museum of Barcelona.

33. Marlene Rodgers, '*Prospero's Books* – Word and Spectacle: An Interview with Peter Greenaway', *Film Quarterly*, Vol. 45, No. 2 (Winter 1991/2), p. 13.

34. Ibid., p. 16.

35. Paul Washington, '"This Last Tempest": Shakespeare, Postmodernity, and *Prospero's Books*' in Heather Kerr, Robin Eaden and Madge Mitten (eds), *Shakespeare: World Views* (Newark: University of Delaware Press and London: Associated University Press, 1996), p. 239.

36. These needn't be film or stage versions. American novelist Tad Williams published in 1994 *Caliban's Hour*, in which the monster gives a very different version of the events in *The Tempest*.

37. Mariacristina Cavecchi, 'Peter Greenaway's *Prospero's Books*: A Tempest between Word and Image', *Literature/Film Quarterly*, Vol. 25, No. 2 (1997), p. 83.

38. Barker, 'A Tale of Two Magicians', p. 29.

39. The books do not appear following their numerical sequence. They are handmade books, profusely illustrated, some of them with tri-dimensional gimmicks.

40. Paul A. Cantor, 'Shakespeare's *The Tempest*: The Wise Man as Idol', *Shakespeare Quarterly*, Vol. 31, No. 1 (Spring 1980), p. 75.

41. Francis Barker and Peter Hulme, 'Nymphs and Reapers Heavily Vanish: The Discursive Contexts of *The Tempest*' in John Drakakis (ed.), *Alternative Shakespeares* (London and New York: Routledge, 1985), p. 203.
42. There are five kinds of spirits: the indigenous inhabitants; Sycorax's domestics; Prospero's library clerks; Prospero's dream creatures and Prospero's prophetic creatures.
43. Ann Griere, 'Reflets et Mirages: De Berio à Greenaway', *Positif*, No. 368 (October 1991), p. 34.
44. Nathaniel Bird, *'Prospero's Books'*, *Films in Review* (February 1992), p. 49.
45. Allarts.
46. Alan Woods, *Being Naked Playing Dead: The Art of Peter Greenaway* (Manchester: Manchester University Press, 1996), p. 109.
47. Bird, *'Prospero's Books'*, p. 49.
48. Jonathan Romney, *'Prospero's Books* (Review)', *Sight and Sound* (May 1991), p. 45.
49. Alain Masson, 'This insubstantial pageant', *Positif*, No. 368 (October 1991), pp. 36–7.
50. Lanier, 'Drowning', p. 191.
51. Romney, *'Prospero's Books'*, p. 45.
52. Lanier, 'Drowning', p. 179.

3

The Red and the Blue: *Jane Eyre* in the 1990s

Lisa Hopkins

Our local radio station recently rang the department to ask if we had an English lecturer who could talk about the classics. The secretary helpfully offered to transfer them to a colleague who works on the cultural influence of Sophocles and Euripides. 'Oh no,' came the horrified reply, 'we mean proper classics. You know, like *Jane Eyre*.' Though considered distinctly *im*proper in its day, *Jane Eyre* (Charlotte Brontë, 1847) has thus, apparently, achieved paradigmatic status as the classic classic, and this is perhaps not inappropriate. Though fulfilling perhaps the first requirement of a 'classic' by being unimpeachably old, it retains both popularity and accessibility, being particularly amenable to new critical approaches such as psychoanalytically informed and feminist readings which have offered it new voices with which to speak; and while clearly flagging its own place in a tradition inaugurated by *Pamela* (Samuel Richardson, 1740–1) it has also proved a seminal text not only in the development of the romance genre but in the inspiration of independent works of fiction such as Jean Rhys's *Wide Sargasso Sea* (1966).

Though the novel itself is thus so securely equipped with both a genealogy and a progeny, however, the various film and television adaptations of it at which I want to look have much less clear points of origin. Both the Franco Zeffirelli and the Robert M. Young versions, I shall argue, owe a considerable amount to texts and discourses other than the original novel. One source to which both clearly pay homage is the 1943 Robert Stevenson film of the novel, starring Orson Welles and Joan Fontaine, and indeed the fact that they both do so serves to enshrine the 1943 film as itself possessing classic status.

The Stevenson film itself, however, is far from being any kind of 'untainted', originary version; one of its most remarkable features is that it not only offers itself as an adaptation of the text, it effectively replaces it, at times even going to the extreme of actual rewriting. The original trailer (released with the video version) shows a woman's hand running along a shelf of 'classic' books that have been turned into films, and explicitly presents *Jane Eyre* as another such. The opening of the film itself continues this emphasis: we see a book whose turning pages bear the cast list. Then we see the first page of the book and both hear and see the words of the first sentence: 'My name is Jane Eyre. – I was born in 1820.' That dash is so perfect, so much in the true nineteenth-century style of punctuation; and yet the words themselves, as any reader of the book instantly knows, are *not* the opening words of *Jane Eyre*. To present them so insistently as if they were is to effect a strange mystification and falsification of the adaptation's origins; for all its anxiety to market itself as *Jane Eyre*, the film seems almost to find the real *Jane Eyre* an embarrassment, which must be replaced. At other points in the narrative pages ostensibly from the book recur, most egregiously when Jane flees Thornfield and we see the appalling sentence 'Going nowhere, I had nowhere to go', which presents itself as the first line of a paragraph of the novel. A notable feature of this and of the other passages of text we see is the brevity of the paragraphs, a feature quite alien to nineteenth-century prose.

Perhaps we need to connect this tendency with one of the other major changes the film makes, which is that Jane does not even attempt to fend for herself after her flight from Thornfield, but instead seeks shelter from Bessie. The fact that it is a woman's hand which ranges along the bookshelf featured in the trailer clearly suggests that this is a 'women's film'; perhaps those women who might see the film without having read the book – and are thus likely to belong to the less educated and less leisured section of society – are not to be exposed to dangerous ideas about women's potential for self-reliance and economic independence. One might also notice how often the camera-angles, particularly when shot/reverse-shot sequences are used, stress that Jane must look up to Mr Rochester, and how her face is habitually fully lit, and thus constantly open to scrutiny, while his is invariably at least partly shadowed, allowing him to preserve his secrets. This is a film, in short, which, while presenting itself as *Jane Eyre*, contains neither of the novel's most famous lines ('Reader, I married him' being also absent), and omits a crucial section of its narrative. In this, I shall argue, as well as in echoes and details, it tellingly foreshadows both the Zeffirelli and the Young adaptations: both of them want to adapt *Jane Eyre*, but both of them find at least one aspect of the text too hot to handle. What they want, I shall suggest, is more to co-opt the original novel's classic status for their own agendas than actually to engage with its most urgently addressed issues.

Though the Stevenson film is curiously ambivalent about its indebtedness to the book, both Zeffirelli's 1995 film and Young's 1997 television adaptation of the novel make no attempt to conceal their own homage to this first screen version. Minimising the preliminary skirmishes which lead to Jane being banished to the Red Room, all three of these retellings focus strongly on that initial horror, and proceed to adopt the same general structure and narrative line. More specific debts are also clearly marked. In both the Stevenson and the Zeffirelli it is Helen Burns's hair which is cut, and in both cases Jane publicly protests (although Zeffirelli typically infuses the moment with a vigour and sensuality absent in the earlier version, having both Helen and Jane provocatively toss their luxuriant locks). In the Young, the dancing china dolls which Mr Rochester presents to Jane recall the puppets with which Adèle plays in the Stevenson film. But there are also significant differences. In the first place, the older film was perforce made in black and white, while in the more recent versions colour is not only an enhancement but, as I hope to show, of considerable thematic importance. And in the second, these 1990s retellings have been structured and reconfigured by contemporary concerns no less pervasive than the 'little woman' slant of the 1940s.

Awareness of other contexts is created partly by the pervasive habit of recycling actors in classic adaptations. Ciaran Hinds, who appeared in Roger Michell's 1995 BBC

Persuasion as Captain Wentworth and was later to steal the show as Bois-Guilbert in Stuart Orme's 1997 BBC *Ivanhoe*, plays Mr Rochester in the Young *Jane Eyre*, improbably marrying the Harriet Smith (Samantha Morton) of Diarmuid Lawrence's ITV *Emma* (1996), after she has stayed in a house where the housekeeper is Gemma Jones – Mrs Dashwood in Ang Lee's 1996 *Sense and Sensibility* – and been looked after by Elizabeth Garvie, the Elizabeth of Cyril Coke's 1979 BBC version of *Pride and Prejudice*, who here plays Diana Rivers. In the case of the Zeffirelli film, the doubling is even more marked. There is a striking overlap between the cast of his film and that of the 1995 *Persuasion*, almost as though Zeffirelli, whose previous attempts at adapting classics such as *Romeo and Juliet* (1968) and *Hamlet* (1990–1) have not met with universal critical acclaim, was seeking to compensate for his own reduced credibility by their accumulated aura of 'classic' prestige. Amanda Root (Anne Elliot) resurfaces as kind but powerless Miss Temple; Fiona Shaw (Mrs Croft) is now widowed, unloved, embittered Mrs Reed, suffering from her late husband's fondness for Jane rather as Mrs Croft perhaps compared her own childlessness with her husband's pleasure in playing with Mary Musgrove's children; and Samuel West (Mr Elliot) has metamorphosed into St John Rivers, whose character, though the part has been swingeingly cut and altered from that in the original novel (where St John is actually given the honour of the closing lines) still retains some of the unctuousness which marked his Regency avatar.

Indeed an unkind commentator might, perhaps, suggest that the Zeffirelli film of *Jane Eyre* actually bears a closer resemblance to *Persuasion* than it does to *Jane Eyre*. As always with Zeffirelli, of whom Ace Pilkington has recently said that 'no modern director has a better claim to the dangerous title of popularizer-in-chief',[1] much has been cut or rearranged. Jane's relations with the Reeds, the Rivers, Helen Burns and Miss Temple have been reduced to the merest of sketches. Characters have been cut altogether, like Diana Rivers,[2] Bessie, and John and Mary, or are merely glimpsed without being named, like Eliza and Georgiana Reed. Most strikingly, time has been telescoped in a number of instances. Helen Burns dies almost as soon as she coughs, and the Jane who rises from mourning at her grave is a decade older than when we saw her last. Later, Jane flees from her abortive wedding straight into an apparently passing coach, and Mr Rochester has barely started to pursue her on horseback when he is called back by some harvesters with the news that the hall is burning; with similar compression, however, he does not have long to wait, for Jane returns to him as soon as she is well, with no intervening period of teaching.

The untried and half-French Charlotte Gainsbourg may seem an improbable choice for the very English Jane, until one hears the ease with which she can speak French to Adèle. The phenomenon of Frenchwomen playing Brontë heroines – Gainsbourg's Jane Eyre having been preceded by Juliette Binoche's Cathy in Peter Kosminsky's 1992 *Wuthering Heights* – also echoes the sisters' own Continental connections, particularly Charlotte's crucial experiences in Belgium.[3] It also usefully reminds British audiences of the extent to which foreign interest in the Brontës has helped shape whole areas of perceptions of Englishness – as is currently being underlined by the widespread panic caused in Haworth by Japanese tourists' threat to boycott it because they feel they receive an insufficiently warm welcome. It is perhaps salutary to look at the Brontës through other eyes, while the entire phenomenon of having a half-French leading actress directed by an Italian and playing against an American co-star serves as a further guarantee that *Jane Eyre* is indeed a 'classic', able to cross cultural divides as well as the intervening years.

It is not Gainsbourg, however, who is marketed as the film's primary draw: top billing goes to William Hurt's Mr Rochester. Some interesting things have been done to the Mr Rochester of this adaptation, who presents a marked contrast with Orson Welles's fiercely overbearing romantic hero. Jane's first encounter with him comes through a painting of him as a child. The image underlines the film's strong interest in representing childhood and its perspectives: trouble has, for instance, been taken over the portrayal of the young Jane, played by the Oscar-winning Anna Paquin, and our strong sense of sympathy for her is echoed in the fact that we are less aware of the frivolousness of Adèle than of the fact that she, too, is young, vulnerable, and sometimes at a loss in an adult world. A society acutely, tragically aware of child abuse has produced a *Jane Eyre* in which the experiences of children loom large, and the fact that our first introduction to Mr Rochester should be as a child is of a piece with that.

This impression of vulnerability is maintained. It is of course merely in line with the novel that the first time we (and Jane) actually encounter Mr Rochester he should fall off his horse and require Jane's help to move, but other emphases are more distinctively the film's own. All Mr Rochester's teasing of Jane is cut; from the outset, we are aware that it is actually Blanche Ingram (played by an imaginatively cast Elle Macpherson, the supermodel) who is being manipulated by him, as his repeated protestations of poverty are seen to irritate her at a stage far earlier than the point at which the Jane of the book, and, through her, the reader, is made aware of the comparable design. Thus we never have a sense of Mr Rochester as powerful or in control of events; after the fire, nothing but shyness or lack of self-confidence seems to hold him back from kissing Jane, which appears to be the outcome towards which the shot is inevitably leading, and he also clearly suggests genuine uncertainty over whether Jane will return to him from the deathbed of Mrs Reed. Most strikingly of all, there is no explanation to Jane after the wedding has been called off and he has finally revealed the existence of Bertha, nor even any real attempt to detain her (though admittedly he hardly has time for one); all he says is, 'I love you. Say you love me.'

Though the adaptation has, perhaps because of strong prejudices against male cross-dressing, omitted any trace of the episode in which Mr Rochester disguises himself as a fortune-teller, he is just as effectively feminised by these words, since the demand that one's partner should say he loves one is, in our culture, so solidly identified as the female role. Similarly, when Jane returns, he takes her to be a dream, and just says, 'Before you go, kiss me', further underlining his passivity. It is also notable that, among the relatively small proportion of dialogue allotted to Mr Rochester, he assures Jane that he is not naturally vicious, and Bertha that he would never hurt her. For all that he puts a bullet through the brain of his rival for Cécile's affections instead of merely through his arm (or lungs, as the Stevenson rather gruesomely has it), Mr Rochester, it seems, has become a New Man, and this softening and sliding over of the original's wildness and potential for violence is further echoed in the toning down of his injuries, with only his eyes hurt and not his hand as well. A man who suffers passionately and has had a string of exotic-sounding mistresses with foreign names may be a stirring and exciting character to meet between the pages of a nineteenth-century novel, but in a film which has already reminded us so powerfully of child abuse, such actions would hover too dangerously on the edges of domestic violence.

It is doubtless for similar reasons of political correctness that the treatment of Bertha differs significantly from that of the book. The question of race receives only the lightest of touches – Mason, seen only briefly, is a very light-skinned black, but Bertha herself is distinguished primarily by her pallor – and there is no mention at all made of her nymphomania, nor of Rochester's assertion that he would continue to love Jane in such circumstances but cannot love Bertha. There is thus nothing in the film to direct our sympathies away from her, and when we first see her, indeed, she looks more pitiable than anything else, cowering close to the fire as if she is cold. Though we are left in no doubt that she is violent, it is by no means so clear that she is malevolent; it would seem absurd to hold such a creature responsible for her actions.

The taming of Mr Rochester and the softening of Bertha are also in line with the overall image pattern of the film. There is a sustained series of alternations between images of redness and of blueness, which, in a crucial instance of the film short-circuiting the contemporaneity and urgency which the novel once had, seem to me to allow it to deflect the representation of those concerns of the novel which the late twentieth century finds the least acceptable from the politically charged arena of race to the ostensibly ideologically neutral one of the aesthetic. The pattern is established from the outset. There is an unusually austere opening shot with no title music; then a voiceover says 'My parents died when I was very young' (another bold jettisoning of one of the most famous opening lines in the history of prose fiction) and the credits roll over a backdrop of unrelieved red, to the accompaniment of the swelling, romantic theme music. To those who know the book, it is easily apparent that this represents the episode in the Red Room, but it is not actually named as such in the film; instead, the emphasis is less on any psychological implications or supernatural resonances of Jane's sufferings than, in keeping with the child-abuse perspective, the viciousness, unjustness and physical violence with which she is treated by the children and Mrs Reed alike. We also see that the Reed house, although large, is bleak and unadorned, while the film is totally faithful to the novel in its presentation of Mr Brocklehurst, who, being lit from behind, does indeed look like a black pillar, and appears almost as sinister to the viewer as he does to Jane in the book.

Mr Brocklehurst removes Jane from the house with the Red Room in it and takes her to a blue world. All the tones at Lowood are cold and muted, signifying both its literal chilliness and its emotional coldness, and this is a phenomenon particularly marked on the night of Helen Burns's death, when snow falls outside and all the events are seen in a harsh, cold, blue light. As well as signalling the coldest and wintriest moment of all Jane's life at Lowood, however, this intense blue also marks the moment when we realise that she will remain unconquered by it. Earlier, Mr Brocklehurst has threatened her with hell; this harshly dominating blue is, at least, the antithesis of that, and indeed can, coupled with the snow, be read as emblematising not only cold but purity and cleansing too. Moreover, Helen's death also becomes, in the visual logic of the film, the catalyst for change and growth in Jane, for when she rises from her friend's grave not only has the film's palette changed to brighter, fresher colours but Anna Paquin, the young Jane, has been replaced by Charlotte Gainsbourg, the older one. In the same shot, we see the first flowers of the film: for Jane, spring has come at last, as is further emphasised by the kindness and cordiality with which Mrs Fairfax (Joan Plowright) welcomes her to Thornfield, and the very great contrast which is quickly marked between the cruelties of her own childhood and the sympathy and care offered to Adèle.

This regeneration allows the image-pattern to insist implicitly that the cold of blue is not merely a contrast to the passion of red, but may also represent a value in itself. Blue light begins to dominate again when Jane awakes immediately before Bertha's attempt to burn Mr Rochester in his bed. When she and he have extinguished the fire by throwing water on it and the red of the flames has thus disappeared, the light reverts to a strong blue, although there is also red on Jane's hands from the thorns on the roses, which she had picked up so that she could throw the water from their vase on the fire. The obvious symbolism of all this underscores very clearly that restraint, too, may have its charms, as well as passion. Though Jane may be shivering with cold, and though we may feel that all the signals in this scene call for it to end with a kiss, the chill blue light of purity holds its own strongly against the red of blood and fire. While the film's careful downplaying of Bertha's racial identity suggests that it may have been reluctant to explore any issues of blackness and whiteness, redness and blueness will, it seems, do quite as well to demarcate an absolute opposition between Jane and Bertha, without carrying any awkward racial connotations.

The pattern of red/blue opposition is continued with the introduction of Blanche Ingram, who, perhaps in a further attempt to avoid any suggestion of the wholesale demonisation of dark women, is here presented as a blonde. The overall impression of the drawing-room, with Blanche standing spectacularly at its heart, is of a glowing red; marginalised in a corner, Jane sits alone on a sofa, wearing blue. In the book, the first hint that Mr Rochester's sight is returning comes when he asks whether Jane is wearing a blue dress, and although that question is omitted from the film, blue is strongly marked as Jane's colour. Alone on the stairs with Mr Rochester, she is seen in a blue light, which darkens virtually to black as she is called on to help care for Mason, a scene during which, in a neat analogue for Jane's inability fully to understand events, we see only by glimmerings. Later, when she and Mr Rochester first embrace, the camera picks out the blue of her cuff, and although after the interruption of the wedding Mr Rochester says that Jane is 'at the mouth of Hell', we remain confident that she will not actually enter it when she flees Thornfield wearing blue. Moreover, the colour serves also to complete the presentation of systematic contrasts between her and Bertha, whom we see immediately afterwards first setting fire to Jane's wedding dress and then jumping into the stairwell as though she were indeed plunging into Hell. Jane wears blue again when she recovers, both when she hears Mr Rochester calling her and again slightly later when she receives St John Rivers's proposal, and she is in blue yet again when she returns to Thornfield (here, in line with the overall muting, merely charred, and thus still habitable, rather than burned to the ground). Having steered a safe course between the extremes of temperature and passion, Jane Eyre can be happy at last, and as she and Mr Rochester stand together in the meadow by the river (echoing the Reeds and Rivers imagery of the original novel), the growth and springtime promised as Jane rose from Helen's grave have finally blossomed into summer.

If Zeffirelli's *Jane Eyre* has affiliations with *Persuasion*, Young's version comes closer to Giles Foster's 1986 *Northanger Abbey*, since it is constantly suggested that what the heroine encounters in the various ancient mansions she inhabits may be the product of her imagination. The Young adaptation has one main interest – the psychological – and one dominant characteristic – heavy-handedness. Sadly, the two all too often occur in conjunction.

In many ways, the similarities between the Zeffirelli and the Young versions are striking; indeed, they even both have 'Jane Eyre' written in virtually identical cursive script on the tape cases. Once again, we see Jane being dragged to the Red Room before the opening credits have finished rolling, and here, too, we have no idea what she has done to deserve it; once again, Mr Brocklehurst is introduced immediately afterwards, and is again lit from behind; once again, the shift from the child Jane to the adult comes immediately after Helen's death, with Samantha Morton looking up from a pencil drawing of Helen. Helen herself, however, is much less securely defined in this version than in the Zeffirelli, appearing only briefly, and her death also registers less forcibly with the viewer, since it has been preceded by the sight of a girl of not dissimilar appearance dead of typhus, and lying in a coffin. Indeed the whole nature of Lowood is less deftly characterised here: though Jane in voiceover *tells* us that it is a terrible place, what we actually *see* is first the kindly face of Miss Temple, and then Jane talking earnestly with Helen. This is of course a marked departure from the novel, where the first-person narration means that we have no external viewpoint to compare with Jane's own. Even the standing-on-a-stool episode has less impact than in the Zeffirelli film since it features not as Jane's cruel and arbitrary introduction to Lowood but, as in the book, as a response to her dropping her slate and disrupting the introduction of Mr Brocklehurst's wife and daughters. Mr Brocklehurst's action is still not reasonable, but it comes closer to being so, and there is no hint here of the gratuitous cruelty of the shorn hair.

The voiceover which gives us Jane's reaction to Lowood is a persistent feature of the adaptation, even at moments of tension such as when Mr Rochester first hints about his feelings for her. Unfortunately, it is an oddly distracting device, for two principal reasons. In the first place, Samantha Morton's pronunciation is horrific: her renditions of 'meagre' and 'vulnerable' grate almost as much as her later appalling French, or as the hopelessly gung-ho St John's declaration that 'I didn't wanna distract you'. In the second place, the adaptation is all too apt to use the words to do the work which film more usually accords to images, for although it does at times share something of the red/blue patterning of the Zeffirelli film, with the red of the first fire contrasting with the blue light playing over the sleeping Jane, it has no consistent visual effects (and no hinting at a possible race issue – Bertha is just a white woman with greying black ringlets). Even the use of the red/blue contrast is undercut by the emphasis on the diegetic lighting provided by the insistent use of candles, which, in accordance with the suggestion of dreams, directs our attention to the characters' own limited perspectives rather than to the overarching directorial one.

Perhaps its best trick is to flirt with blurring our perspective with Jane's own, which is done to considerable effect on two notable occasions. When Bessie enters the Red Room, we see her first from under the bed, where Jane lies asleep. Much later, our first view of St John again presents him as we would see him if we shared the viewpoint of Jane, who is lying on the bed, once more asleep. What is particularly interesting about these shots is that both are taken from Jane's perspective, yet each time she is asleep. Technically, she ought thus to be unable to have a perspective at all, since her eyes are closed and her senses, literally, dormant; the effect is, therefore, to figure what we see as effectively a product of Jane's unconscious mind, her dream-state. The same thing is, moreover, suggested on many other occasions. It is first seen when Jane is locked into the Red Room. Though the room is not even, in this adaptation, particularly red, it nevertheless has an extraordinary effect on Jane's psyche: we hear weird wailings and we see a corpse in the bed, but we are insistently aware that these may be products of Jane's imagination rather than of reality. There is a marked difference here from the Stevenson film, where we see a door rattling and are also shown some scenes at which Jane is not present, leaving us in no doubt of their external reality. We are not, though, consequently asked by the Young version to judge Jane as neurotic, for subsequent events make it plain that she does indeed live in a world where strange things may happen. Though the Reeds are externally a much more secure and comfortable family than in Zeffirelli's version, with an elegant house and luxurious clothes, Mrs Reed verges so closely on the unbalanced and hysterical that even Mr Brocklehurst visibly registers the oddity of her behaviour.

This offers a considerable contrast with the grim, angular psychology of Fiona Shaw's Mrs Reed in the Zeffirelli version, and the difference is accentuated by the fact that we do not see Mrs Reed again. The suggestion of the uncontrolled in Mrs Reed's behaviour is, moreover, echoed by the sinister demeanour of Mrs Fairfax outside the locked door to the West Wing; whereas Joan Plowright in the Zeffirelli version looks a model of solid respectability who finds the whole attic business exceedingly distasteful, Gemma Jones hovers behind Jane like some noiseless supernatural creature.

The character who suffers most from this lack of subtlety is undoubtedly Mr Rochester. Like William Hurt, he gets top billing, and is thus obviously considered to be the adaptation's major attraction, and yet it seems hardly to know what to do with him. The case of the video version refers to him as 'Mr Rochester (CIARAN HINDS – *Ivanhoe, Cold Lazarus, Persuasion*), an impenetrable man with a mysterious past and harsh manner'. This is a definition which comprehensively undoes itself, for the Mr Rochester thus introduced to us is, in one sense, not a man with a mysterious past at all, but one whose history we are explicitly invited to track in terms of the most relevant and notable achievements on his CV. This lack of clarity is symptomatic of the presentation of Mr Rochester throughout the adaptation. Our initial introduction to him figures him, like so much else in the adaptation, as essentially the product of Jane Eyre's imagination: she has just been saying that Thornfield is too tranquil when we suddenly see her standing beside a waterfall, in a storm, and with Mr Rochester thundering towards her on his horse. The accident, too, is much more dramatic than in the Zeffirelli version, with echoes of Willoughby's first introduction to Marianne in Ang Lee's 1996 *Sense and Sensibility*.

Even less Brontë-esque is the language of this adaptation. 'Edward, you said you were going to let Grace Poole go,' says Jane, as no nineteenth-century woman ever could have done, before breathing piously, like a modern tabloid reporter, 'Surely it's only a matter of time before a tragedy occurs.' This use of neologism finds its darkest hour in the psychobabble which both Rochester and Jane start to spout after Mason's interruption of the wedding, beginning with the former's explanation that 'I tried the best doctors; I sought alternative methods'. (Aromatherapy? Reflexology?) He rants to Jane, 'You were never in love with me ... You're no better than Blanche Ingram ... I thought you were mature' (a good slur coming from a man who has just thrown her bags downstairs). Jane quickly proves herself equally fluent in New Age self-discovery-speak, riposting that '[y]ou led me to believe you were one person but you are really another'.

They are even more of the twentieth century than of the nineteenth in their frank discussion of sex. Rochester pants, 'You want me – I can feel your passions are aroused – Say you want me! Say it!' What Jane actually says, though, is, 'How can I lie with you knowing that I am not your wife?', adding in the true spirit of an advert for L'Oréal that 'I am worth more than that.' To this he, reverting to psychobabble, angrily responds, 'Do you think what we have is nothing?' And an even more egregious instance of such language occurs when Jane returns after the fire (of which, as in the novel, we have had no prior notice) and, finding Mr Rochester blind, soothingly tells him that, 'You are not your wounds.' Actually, blindness is probably grist to her mill; she is quite likely disappointed that here, as in the Zeffirelli, his hand is not damaged too. Virtually the only thing here which is in the spirit of the original is that Mr Rochester still bullies and hectors her.

Though Jane may sound like the veteran of some depressingly formulaic counselling, she does retain a surprising amount of her original grit – in some ways, indeed, more so than in the Zeffirelli adaptation. Though she recoils from the religion of Mr Brocklehurst, she tells Mr Rochester that she has 'studied the Bible since and found my own faith in the Lord'. Here, she sounds a genuinely nineteenth-century note, as she does again later when she lists her accomplishments for him because 'it's a fact'. Unlike the Zeffirelli, this adaptation also retains Jane's postbetrothal independence of mind on the subject of clothes and presents, and, again unlike the Zeffirelli, we have glimpses of Jane's suffering and endurance on the moors, of her teaching career, of her attempts to learn German, and of her serious entertainment of St John's proposal of marriage and a joint missionary career. The only counter-indications are that here, unlike the Zeffirelli, she gains neither fortune nor family: the Rivers family are not revealed to be related to her, nor does she inherit money from a long-lost uncle. But then, we are in any case less aware of a prevalence of fragmented families: Mr Rochester here is warm towards Adèle, whom he affectionately *tutoies*, and the presence of Bessie joins with a less powerless Miss Temple to make us feel Jane's own orphaned state less poignantly.

If the Jane of this adaptation has a better developed sense of her own ego, however, she also unquestionably has a more pronounced id. Though she has not, in this version, cut her hand on the roses, she nevertheless has a sudden horror of giving it to Mr Rochester, and shivers uncontrollably. As in the Zeffirelli, she is lit in blue at this point; she also wears a blue dress the next day, and is bathed in blue light once again when she hears the noises of Bertha's attack on Mason. At first, those noises sound like her heartbeat, and this suggestion that we are in the Gothic realm of the unconscious is further reinforced when Mason exclaims that, 'She sucked the blood from my shoulder like a vampire', while Jane's horror is clearly signalled when she hides behind the door as Grace Poole enters to check on Mason. All in all, the treatment of the whole episode thus hints strongly that we may, on one level, see these events as rooted in Jane's subconscious.

This is even more true of the proposal scene, in which Ciaran Hinds exhibits a roughness quite alien to William Hurt's 1990s Man, and we then cut to Jane asleep, as though the scene had been her dream rather than reality – as indeed she says she fears. The same technique is applied to the tearing of the veil: Jane stares sleepily as it is ripped, and we cut straight to Mr Rochester saying 'must have been a dream, Jane', which posits for Jane a psyche strikingly similar to that of the Clarissa in Robert Bierman's 1991 BBC adaptation, who dreamed of Lovelace cutting through her veil. Even Mr Rochester thinks he may be dreaming when he hears Jane's voice in his blindness. In choosing how to plot the fine line which the novel treads between realism and Gothic, this adaptation has clearly veered towards the Gothic, but it has done so unsystematically and without understanding that the Gothic works best when it has something to suggest, rather than as a mechanical device used in isolation and in the absence of any compelling psychological or visual agenda.

These two adaptations, then, encapsulate virtually opposite approaches to the issues of adapting a classic text for screen. The Zeffirelli exemplifies the idea that a text can be changed and updated if the reshaping is performed in the context of a coherent guiding project; it offers a *Jane Eyre* retold to address the concerns of the 1990s, an age ridden with guilt and fear about its children, and it controls both its retelling and audience response through a strongly developed visual pattern which substitutes well for the novel's manipulative tools of tone and pace. Above all, it understands that a classic was not always a classic; once it was new, and *urgent*, and in order to feel the full flavour of its power, it needs to be made so again, which is what Zeffirelli does with his use of big names such as Elle Macpherson and William Hurt who are strongly associated with highly contemporary cultural forms, and by his tapping into distinctively 1990s concerns.

The Young adaptation, on the other hand, illustrates the dangers of treating a classic text merely *as* classic. Moreover, the novel suffers from being treated not only as a classic but as a celebrated romance, for where the Young adaptation does update, as in its use of the currently popular language of feeling, it does so not in the realm of issues but of emotions, which are presumably conceived of as timeless, transcending culture, with *Jane Eyre* merely as a particularly good repository of them. Since our own culture allows for more heightened expression of emotion and of sexual feeling, the language of passion is consequently injected into the story, presumably on the assumption that it had been latently there all the time and that to allow it be more fully heard is indeed to do the book a favour. But for those who do believe in the shaping influence of cultures on psyches, what the Young adaptation thus offers tells us neither about the Brontës' society nor about our own. Though the Zeffirelli may jettison significant original parts of the novel, it does at least offer new and reshaped concerns to replace them, but the Young version appears to think that a classic is merely something old, and dead.

Notes

1. Ace Pilkington, 'Zeffirelli's Shakespeare' in Anthony Davies and Stanley Wells (eds), *Shakespeare and the Moving Image* (Cambridge: Cambridge University Press, 1994), p. 164.
2. The Young version also has only one Rivers sister, but here it is Mary who is cut and Diana who remains.
3. While attending school in Belgium, Charlotte had fallen unhappily in love with her teacher.

4

Transcultural Aesthetics and the Film Adaptations of Henry James

Martin Halliwell

The recent emergence of a number of cinematic adaptations of Henry James's novels – *The Portrait of a Lady* (Jane Campion, 1996), *The Wings of the Dove* (Iain Softley, 1997), *The American* (Paul Unwin, 1998) and *Washington Square* (Agnieszka Holland, 1998) and forthcoming *The Golden Bowl* (James Ivory, 2000) – provides an interesting focus for addressing a series of cultural issues concerning the status of national cinema, the vogue for literary or 'heritage' adaptations and the place of James's nineteenth-century transatlantic imagination in late twentieth-century culture. All of these Jamesian films, together with earlier adaptations, such as *The Heiress* (William Wyler, 1949) and *The Innocents* (Jack Clayton, 1961),[1] could be labelled 'costume dramas' in their attention to period dress and use of realistic *mise-en-scène*, but, as Stella Bruzzi argues, this umbrella term, deployed by Andrew Higson in relation to 'heritage cinema', does a great injustice to the stylistic differences between such films, ignoring their historical content and emphasising the cinematic pleasures of literary spectacle.[2]

James's status as a 'classic' writer was first established in the inter-war period and consolidated in 1948 by F.R. Leavis, who included James in his 'Great Tradition' of writers whose work displays their awareness of the 'possibilities of life' and helps to 'change the possibilities of art for practitioners and readers'.[3] Although his analysis of James's writing rarely rises above the level of admiration, what Leavis describes as the mixture of 'serious art' and 'overt attractions' corresponds to Philip Horne's claim that James is 'the current classic literary adaptee of choice for the English-speaking film world'.[4]

Although there are marked similarities between the recent Jamesian films and the adaptations of E.M. Forster's and Jane Austen's fiction in the 1980s and early 1990s – what Higson calls 'middle-class quality products, somewhere between the art house and the mainstream' – most of the adaptations of James's transatlantic work clearly cannot fit with the notions of English heritage which Higson argues are central to the audience appeal of British costume dramas.[5] Forster's and Austen's fictions most often represent a 'fragment of England',[6] whereas James is more interested in the clash between three cultures: English, European (most often French and Italian) and American. James explored this triangular relationship throughout his writing and, although he leaned increasingly towards Europe, as a writer of international fiction, he did not fully reject either American or European culture as he continued to explore their relationship with, and dependency upon, each other.[7]

The simplistic equations of American innocence and European experience often attributed to James do not account for the complex gradings of his literary symbolism. Indeed, in 'The Art of Fiction' (1884), James asserted that 'the successful application of any art is a delightful spectacle', but he also suspects that 'there has never been a genuine success that has not a latent core of conviction.'[8] This combination of 'spectacle' and 'conviction' is lost in the rhetoric of the 'costume drama', a term which this chapter rejects in favour of 'transcultural aesthetic' for defining both James's fiction and the recent adaptations of it. The term 'transcultural' is most often located in postcolonial studies as a means for describing both the encounter with new cultures (acculturation) and the gradual loss of old bearings (deculturation). For the critic Nicholas Mirzoeff, transcultural studies offer a way of analysing 'the hybrid, syncretic global diaspora in which we live'.[9] But, rather than locating transcultural identities squarely within postmodern parameters, James's fiction explores the problematic site of transatlantic exchange in the late nineteenth and early twentieth centuries, when American writers were beginning to reassess the complex relationship between the New and Old Worlds.

In order to develop these ideas, this chapter addresses the way in which three recent film adaptations explore and develop James's transcultural aesthetics: firstly, by focusing on the destabilisation of national identity and, secondly, by interrogating the status of characters who are uncertain and, at times, paralysed in the face of historical change. The three films deal with the abrasive clash between European and American cultures and together bridge James's output of inter-national fiction produced over three decades: *The American* (1877), *The Portrait of a Lady* (1881), and *The Wings of the Dove* (1902).[10] The adaptations of these three novels are reasonably faithful in terms of plot and characterisation, but highlight particular features of the texts: *The American* is adapted into a Gothic melodrama; *The Portrait of a Lady* develops a cinematic version of the transcultural travelogue; and *The Wings of the Dove* offers a film noir plot at the expense of some of James's psychological detail.[11] Despite these directorial decisions, the screenplays cohere to James's literary project (which, of course, had 'not one window, but a million') by stimulating what Brian McFarlane describes as 'the viewer's memory of the original text without doing violence to it'.[12]

In his recent book on *British Cinema in the 1980s* (1999), John Hill surveys the rise of British heritage drama 'as an important economic activity and a significant part of the new "enterprise" culture' during the Thatcher years.[13] In the respect that British heritage films tend to portray nineteenth-century culture as a historical phase of relative stability, James's genteel fictions share with other literary adaptations a 'fascination with the past and the role that this plays in relation to the present'.[14] But, rather than seeking comfort in nostalgia, where the past is treated as a 'refuge', and in con-tradistinction to Higson's claim that costume dramas tend to result in 'museum' or 'showcase' pieces, this essay argues that by emphasising certain aspects of James's aesthetics the recent adaptations preserve a critical vantage point to deal with such current cultural issues as historicity, nationhood and gender politics.[15] Hill claims that the heritage film is actually a much wider international phenomenon than Higson credits, but he admits that it is difficult to defend the films from the charge that they are little more than symptoms of postmodernist 'hyper-history', in which the past becomes a shallow filmic simulacrum.[16] However, in the later phase (the mid- to late 1990s), rather than delighting only in their own spectacle, post-heritage films – of which I argue the Jamesian adaptations are examples – can be viewed less as symptoms of the collapse of historical meta-narratives and more as critical interventions into the problems of historical authorship, in much the same way that James was concerned with developing his fiction further than the constraints of nineteenth-century historiography.[17] For these reasons, here I will argue that, while the current crop of Jamesian adaptations buy into the heritage label as part of their marketing strategy and, on the whole, replicate what Ginette Vincendeau calls a 'classical European film style', they emerge as self-conscious explorations of the constraints of the heritage film, both in terms of their international subject matter and their tangible, yet shifting, preoccupation with transcultural aesthetics.[18]

In *Women Intellectuals, Modernism and Difference* (1997), Alice Gambrell describes one of the defining features of transatlantic modernism as an 'insider–outsider activity', which consists of a 'simultaneous distance from and intimacy with the subjects of their own inquiry'.[19] While Gambrell uses the 'insider–outsider activity' to discuss the generation of early twentieth-century female intellectuals, this notion of cultural traffic is particular apposite for considering a range of American modernists in Europe: from Henry James and James Whistler in the late nineteenth century to Gertrude Stein and Ernest Hemingway in the 1910s and 20s. The transatlantic journey was not a simple one-way affair for any of these artists (even though Stein chose not to return to America to live), but provided a fluid symbolic site to investigate the complex interaction between European and American culture. The notion of 'familiar strangeness',[20] which Gambrell appropriates from the Harlem Renaissance writer Zora Neale Hurston, characterises the work of all these artists as a simultaneous intimacy with, and distance from, a single cultural perspective. Iain Chambers extends this analysis of cultural traffic in *Migrancy, Culture, Identity* (1994) in his argument that the displacement of ideas in modernity creates a geographical and figurative zone of 'transit' which not only disables the symbolic trajectory of the journey, but makes 'completing the story', or the final homecoming, 'an impossibility'.[21] Deploying similar language to Gambrell, Chambers argues:

> to come from elsewhere, from 'there' and not 'here', and hence to be simultaneously 'inside' and 'outside' the situation at hand, is to live at the intersections of histories and memories, experiencing both their preliminary dispersal and their subsequent translation into new, more extensive, arrangements among emerging routes.[22]

Such themes of transit, cultural translation and the relocation of the journey are central to modernist aesthetics – suggesting that space is as important as time for defining the philosophical subtext of American modernism – by inscribing what Gambrell calls the 'insider–outsider' complex and what Chambers calls the 'drama of the stranger' as central to understanding both James's fiction and the way in which the recent Jamesian films circumvent the common alignment of heritage with the perspective of the insider, the collapse of 'real' history and stories of parochial homeliness.[23] In the same vein, the critic Kelly Cannon argues that James's fictions are full of 'in-between' characters who 'must learn both the limitations and the potential' of their habitat.[24] On this model, Jamesian narratives exploit what Paul Gilroy has defined as the symbolic fluidity of the Atlantic (and the Pacific, in the case of the New Zealand director Jane Campion's *The Portrait of a Lady*) as a space of cultural multiplicity, simultaneously a place of expanding possibilities and a zone of threat and strangeness: a place of fictional 'wandering between geographical, sexual, and ideological worlds'.[25] As I will argue, the recent Jamesian adaptations develop strains of cultural and historical ambivalence in order to re-emphasise the quality of James's aesthetics from the shifting and, in retrospect, 'classic' experience of modernity.

The American

In his Preface to *The American* (1907) James describes the tale as an 'arch-romance', in which Christopher Newman, an eligible and self-made American, who has acquired his fortune in speculation (described by James's narrator as 'an intensely Western story'), desires to find a wife during his sojourn in Paris in the late 1860s.[26] Although Newman (as his name suggests) acts as an innocent check to the corrupt machinations of the aristocratic Bellegardes – in the mode of Herman Melville's 'Benito Cereno' (1856) and Mark Twain's *Innocents Abroad* (1869) – he is the victim of the narrator's subtle criticism, in this case, of the American inability to value art as anything other than the target of material acquisitiveness. Newman's first word in the novel is '*Combien?*' (p. 8), which not only 'constituted the strength of his French vocabulary' (pp. 7–8) but, for Virginia Fowler, helps to establish his 'aggressive and wholly materialistic masculinity'.[27] Whilst Newman's materialism is undeniable, Fowler's comment that America has been 'blighted and destroyed' by the wilfulness of this kind of 'masculine energy' is borne out neither in James's novel nor in Paul Unwin's 1998 adaptation of it.[28] Like the novel, a combination of self-confidence, 'aesthetic verdancy' and ignorance of social customs best describes Newman's attitude to Parisian culture in the film. Nevertheless, Newman (Matthew Modine) is certainly an opportunist: his courtship of Claire de Cintré (Aisling O'Sullivan) is forceful and, on discovering a 'beautiful Gothic tower' in Brussels whilst on tour in Central Europe (a sequence omitted from the film), he 'wondered whether it would not be possible to "get up" something like it in San Francisco' (p. 55; p. 58). In the film version, Newman's character is established primarily in his relation to the Tristrams, an American couple who have largely assimilated into Parisian life, Noémie, a hack painter, and her father, M. Nioche. Newman is comfortable in business matters – he feels 'rich in the possession' (p. 43) of a second-rate Madonna painted by Noémie – but he is uncertain about what is expected of him by French society and bored with genteel niceties. However, the novel goes further than this depiction of cultural contrasts. Whilst on tour, Newman meets a young New Englander, Benjamin Babcock, who is deeply appreciative of European culture and is critical of Newman's Western devotion to 'the pleasures of the hour' and his ignorance of 'the immense seriousness of Art' (pp. 64–5).

James's narrative establishes itself very quickly as a comedy of manners, with Newman and the Bellegardes being representative types of the naïve American abroad and the corrupt European aristocracy, whereas Unwin's film begins with a much darker Gothic episode in a scene depicting the death of M. Bellegarde and the deliverance of their daughter Claire by Bellegarde's wife (Diana Rigg) to the grotesque M. de Cintré. The lyrical music and tapestried curtains in the title sequence do little to hide a seething concoction of denied wishes and 'abominable acts'.[29] Although the motives behind these deeds are not made clear until much later, the opening mood pervades the whole film, in contrast to the slow darkening of James's narrative. The spirit of freedom which Newman embodies in the first section of the narrative – the freedom to travel and to 'complete himself' (p. 106) by choosing a wife – is replaced in the film adaptation by the claustrophobic interiors and psychic confines of the Bellegarde estate. The gloom of the opening foreshadows Newman's doomed courtship of Claire de Cintré, whereas, in the novel, the narrator gently conveys Newman's first 'unusual, unexpected sense of having wandered into a strange corner of the world', even though he was 'not given … to anticipating danger, or forecasting disaster' (p. 74). Indeed, James's mediating narrator, who constantly hovers on the edge of irony, is crucial in exposing Newman's social naïveté and cultural myopia, whereas the film, lacking recourse to narrative viewpoint, has to rely much more on establishing a mood which conflicts with his childlike optimism and self-serving obstinacy. In James's *The American*, the ambivalence of 'insider–outsider activity' is crystallised in the shifting narrative voice: an intermediary zone distinct to literary fiction, for which the film director must devise a cinematic equivalent. On this issue, Unwin's *The American* shares a reliance upon the juxtaposition of mood, setting and character perspective with, for example, Martin Scorsese's adaptation of Edith Wharton's *The Age of Innocence* (1993) and Christopher Hampton's version of Joseph Conrad's *The Secret Agent* (1996), in order to convey something of the dramatic and verbal ironies of the respective novels.[30]

Of the three adaptations considered here, Unwin's *The American* is the least successful in finding a mode of presentation which replicates the narrative tone of James's novel. Nevertheless, one way in which the film creates a comparable zone of 'in-betweenness' is by focusing as much on the personality differences and growing fraternal relationship between Newman and the young Valentin de Bellegarde (Andrew Scott) as it does on his love match with Claire. Valentin and Newman are symbolic counterparts who cast each other into structural relief, particularly as regards their relationships with Noémie Nioche. Both men share an interest in Noémie but, whereas the novel only implies a fleeting engagement between Newman and the painter, the film depicts a number of sexual liaisons between the two (of which Newman soon tires), followed by a passionate relationship between Valentin and Noémie (mirroring the cross-class courtship of Newman and Claire). In contrast to Newman's respect only for monetary value, Valentin appreciates Noémie from an aesthetic perspective 'as he would have listened to a piece of music', even though the reader is told that he was just practising 'good manners' (p. 132). Valentin also acts as the go-between for Newman and Claire: at one point he 'stood looking from his sister to our hero' as a cultural and symbolic mediator between the two (p. 170). Valentin's complex mixture of wit and direct emotion, aristocratic *ennui* and passionate confrontation, European '*raffiné*' and attraction to American mercantilism are conflicting qualities which provide dramatic counterpoints to the trajectory of Newman's story.[31] Moreover, the duel between Valentin and M. Kapp over Noémie, leading to the young Bellegarde's death in Geneva, is described as a 'wretched theatrical affair', in which Valentin's recognition of his 'mock-heroism' (p. 216; p. 210) contrasts favourably with Newman's own sense of heroic importance as he attempts to force the hand of the Bellegardes over his designs to marry Claire.

Before he dies, Valentin mentions the Bellegarde secret to Newman: a story from the past which is elaborated upon by the servant Mrs Bread, who is another symbolic mediator as a working-class Englishwoman. Newman's realisation that M. de Bellegarde has been the victim of a murder conspiracy between his wife and the elder son, Henri, because he forbade the marriage of Claire to the noble, but morally wretched, M. de Cintré, provides a 'thunderbolt' (p. 273) to avenge himself against the family after they close their doors to him and Claire retreats to a convent. Most interestingly, the history of the incident is not told as authentic fact, but explicitly in terms of storytelling: the lowly Mrs Bread is described as 'the most artistic of romancers'; whilst he is listening Newman 'made a movement as if he were turning over the page of a novel'; and the note written by M. de Bellegarde before his death has to be translated before the truth is laid bare (p. 281). Whereas in the novel Newman discloses his knowledge of the deed to the Bellegarde conspirators and then travels to Britain and America before returning to Paris, in the film he humbles Madame de Bellegarde and then prepares to leave with Claire, before Henri ruins his plans by maliciously telling his sister of the circumstances of her first marriage. Nevertheless, the film also ends with storytelling: after Claire has shorn off her hair and vows to stay in the convent, the final scene presents the two lovers parting with Claire's promise that she will remain with Newman spiritually as he rides across the prairies and dances on Independence Day.

Although it seems that Newman will publicly expose the Bellegarde secret and then fulfil his desires, neither film nor novel ends with a satisfactory denouement: Claire has also been poisoned by her realisation of the past and Newman feels 'like a widower' (p. 307) without ever having taken a wife, suggesting a moral scarring ('a stubborn ghost', p. 319) which denies the narrative healing of closure. As such, the visual memories of the Bellegardes cloud Newman's future-oriented vision at the close of the film, but to what extent the viewer must guess. Similarly, as Newman burns the paper which M. de Bellegarde wrote on his death bed, the ambiguity of the final sentence of the novel – 'Newman instinctively turned to see if the little paper was in fact consumed; but there was nothing left of it' (p. 325) – problematises the nature of 'consumption' and whether, in fact, the paper has actually disappeared, perhaps to emerge in another story. Indeed, Newman's increasing sense of strangeness – on returning to America in the novel he feels disturbed as the story 'murmured in his ears and hovered perpetually before his eyes' (p. 319) – prohibits any final homecoming which this 'arch-romance' may at first have promised. Like many 1940s literary adaptations, such as David Lean's *Great Expectations* (1946), Unwin's *The American* deploys Gothic elements not only to amplify the psychological drama of the central characters, but also to problematise the past as purely a site of nostalgic spectacle for the viewer. In this sense, in both the novel and film version of *The American*, the intertwining of personal and national histories transmutes into a complicated transcultural story which the reader/viewer realises cannot be told straight, nor concluded satisfactorily.

The Portrait of a Lady

The transatlantic trajectory of Unwin's *The American* works both in terms of content and production: sponsored by Investment Incentives and the Government of Ireland for the Irish Film Industry, the BBC and WGBH Boston, the film was shot in Ireland (to lower costs) and contains a mixture of British and American actors. Jane Campion's stylish adaptation of *The Portrait of a Lady* (1996) also shares a transcontinental perspective: both she and the screenwriter, Laura Jones, are Australasian (collaborating previously on the Australian film *An Angel at My Table* (1990), an adaptation of Janet Frame's autobiography); finance and production came from Polygram in America; and the film uses a combination of British, American, European actors and, in the case of Nicole Kidman who plays Isabel Archer, a Hollywood star with an Australian background. In her preface to the screenplay, Laura Jones discusses how the genesis of the film began as a personal venture between Campion and herself: 'Jane and I talked about why we loved the novel ... I remember our working our way toward understanding Isabel, not only in her world, but for us in our own pasts and in our understanding of what it is like to be a girl like Isabel, in any time.'[32] The homology between the trans-Pacific and trans-Atlantic experience is emphasised in the opening sequence of the film in which the viewer is visually presented with a group of Australian teenagers 'on the brink of their lives' dancing in a wooded glade who are, paradoxically, both within a twentieth-century history of female solidarity and outside history in a mythic cinematic space.[33] Isabel Archer is thus established as a prototype of modern 'independent' womanhood, both real and fictional: a bridge between the experimental modernist artist 'with delicate, desultory, flamelike' spirit and a late twentieth-century global sisterhood.[34] The opening and Jones's commentary lend the film a contemporary cultural agenda, but also problematise the realistic geographical scenes of the story. Behind the façades of Florence and Rome are other unrepresented places, complicating the visual spectacle of the costume drama and inviting the viewer to ask whose heritage is being explored.

One of the female voices in the opening sequence speaks of 'finding a mirror … the most loyal mirror', with which to articulate her desires and emerging sexual identity. On this level, rather than seeking absolute verisimilitude or slavish conformity to the flow of James's narrative, Campion develops a more flexible filmic aesthetic: the cinematic mirror fluctuates between realistic depiction, the interior mirrors of Isabel's own fantasies, and the exterior mirror of cultural travel. Yet this aesthetic is, in itself, intensely Jamesian; as James states in his Preface to the novel, 'the interest was to be raised to its pitch and yet the elements to be kept in their key; so that … I might show what an "exciting" inward life may do for the person leading it even while it remains perfectly normal'.[35] Although the film compresses the first 100 pages, the screenplay is not only faithful to the visual moods and nuances of James's narrative, but actually quotes him directly in order to set scenes and to introduce characters, reinforcing Ken Gelder's argument that here film and fiction are inextricably intertwined.[36]

Developing the spirit of James's narrator, the film periodically disturbs the viewer's critical perspective, provoking as many questions about the art of fiction as it does about the themes of cultural difference and gender identity. For example, after the titles have dissolved, the camera presents a close-up of Isabel's face, so close that we see her facial blemishes and bloodshot eyes, which are red from crying as the result of Lord Warburton's (Richard E. Grant) proposal.[37] Rather than providing an aesthetic distance to frame Isabel's portrait (which is the usual mode of presentation for costume dramas), the viewer is disturbed by the intense close-up of Isabel's face, which, in terms of portraiture, would have more in common with James Whistler than John Singer Sargent. Although the film deploys such lingering shots sparingly to establish a realistic story of a young American woman in Britain who is left a legacy by her uncle, Daniel Touchett (John Gielgud), so that she may begin her adulthood 'by getting a general impression of life', this post-heritage film returns to unexpected or fantastical images that disturb the realistic frame of the film.[38] As James argues in his Preface, it is precisely the 'disposition to reflect and project' which makes a certain kind of art 'appear more true to its character in proportion as it strains, or tends to burst, with a latent extravagance, its mould'.[39]

There are significant parallels between Christopher Newman and Isabel Archer as young Americans abroad with an, at times, inflated sense of their own self-importance, but, whereas Valentin is established as the major 'in-between' character in *The American*, Isabel acts as the barometer by which the other characters' emotions and designs can be assessed. The opening phase of the novel and the film establishes three suitors: the aristocratic Lord Warburton, the sick cousin Ralph Touchett (Martin Donovan), who engineers his father's legacy so that Isabel may meet 'the requirements of her imagination', and Caspar Goodwood (Viggo Mortensen), the enigmatic American, who periodically returns to remind Isabel of her national past.[40] While Isabel is largely a representative type like Newman, she is no 'model' of virtue (by her own admission) and possesses an imaginative exuberance and depth of character which distinguish her from her fictional predecessors: her thoughts are described as 'a tangle of vague outlines' and her opinions 'had led her into a thousand ridiculous zigzags'.[41] This inner life is dramatised early in the film in a fantasy sequence in which she imagines being caressed on her bed by all three suitors: a scene which recalls the sexuality of the Australian girls in the opening sequence. Although there is no equivalent to this scene in the novel, the interiority of such sequences goes some way to replicating James's narrative style which hovers between realistic description and probing psychodrama. Campion and Jones not only adopt a similar cinematic aesthetic, but develop one of James's chief themes: the opposition between the static portrait which most of Isabel's male suitors would make of her – especially the malevolent Gilbert Osmond (John Malkovich) who wishes to transform Isabel into an art object – and the dynamic inner portrait of Isabel which continues to 'burst its mould', even when she is forced to wear the mask of the 'lady'.

The section of the film which most obviously brings together the twin themes of travel and identity is the bridging travelogue section (entitled 'My Journey, 1873'), which occurs immediately after Isabel has been seduced by Osmond in Florence (in a joint plan with his ex-lover Madame Merle (Barbara Hershey) to entrap Isabel for her money). Here the cinematic frame is disrupted not just by the compression of Isabel's travels – partly in Europe and partly in Africa – but by the monochromatic production of the sequence to resemble an early silent film. The sequence dissolves from an expressionistic portrait of Isabel on a boat with the leering Madame Merle behind her, to an image of Osmond's open hand around Isabel's waist which pans upwards to reveal the tempter coiled around his prey. During a series of brief desert scenes in Arabia, the repetition of Osmond's whispered declarations of love materialises into a surreal image of several miniature lips pushed around a plate by a fork (seemingly a homage to Luis Buñuel's and Salvador Dali's *Un Chien Andalou* (1928)) and a psychedelic scene with disorienting spirals, with the upright image of Osmond and a full naked portrait of Isabel superimposed over him (an image which would not be out of place in Alfred Hitchcock's *Vertigo* (1958)). Although the deliberate anachronism of these styles may cause critics like Brian McFarlane some concern, the images not only jolt the viewer out of the melodramatic frame of Osmond's villainous seduction of Isabel, but once more suggest a cultural lineage of which Isabel is a prototype: in the words of James's narrator, this provides the reader/viewer with 'a little corridor leading out of the past'.[42] Although the film is much more deliberately experimental than James's novel, such a sequence emphasises the strangeness of Isabel's European experience on geographical, symbolic and emotional levels.

The parallels between *The American* and *The Portrait of a Lady* on the level of plot are numerous – for example, the secret of Pansy Osmond's heritage, her being sent to a convent and Isabel's silent revenge – but the later novel (and its cinematic counterpart) goes much further in developing an 'in-between' world which interweaves a study of social manners and cultural difference with the pulsating inner life of a character who eventually learns to refuse the static role which Gilbert Osmond would have her adopt. Towards the end of Campion's film, Isabel appears as a double image, suggesting either that she has discovered hidden resources to escape from Osmond's sadistic snare or that she has indeed become a stranger to herself. But rather than answering this question satisfactorily, like *The American*, the ending of *The Portrait of a Lady* is interesting in its refusal of closure. After Isabel has left Osmond to tend to her dying cousin in Britain, she encounters once more the attentions of Caspar Goodwood and, for the first time, experiences 'the hot wind of the desert' and 'the sweet airs of the garden ... as if something potent, acrid and strange, forced open her set teeth'.[43] But, rather than a harmonious ending, in the novel Isabel returns to Rome on unfinished business while Goodwood is forced to wait for her once more (even though he may at last have discovered 'the key to patience') and in the film Isabel stands alone with her hand 'on the door latch' looking 'into the dark snowy grounds' of Gardencourt on the brink of her future life.[44] Whereas the ending of *The American* combines melancholy with ambiguity, both versions of *The Portrait of a Lady* end by opening up future possibilities, but without the promise of a happy ending.

The Wings of the Dove

In his late phase of fiction, James withdrew from the relatively stable social scenarios of *The American* and *The Portrait of a Lady* to enter a complex psychological world in which, as Peter Brooks argues, 'unarticulated motives and interpretations'[45] characterise a narrative mode which undermines the privileged perspective of the reader. In the first novel of his late phase, *The Wings of the Dove* (1902), James's interest in the fringes of consciousness gave rise to an intensely interior novel which does not lend itself easily to the third-person perspective of film. Hossein Amini, the screenwriter for the British director Iain Softley's 1997 adaptation of *The Wings of the Dove* (made for Miramax with a mixture of American and British actors), admits that the novel is 'completely uncinematic' and he expresses his frustrated attempts to do justice to it: 'my early drafts were more faithful to the book [than the final version] and almost always a disaster as screenplays. They were either too long or too stiff'.[46] As a result, in the final screenplay Amini concentrates on the themes of deception and betrayal to create what he calls 'a film noir in costume'.[47] He characterises his 'irreverent' version as 'something of a mongrel: part literary adaptation and part film noir homage'[48] which risks losing touch with the original, not only in the paring down of psychological detail but also the invention of noirish scenes such as an opium den and a Venetian carnival and the omission of critical scenes such as Milly Teale's encounter with Bronzino's *Portrait of Lucrezia Panciatichi* when she finally confronts her own mortality. Although the finished product is a lavish and, at times, an innovative post-heritage film which preserves James's interest in transcultural aesthetics, it often works best on the level of visual spectacle rather than as an exploration of the novel's 'insoluble mysteries'.[49] However, Amini's interesting use of the word 'mongrel' to describe the screenplay aligns him with James in an exploration of the 'in-between' worlds which the characters encounter.

In his Preface to the novel (1909), James admits that the storyline is essentially melodramatic, involving a triangular relationship between the British lovers Kate Croy (played by

Helena Bonham Carter in the film) and Merton Densher (Linus Roache) and the American heiress Milly Teale (Alison Elliott). James acknowledges that only the struggle to represent 'the precious experience' of his characters – by moving in 'narrowing circumvallations' from the 'outer ring' of action[50] – enabled him to elevate his story above the level of melodrama. By choosing to develop the story as a film noir plot, Amini and Softley have created difficulties in penetrating further than this 'outer ring' of action. However, as E. Ann Kaplan argues in her introduction to *Women in Film Noir* (1978), one of the chief differences between melodrama and film noir is that in the former the ideologies of the patriarchal family are paramount, whereas the latter deals with 'negative or absent' families.[51] Although Kate Croy's aunt (Charlotte Rampling) and father (Michael Gambon) are central to her financial dilemma – her aunt provides her with wealth on the condition that she has nothing to do with her father or her lowly lover Densher – the film is notable in its fragmentation of family: for example, Kate visits her dead mother's graveyard, and Milly's and Densher's parents are absent. Thus, rather than focusing explicitly on the role of money and inheritance within the family structure, as does *Washington Square*, the film version of *The Wings of the Dove* uses the restrictions which Aunt Maud places on Kate as a means to explore the darker side of love, admiration and obsession. Moreover, these noirish elements parallel James's interest in playing off 'picture' against 'drama' – in which 'each baffles insidiously the other's ideal and eats round the edges of its position'[52] – and prove more interesting in an analysis of the film than its frustrated attempts at fidelity.

Although most of the plotting derives from Kate's attempts to preserve her fortune and keep Densher by encouraging him to court the dying Milly in Venice, it is Milly who symbolically embodies the dove of James's title. Like Isabel Archer and, to a certain extent, Christopher Newman, James describes Milly as the 'heir of all the ages' whose appetite for 'boundless' experience characterises a young woman on 'the threshold of a life'.[53] These possibilities are limited when Milly contracts a mysterious illness, which is not defined, but shares with consumption a heightening of her senses and a spiritualising of her bodily form. Thus, Milly gradually transforms into the 'dove' of the title, only to finally materialise into the bird after her death. The two lovers try to describe Milly in painterly images: Densher realises that Milly fills 'more of the foreground' of his world 'picture' than he had previously realised and he later attempts to describe her in regal and celestial terms 'as a princess, as an angel, as a star', but it is Kate's metaphor of 'dove' which symbolises Milly's life most powerfully.[54] However, these attempts to 'frame' Milly cannot contain her 'charm', which 'turned on them a face that was cold in its beauty, that was full of poetry never to be theirs, that spoke in an ironic smile of a possible but forbidden life' (p. 323). Both James's novel and, less successfully, Softley's film gesture towards the margins of representation and hints of a mysterious world beyond Newman's story of American self-reliance and Isabel's realisation that her worldly destiny is not what she had expected. The strangeness both characters encounter is heightened in *The Wings of the Dove*, as Milly provides an irresistible lure which forces Kate and Densher to face the indecipherable meanings which 'hung ... upon her, hovering, dropping and quavering forth again, like vague faint snatches, mere ghosts of sound' (p. 349).

The film version does not offer direct images of Milly as a dove, but subtly contrasts the social iron cage in which Kate and Densher find themselves entrapped (imaged in the 'prison bars' of the London Underground lift early in the film and the cage of Aunt Maud's room in the novel) with the scenes when Milly wishes to climb above Venice to secure an aerial perspective on the world, mirroring James's use of aesthetic 'windows and balconies' in his novel.[55] Indeed, the film continually plays with images of verticality: from the early aerial shots in which Merton and Kate seem pinned to the earth, to the passionate embrace which ensues after Merton follows Milly up a church scaffold. The equivalent image in Kate's relationship with Milly occurs when the pair hold hands between two Venetian gondolas, in a ghostly scene which emphasises their white dresses against the background of the dark canal (repeated in the final moments of the film as a memory sequence). The film uses these images of doubling to suggest a kinship between the three (despite

Kate's and Densher's plans to use Milly for their own ends) but also of confused identities and, at times, ambivalent gender roles (Kate dresses as a boy in the carnival sequence of the film). But these images, together with the numerous mirrors which reflect Kate's pale face, suggest an existential angst which lies only partially covered behind the veneer of this story of money, jealousy and betrayal. Replicating the indirect style of James's novel, Softley's film uses these almost post-Impressionist scenes to chart the transformation of Kate's and Densher's feelings for Milly, while she remains nebulous and insubstantial outside their perceptions of her. Where the European settings of the previous two novels are used primarily as cinematic topi for exploring the experiences of Americans abroad, Venice in *The Wings of the Dove* is, in turn, magical, unpredictable, exotic, drab and disappointing: to begin with 'the sun on the stirred sea-water, flickering up through open windows, played over the painted "subjects" in the splendid ceilings', but later it becomes 'a Venice all of evil ... of cold lashing rain from a low black sky, of wicked wind raging through narrow passes' (p. 311; p. 403). Just as Thomas Mann was to explore in *Death in Venice* (1912) a decade after James, Venice is a place of mystery but also of mortal peril. But, whereas the moral decline of Mann's Gustav von Aschenbach is compounded by the pestilence of Asiatic cholera, the heightened spirituality of Milly's illness is thrown into relief by the darkening scenes around her and also facilitates the shedding of her national past to the extent that she becomes a celestial icon for her two admirers. In this sense, the 'in-between' world which the three characters experience is more metaphysical than geographical, serving to radically challenge their view of material reality.

As the novel and film progress, the intricacies of the triangular relationship draw the reader's/viewer's attention away from national and class tensions into a mythical story which enchants as spectacle, but also provokes serious questions about the interweaving of myth and history and the nature of storytelling. Although an intensely modern story (emphasised by the London scenes in the film), *The Wings of the Dove* becomes increasingly mythical in its transcendence of worldly values, suggesting a modernist recycling of myth on the same level as James Joyce's *Ulysses* (1922) or Hermann Broch's *The Death of Virgil* (1945). Moreover, the stories the three characters tell each other in love scenes and in letters to each other suggest a seamless interweaving of fiction and reality, in which history can no longer be extracted from desire. This is best illustrated in the final scene of the novel after Milly's death, in which Merton agrees to marry Kate only without Milly's money. Rather than consenting to this condition, Kate asks Densher to promise her that he is not in love with Milly's 'memory' (p. 509). Although he does not answer her directly, his apostrophe, 'Oh – her memory!' (replaced by silence in the film) prohibits the couple from making the choice which would propel them into the next phase of their history together: in the novel, Kate proclaims, 'We shall never be again as we were!' (p. 509) and in the film Densher returns mentally to Venice with memories of Milly ringing in his head. In this way, Kate and Densher are dragged out of reality by their experiences with Milly and are thrown back into history without the capacity to act.

Here, James's transcultural aesthetic develops the themes of his previous novels by propelling the two lovers towards, to recall Iain Chambers, 'the intersections of histories and memories' to the point where they are 'simultaneously "inside" and "outside"' reality. Similarly, rather than the Jamesian adaptations being branded (or even dismissed) as heritage films or costume dramas, their exploration of 'in-betweenness', as John Hill discusses, mirrors the themes and 'formal strategies' of more politically and racially aware films of the 1980s and 90s, such as *My Beautiful Laundrette* (Stephen Frears, 1985) or, more recently, *Central Station* (Walter Salles, 1998), both in their postmodern exploration of 'identities ... no longer grounded in an identification with place' and their dramatisation of the classic, but disturbing, modern dilemma of knowing when and how to act in an unstable world.[56]

Notes

1. *The Heiress* is a period adaptation of *Washington Square* (1881) and *The Innocents* a sinister version of *The Turn of the Screw* (1898).

2. Andrew Higson, 'The Heritage Film and British Cinema' in Andrew Higson (ed.), *Dissolving Views: Key Writings on British Cinema* (London: Cassell, 1996), p. 232. Stella Bruzzi, *Undressing Cinema: Clothing and Identity in the Movies* (London: Routledge, 1997), p. 35.
3. F.R. Leavis, *The Great Tradition* (Harmondsworth: Penguin, 1993), p. 10.
4. Leavis, *The Great Tradition*, p. 177. Philip Horne, 'The James Gang', *Sight and Sound* (January 1998), p. 16.
5. Higson, *Dissolving Views*, pp. 35–6.
6. E.M. Forster, *Howards End* (London: Penguin, 1989), p. 170.
7. James's return visit to America in 1904 after a 20-year absence is documented in *The American Scene* (1907). However, this expression of his increasing alienation from America was written towards the end of his career as a fiction writer.
8. Henry James, 'The Art of Fiction' in Roger Gard (ed.), *The Critical Muse: Selected Literary Criticism* (Harmondsworth: Penguin, 1987), p. 187.
9. Nicholas Mirzoeff, *An Introduction to Visual Culture* (London: Routledge, 1999), p. 131.
10. It is generally accepted that James's first phase of fiction writing, characterised by pictorial realism, ends with *The Portrait of a Lady* and the second phase, influenced by the naturalism of Zola and Turgenev, begins with *The Bostonians* (1886). However, the transition between these phases is much more fluid than this model suggests. See David Timms's discussion in 'Hawthorne, James and History' in Gavin Cologne-Brooks *et al.* (eds), *Writing and America* (London: Longman, 1996) pp. 196–8.
11. For a digest of all the James film adaptations, see Horne, 'The James Gang', pp. 16–19.
12. James, 'Preface to *The Portrait of a Lady*', in *The Critical Muse*, p. 485. Brian McFarlane, *Novel to Film: Introduction to the Theory of Adaptation* (Oxford: Clarendon, 1996), p. 21. I do not discuss in detail Agnieszka Holland's *Washington Square* because, being wholly set in America, it does not raise transcultural issues as centrally as the other three films.

13. John Hill, *British Cinema in the 1980s* (Oxford: Clarendon, 1999), p. 73.

14. Hill, *British Cinema*, p. 74.

15. Ibid., p. 74. Higson, *Dissolving Views*, p. 36.

16. Hill, *British Cinema*, p. 76.

17. See Roslyn Jolly, *Henry James: History, Narrative, Fiction* (Oxford: Clarendon, 1993) for a discussion of this topic.

18. Ginette Vincendeau, 'Issues in European Cinema' in John Hill and Carol Church Gibson (eds), *The Oxford Guide to Film Studies* (Oxford: Oxford University Press, 1997), p. 446.

19. Alice Gambrell, *Women Intellectuals, Modernism and Difference: Transatlantic Culture, 1919–1945* (Cambridge: Cambridge University Press, 1997), p. 5; pp. 4–5.

20. Gambrell, *Women Intellectuals*, p. 9.

21. Iain Chambers, *Migrancy, Culture, Identity* (London: Routledge, 1994), p. 4.

22. Ibid., p. 6.

23. Ibid., p. 6. Even though Forster's fiction and the film versions of *A Room With a View* (1985), *Where Angels Fear to Tread* (1991) and *Howards End* (1991) explore the conflict between Central European culture and ideas of Englishness, they all end with closure and symbolic homecoming.

24. Kelly Cannon, *Henry James and Masculinity: The Men at the Margins* (London: Macmillan, 1994), p. 8.

25. Paul Gilroy, *The Black Atlantic: Modernity and Double Consciousness* (London: Verso, 1993). Cannon, *Henry James and Masculinity*, p. 5.

26. Henry James, 'Preface to *The American*', in *The Critical Muse*, p. 468. Henry James, *The American* (London: Penguin, 1995), p. 20. Subsequent references to the novel are included in the text.

27. Virginia Fowler, *Henry James's American Girl: The Embroidery on the Canvas* (Madison: University of Wisconsin Press, 1984), p. 53.

28. Fowler, *Henry James's American Girl*, p. 26.

29. In James's novel the withholding of M. de Bellegarde's medication leads to his death, whereas in Unwin's film a poisoned glass (an image of which accompanies the title

of the film) is administered by his wife. This is just one example of the overstating of certain aspects of James's novel in which the film indulges as dramatic shortcuts.

30. Unwin uses a narrative voiceover sparingly at the beginning and end of *The American*, whilst Scorsese uses the ironic interventions of Wharton's narrator to much greater effect in *The Age of Innocence*.

31. Valentin suspects 'the charms of shopkeeping' have a 'romantic, picturesque side' which would 'look well' in his 'biography'. James, *The American*, p. 208.

32. Laura Jones, *The Portrait of a Lady: Screenplay* (London: Penguin, 1997), p. vi.

33. Lizzie Francke, 'On the Brink', *Sight and Sound* (November 1996), p. 6. Jones, *The Portrait: Screenplay*, p. 1. In a recent article on Jane and Anna Campion, Suzie Mackenzie discusses the 'fascinating feminised spaces' of Campion's films, in which she explores 'the limbo between sleep and wakefulness'. Suzie Mackenzie, 'Beloved Rivals', *Guardian Weekend* (5 June 1999), p. 12.

34. Jones, *The Portrait: Screenplay*, p. 1.

35. James, *The Critical Muse*, p. 493.

36. Brian McFarlane complains that Campion's film 'is at its least impressive when it seems most earnestly straining to be "cinematic"', whereas Ken Gelder is more interested in exploring the 'undecidability inhabiting' the relationship between novel and film, which 'enables the latter to be faithful and independent, monogamous and promiscuous, restricted or compromised by the source novel and yet "separate" or autonomous from it, all at the same time'. Ken Gelder, 'Jane Campion and the Limits of Literary Cinema' in Deborah Cartmell and Imelda Whelehan (eds), *Adaptations: From Text to Screen, Screen to Text* (London: Routledge, 1999), pp. 169–70.

37. Not only does the film begin *in medias res*, but the first image of Lord Warburton is 'a pair of male legs, seen from below the knee ... The tree's foliage hides the owner of the boots.' Jones, *The Portrait: Screenplay*, p. 2.

38. Jones, *The Portrait: Screenplay*, p. 6.

39. James, *The Critical Muse*, pp. 484–5.

40. Jones, *The Portrait: Screenplay*, p. 26.

41. James, *The Portrait of a Lady* (London: Penguin, 1986), p. 206; p. 104.
42. Quoted in Jones, *The Portrait: Screenplay*, p. 43.
43. James, *The Portrait*, p. 634.
44. James, *The Portrait*, p. 637. Jones, *The Portrait: Screenplay*, p. 132. It is interesting that the final scenes of the screenplay, in which Goodwood arrives to find that Isabel has returned to Italy in order to rescue Pansy, were not included in the film version, perhaps because they would have restricted the openness of the ending.
45. Peter Brooks, Introduction to *The Wings of the Dove* (Oxford: Oxford University Press, 1984), p. vii.
46. Hossein Amini, *Henry James: The Wings of the Dove: Screenplay* (London: Methuen, 1998), p. vi; p. v.
47. Amini, *The Wings*, p. v.
48. As Philip Horne notes, the film also transports the scene of the story from 1901 to 1910, perhaps in order to emphasise the 'modern' dilemmas of the characters. Horne, 'The James Gang', p. 19.
49. James, 'Preface to *The Wings of the Dove*' in *The Critical Muse*, p. 548.
50. James, *The Critical Muse*, p. 547; p. 552.
51. E. Ann Kaplan, *Women in Film Noir* (London: BFI, 1978), p. 4.
52. James, *The Critical Muse*, p. 555.
53. James, *The Critical Muse*, p. 550. James's Notebook IV (3 November 1894), reprinted in *The Wings*, p. 511.
54. James, *The Wings*, p. 225, p. 341, p. 508. Subsequent references to the novel are included in the text.
55. Amini, *The Wings*, p. 2. James, *The Critical Muse*, p. 562.
56. Hill, *British Cinema*, p. 216; p. 215.

5

'Hystorical' Puritanism: Contemporary Cinematic Adaptations of Nathaniel Hawthorne's *The Scarlet Letter* and Arthur Miller's *The Crucible*

Sergio Rizzo

Standard reading in American high schools and colleges for decades, Nathaniel Hawthorne's *The Scarlet Letter* (1850)[1] and Arthur Miller's *The Crucible* (1953)[2] are firmly established as 'classics' of American literature – both within the American academy and the popular culture more generally. In the case of the former, they are ratified by the kind of professional attention such as seminars, scholarly articles, monographs, and dissertations one would expect of texts that are highly valued in a society where the production of literature and literary value is fully institutionalised. In the case of popular culture, their ratification occurs by a less quantifiable and more allusive means. Both the professional and popular recognition of this literature enshrines their very similar critiques of Puritanism, lending them, too, a 'classic' status. Even for those who have not read the works, their depictions of the Puritans as dour and pale patriarchs administering a repressive and often hypocritical sexual morality are readily comprehensible and recognisable. And if one agrees, as many do, that Hawthorne's Hester Prynne presents a picture of idealised femininity while a hundred years later Miller's Abigail Williams presents a picture of demonised femininity, then these characters are also recognisable as 'classic' female types: specifically, Hester Prynne as the fallen woman who redeems herself (Julia Roberts in *Pretty Woman* (1990)) and

Abigail Williams as the fallen woman who cannot or will not redeem herself (Glenn Close in *Fatal Attraction* (1987)).

Recent Hollywood adaptations of Hawthorne's novel and Miller's play have tried to capitalise, in both the artistic and monetary senses of that word, on the classic status these works enjoy. If a movie company can gross nearly $150 million from a screen version of James Fenimore Cooper's *The Last of the Mohicans* (1992),[3] the logic of putting its star, Daniel Day-Lewis, in an adaptation of *The Crucible*, much more widely read and recognised than Cooper's novel, becomes irresistible.[4] The intimate connection between literary and film narrative has been explored and maintained by many film theorists. And in turn the 'classic' film style, represented by Hollywood studio films produced between the 1930s and 1950s, is seen as the definitive expression of literary film-making. However, the classic film style does not primarily use, let alone require, classic literature. Indeed, as Dudley Andrew puts it, 'Well over half of all commercial films have come from literary originals – though by no means all of these originals are revered or respected.'[5] Indeed, works that are 'revered or respected', like *The Scarlet Letter* and *The Crucible*, that is to say literary classics, form their own genre when adapted by Hollywood – much like other literary genres such as the detective, romance or historical novel. The recent pressure to exploit classic literature, as a genre, has come to the attention of more than one movie reviewer. In his review of *The Crucible*, Jonathan Coe of the *New Statesman* complains:

> In the past few months I've done nothing but re-read classic novels and plays. My desk groans under the weight of *Cole's Notes* and old school essays, as I desperately refamiliarise myself with Hardy, Jane Austen and, of course, William Shakespeare every one of whose plays seems to have been filmed at least twice this year.[6]

As Roland Joffé's *The Scarlet Letter* (1995) and Nicholas Hytner's *The Crucible* (1996) demonstrate, Hollywood's ability to exploit this genre can vary widely. Nonetheless, despite the critical success of the latter, both films represent a postmodern film-making that fails to transcend the limits of the literary classics it attempts to appropriate.

The films fail because of two distinct yet closely related aspects of their postmodern condition. The first is seen in their efforts to represent the past or history; the second is seen in their efforts to represent feminine difference. What should be, and sometimes is in other postmodern texts, a productive blurring between the fictional nature of history and the historical nature of fiction results in two different forms of overdetermined history. In the case of Joffé's *The Scarlet Letter*, this overdetermined history is self-apparent and attains an unintentional level of parody and campy excess. In the case of Hytner's *The Crucible*, on the other hand, the painstaking historical detail ironically loses historical depth and gives way to a closed and literary 'realism'.

The second aspect of their postmodern film-making involves sexual difference and the star system. In order to bash the present with the past, both authors fabricate out of Puritan history a feminine excess that is simultaneously historical and hysterical – Hawthorne's Hester and Miller's Abigail. Clearly indebted to feminist revisions of history, Joffé and Hytner's films highlight the problems with Hawthorne and Miller's 'hystorical' women. And yet, like their literary fathers,[7] Joffé and Hytner reinscribe these fictional women at the expense of 'real' women. For Joffé and Hytner, the real women they rely upon are Demi Moore in the role of Hester and Winona Ryder in the role of Abigail. Representing two types of postmodern femininity, neither star can escape the masculine scripts their directors provide for them. In an uncanny return of the repressed, their situation imitates that of the characters they play. Whether it is the sympathetic romanticism of Hawthorne, the alienated modernism of Miller, or the postmodern film-making of Joffé and Hytner, we see a feminine history that cannot escape the literary designs of its male authors.

In what follows, I'm not trying to locate the 'real' Winona Ryder or Demi Moore. Instead, to illustrate the process by which their respective films limit or compromise their feminine self-expression, we need to look at their roles – both personal and professional – outside and before the films. In short, we need to historicise their stardom to better understand how it is put to use by the film-makers.

Two of Hollywood's most successful actresses of the past decade, Moore and Ryder came to prominence in the mid- to late 1980s (Moore in *St Elmo's Fire* (1985), Ryder in *Beetlejuice* (1988) and *Heathers* (1989)). Their careers have two distinct tracks. In terms of recognition and money, Moore has left her fellow brat packers far behind. Whatever the critical success of her movies, over the past two years they have brought in 21 million dollars for her, giving her the distinction of being the only movie actress on the Forbes list of top-earning entertainers.[8] Ryder and her career, on the other hand, are not defined by box office success to the same extent. In keeping with this distinction, Moore's films have tended towards 'lowbrow' popularity (*Ghost* (1990), *Indecent Proposal* (1993), *Disclosure* (1994), *Striptease* (1996)) while Ryder's are scrupulously 'highbrow' (*Edward Scissorhands* (1990), *Little Women* (1994), *How to Make an American Quilt* (1995)). Consequently, a celebrity profile in *People Weekly* can proclaim that Ryder is 'a classic'[9] – a term that one would hesitate to use for Moore. Director Joel Schumacher makes clear that the popular sense of Ryder as a 'classic' has to do with her perceived ability to embody the past: 'She looks almost Pre-Raphaelite, from a long time ago ... But at the same time she is contemporary.'[10] It would be hard to imagine a director admiring Moore as evocative of any era other than the present. Indeed, she is entirely, almost ruthlessly, a contemporary woman.

In a discussion exploring the differences between stage and screen, Leo Braudy provides a useful theoretical context for understanding these differences between Ryder and Moore.[11] In Braudy's terms, Ryder's stardom – artistic, highbrow, evocative of the past – represents a stage-style form of acting that is primarily concerned with and identified by 'virtuosity'. Moore's stardom – commercial, lowbrow, contemporary – represents a film-style form of acting that is primarily concerned with and identified by 'personality'. The common assumption is that the stage actor is superior to the film actor, which Braudy questions: 'The film actor emphasizes display, while the stage actor explores disguise. But stage acting is still popularly considered to be superior to film acting. An actor who does a good job disappears into his role, while the bad (read "film" actor) is only playing himself.'[12] Certainly, the critical response to Ryder and Moore reflects this largely unquestioned privileging. Besides helping us to understand the sources of this bias, Braudy's distinction between the stage actor's concern with 'disguise' and 'disappearing into a role' versus the film actor's concern with 'display' and 'playing herself' can also help us understand their careers in terms of their femininity. For women within patriarchal culture, stratagems of disguise and display are part of a social drama much larger than any stage or screen.

Moore's display of what she calls her 'goodies'[13] both on and off the screen is carefully enumerated by an article in *People* magazine:

> Beginning with her first major picture, 1984's *Blame it on Rio*, and now with *Striptease*, Moore has appeared topless six times on the screen. There were her notorious nude *Vanity Fair* covers in 1991 and '92, and at this moment a photo in *Arena* magazine of Moore – made up as a man and baring her breasts – is causing a stir in Britain.[14]

Ryder, in comparison, has been almost prudish with her body: no startling photos on the covers of magazines and she consistently plays characters whose physical presence evokes a tomboyish girlhood and whose expression of sexuality, if any, occurs primarily through the face and not the body. David Seltzer, who directed Ryder in one of her first films, *Lucas* (1986), describes his discovery of the actress: 'There was Winona ... this little frail bird. She had the kind of presence I had never seen – an inner life. Whatever message was being said by her mouth was being contradicted by her eyes.'[15] Playing the child bride of Jerry Lee Lewis in *Great Balls of Fire* (1989), Ryder describes her performance in the wedding night scene in the following manner:

> No part of my body is exposed, it's just that the camera is on my face a lot, especially during the pain part. And then she starts to enjoy it, and that was the really embarrassing

part. The face I chose is really revealing – I couldn't believe it was me. It looks really weird to me: Dennis is so big, and I'm so little ... I was just going by what I thought it would feel like. I watch these other people's love scenes, everybody's so sexy, everyone tries to be really subtle. With me, it's very different. I don't think I was very sexy.[16]

Although her appearance in *The Crucible* marks a departure from the vulnerable virgin or androgynous tomboy role, one can hear in a recent television interview with Charlie Rose her self-effacing and almost apologetic attitude towards her diminutive stature.[17] This attitude can still be felt, even when she attempts to play stronger and/or evil women, such as the wantonly destructive Abigail in *The Crucible*. Ryder's attitude towards her body should not be too surprising if we remember that her professional role-playing, perfecting disguise and a loss of self, draws upon well-defined social roles that women within patriarchal culture have been practising for centuries.

Like Ryder's artful strategy of disappearance, Moore's apparently artless strategy of display also has its risks and point of diminishing return. Moore's display of femininity and strength, regardless of whether the characters are seen as 'good' or 'bad', risks alienating her audience. Commenting on Moore's marketability, one film producer said, 'Audiences have an abiding affection for actresses who play vulnerable characters, like Julia Roberts ... but it's a different situation for Demi.'[18] Another quotation from the same article suggests that if she risks alienating men with her portrayals of strong women, she also risks alienating women with her willingness to display her body. A writer in *Allure* magazine described her as the 'famously buff mother of three [who] is despised by unbuff mothers of three everywhere'.[19] But whatever the risks involved with her combination of strength and feminine objectification, it works – meaning it sells – and to the tune of 12.5 million dollars per picture, despite the qualms of nervous movie executives and the smouldering resentment of 'unbuff mothers'.

Moore's cinematic maturation from brat pack angst in *St Elmo's Fire* to a self-assured single mother who strips for a living in *Striptease* parallels a personal strength and maturity gained over the years in Hollywood. From the early days of *St Elmo's Fire*, when her drug and alcohol abuse almost got her fired, Moore has evolved into an actress who is not afraid to stand up to the men who run Hollywood. Adrian Lyne, who directed Moore in *Indecent Proposal*, makes complaints that others have put more discreetly: 'If you want her to sit down, she tends to stand up. Or she wants to know why you want her to sit down,' and giving a piece of advice to other directors, he adds, 'put on a suit of armor. She's a very tough ride.'[20] In contrast to Moore's determination, Ryder's enduring affability was spotted in an early *Rolling Stone* article that describes the young Ryder as 'Precocious enough to hold her own with adults, she radiates the qualities of a child who has always been encouraged: a chatty, optimistic disposition and an unself-conscious creativity.'[21] If Moore has a reputation as Hollywood's shrewish daughter, Ryder is its innocent Bianca.

Moore's 'tough girl determination'[22] and Ryder's 'optimistic disposition'[23] come from backgrounds that have some similarities and yet illustrate the class divisions inherited from their parents and the 1960s generation. Moore is a 'trailer park kid',[24] as she calls herself, and Ryder is a child of a hippie commune. Moore's working-class parents were trapped in poverty and substance abuse, while the anti-materialism and experimental drug use were a conscious choice for Ryder's parents – 'hippie intellectuals and psychedelic scholars', as Ryder's godfather, Timothy Leary, called them.[25] Their different backgrounds inform their two careers – Moore's stardom of 'personality' and Ryder's stardom of 'virtuosity'.

Furthermore, their lives and careers can represent the two feminisms that have come to dominate the 1980s and 1990s and the different sides of the debate about what the feminism of the 1960s and 1970s means to the younger generation of women like Moore and Ryder. Moore's brand of feminism favours integration into the male mainstream and corporate culture, and sees liberation almost entirely in terms of personal income and mobility. As Andrew Bergman, Moore's director in *Striptease*, points out, 'Everything is a matter of Demi trying to have a sense of empowerment ... Given her early life, you can understand it.'[26] Ryder's feminism is a more liberal or radical feminism that wants to continue to use the identity politics of the 1970s to challenge and change the patriarchal structure of society.[27] When represented by Moore and Ryder, the choice may not be an easy one for many women to make. Moore's 'tough girl' personality both on and off the screen makes her an appealing figure, even in spite of her commercialism and the narrowness of her political vision. And in spite of Ryder's feminism, her preference for artful disguise and 'virtuosity' weaken her ability to challenge traditional models of femininity.

Although movie reviewers were consistent in their condemnation of Joffé's *The Scarlet Letter* and praise for Hytner's *The Crucible*, the extended description of Moore's and Ryder's separate yet complementary careers will put the categorical pronouncements about the films in a broader context. Even though it is easy to see why *The Scarlet Letter* is a 'bad' film and *The Crucible* is a 'good' film, exploiting their respective female leads, more can be said about the process which made the failure and success of each so apparent to most viewers.

Once Joffé's *The Scarlet Letter* is put in relation to Moore's career another statement about feminism in the 1990s, rather than the muddled one which is the 'message' of the film, begins to appear. Joffé's film provided Moore with her first starring role in a movie that encompassed both American history and literature. As a high school drop-out one can imagine she had less access to and was less comfortable with the literary canon than Ryder who was raised by 'hippie intellectuals and psychedelic scholars'. Perhaps more imposing than the literary heights of Hawthorne's novel was the sense of American history that it presents. Since they are so often perceived as the objects rather than the subjects of history, playing historical roles holds forth particular challenges for women. And for Moore, whose stardom is based on her image as a contemporary woman, the risk of being perceived as 'out of place' probably made the role even more intimidating.

Not only did the film present a new cultural terrain, its explicit political agenda was also new for Moore. Joffé expressed his political take on the story when he commented that the film wasn't so much about religion as '"the relationship between men and women politically"' and an associate of Moore's explained to *Vanity Fair*, '"we liken Hester Prynne a lot to Anita Hill"'.[28] On CNN's *Showbiz Today*, Moore expressed her personal attachment to the role, claiming that she 'aspired to be Hester Prynne, [by] removing self-imposed limitations in her own life ...' Unfortunately, as several reviewers point out, these good intentions only result in a facile political correctness which blames the past for not being the present.[29] More than just the failure of a movie, *The Scarlet Letter* was the failure of a new direction for Moore, one which included more 'serious' or overtly political characters and projected her onto the highly respected cultural terrain of American history and literature.[30] The failure of *The Scarlet Letter*, along with *The Juror* (1996) soon after, may explain her return to a movie like *Striptease*. If audiences were not interested in her mind, she would try to win them back with her body.

Of the many travesties Moore and Joffé's adaptation visits upon Hawthorne's story, perhaps the one that is the most upsetting to English teachers, or others who see their job as reaffirming the 'classics', is the happy ending given to Hester and Dimmesdale's relationship. I was in an awkward position as I watched Moore and Gary Oldman triumph over rigid Puritans and murderous Indians. Dimmesdale, on the gallows for adultery, is rescued at the last second by an Indian attack. After much carnage, the couple along with Pearl take their leave of the stunned elders, and as their wagon departs the camera does a close-up of the scarlet letter which Hester unfastens and lets drop onto the muddy ground. On the one hand, I condemned the ending's irritating improbability and corniness. On the other hand, watching the triumphant New World family leave their hypocritical and heartless kinsmen, I was reminded of a graduate paper I wrote excoriating Hawthorne for preventing the couple's love, which the paper argued was proof of the author's inability to rise above the patriarchal insensitivity he set out to critique.

Of course, what inspired Joffé's revision of the novel's conclusion had less to do with sentiment or feminist literary criticism than with the 40 million dollars invested in the film. Nonetheless, this fact, along with the movie's often laughable revisions, should not prevent us from seeing any critical value in the film's happy ending. Moore herself, on Jay Leno's *The Tonight Show*, made a good case for the critical value of the film's ending by debunking notions of the literary work as some sort of sanctified text, permanent and unchangeable. And as anyone who has taught the book knows, the desire for a happy or happier ending to *The Scarlet Letter* is shared by many if not most of the students who read the novel for the first time.

One could dismiss their desire for a happy ending as a desire for the classic narrative pattern (a state of equilibrium introduced, then disrupted, then re-established) which the classic Hollywood film narrative promoted and disseminated as no other medium before it could.[31] And part of what makes Hawthorne's novel an 'American classic' is its departure from the classic narrative pattern: from the author's satiric 'Custom-House' Introduction, followed by a 'love plot' that begins after the lovers' fall to the separation which the lovers never overcome. All of this is dispensed with by Joffé who gives Hester and Dimmesdale a 'proper love story': introduction (the lovers meet) – climax (they consummate their relationship) – resolution (their love triumphs and they live happily ever after). One of the ironies, however, is that in using a classical narrative to rewrite Hawthorne, the film achieves an unintentional excess that works against the (literary) unity and transparency of the classic film narrative and the 'passive adhesion'[32] of the movie audience.

The film's excessive character is directly related to a more gender-specific genre, that of popular romance – a genre which, more than classical narrative, Hawthorne had in mind and was writing against.[33] The movie's scriptwriter, Douglas Day Stewart, is best known for such successful Hollywood romances as *The Blue Lagoon* (1980) and *An Officer and a Gentleman* (1986). In these earlier films, which are not trying to adapt history or literature that is 'revered and respected', Stewart is able to achieve the unity, transparency and adhesion that classical film desires. In *The Scarlet Letter*, however, what results is a romantic excess that seems more picaresque than classical. Ultimately, its romantic excess provides another level of feminist awareness above and beyond the politically correct message(s) of the film.[34]

In Stewart's revision, popular romance takes its revenge upon Hawthorne's (masculine) literary highmindedness. As already mentioned, the film allows the lovers to fall in love; the moral ambiguity of Hawthorne's characters is replaced by their moral simplification and sexualisation (Dimmesdale's swim in the nude, the couple's love scene); the dreary New England colony becomes a bustling community surrounded by 'exotic' Indians and breathtaking nature; the character of Pearl, whose erratic behaviour is part of Hawthorne's anti-sentimentalism, becomes the film's narrator whose childlike voiceover unabashedly sentimentalises the film. But above all of this, there is the character of Hester who, like Moll Flanders, goes through one harrowing adventure after another – homesteading, childbirth, imprisonment, single motherhood, attempted rape – proving herself to be stronger than both Dimmesdale (her good lover) and Chillingworth (her bad husband), while never losing her femininity.

It is Moore's star personality that gives vitality and coherence to the film's revision of Hester. Although in the minority, Richard Corliss, in an otherwise disparaging review of the movie, appreciates Moore's strength of personality: 'The stars are actually pretty good – Moore holds the camera's gaze as securely as any actress.'[35] However, for most critics, Moore's personality and inability to lose herself in the role make her 'annoyingly contemporary' and full of 'feminist posturing'.[36] Neither view is wrong. They indicate the strengths and weaknesses of Moore's type of acting and stardom.

Although the film realises a sense of feminine empowerment that goes beyond 'feminist posturing', the critics are quite correct to point out that not only does the film make a muddle of Hawthorne's story, it also makes a muddle of its own story. Too many historical allusions are evoked to assist Hester's new role as romantic heroine: Ann Hutchinson and Ann Hibbens (who become 'Harriet Hibbens'), Tituba (who becomes 'Mituba') and the Salem witch trials, Metacom and King Philip's War, are crowded together with Hawthorne's characters.[37] Perhaps this overdetermined use of history becomes most blatant when it crosses and interferes with the climax of the love plot. In what would otherwise be a fairly successful erotic scene, the film-makers weigh it down with such overdone symbolism that it becomes embarrassing to watch. Mituba, Hester's black deaf-mute servant, sees her mistress and Reverend Dimmesdale go off together to consummate their relationship. Inspired by what she sees, she overcomes a superstitious fear of bathtubs and abandons herself to a sensual bath. Her bathing is then inter-spliced with their lovemaking. Add a little red bird and a candle to this already loaded, if not insulting, imagery, and you get some idea of the scene's symbolic overkill.

The overdetermined use of history and symbols disrupts narrative transparency, unity and adhesion, but it also disrupts any coherent understanding of the past it tries to represent. Jill Lepore in an interesting review of *The Scarlet Letter*'s contortion of historical fact and fiction compares it to Disney's *Pocahontas* (1995). Both films, she claims, are like a 'fetid distillation of recent scholarship'[38] that re-evaluates the early European colonisation in terms of race, gender and crosscultural encounter. But in the process, Lepore says, these films tell us more about ourselves than they do about the history they use:

> for all their flirting with historical fact and fiction, *Pocahontas* and *The Scarlet Letter* ultimately tell a story about the origins of our late twentieth-century selves. Smith and Pocahontas, Dimmesdale and Prynne, are presented as our Adam and Eve, transcending a violent historical legacy of racism, patriarchy, and prudery to found our more enlightened age.[39]

The Scarlet Letter certainly does use history as escapist wish fulfilment. But it also, albeit unsuccessfully, attempts to empower Hawthorne's Hester by turning her into the con-ventional heroine of popular romance and provides its female star with a vehicle for a new feminine persona.

When *The Crucible* is added to these other late twentieth-century efforts to locate the origins of contemporary race and gender relations in history, the failure of a film like *The Scarlet Letter* is all the more glaring. However, if *The Scarlet Letter* fails because it is too artless and at odds with Moore's personality, it can also help to illustrate how *The Crucible's* artistry and dependence on Ryder's virtuosity undermine its apparent success. Keeping in mind that it is not just the seventeenth century that interests both Hawthorne and Miller, but more specifically feminine hysteria within the seventeenth century, it becomes easier to see ways in which *The Crucible*, too, like its inferior counterparts, also fails.

Given the 81-year-old Miller's antipathy to film[40] and the fact that his last notable screenplay was for *The Misfits* (1961), his ability to work with director Nicholas Hytner (*The Madness of King George*, 1995) in 'opening out' his play is all the more remarkable. As critics point out, the reason for his success was his ability, as Miller himself says, to 'put the play out of mind as much as possible and to proceed as though it never existed'.[41] This meant cutting back on the play's dialogue – the screenplay is about half the length of the original – and letting the camera 'narrate' the action.

While Miller was forthcoming and enthusiastic about the formal challenges of adapting his play to film, when it came to the thematic reasons he was vague or inconclusive. Miller's indecision is noteworthy because in the past he was not so uncertain about what he would say if he were to rewrite the play. In the introduction to his *Collected Plays*, written in 1957, four years after writing the play and after he himself had been called before Senator McCarthy's House Un-American Activities Committee, he said that he would expand on the 'evil' represented by the Salem judges.[42] However, in the 1996 film version this aspect of the play is severely diminished as the courtroom scenes are significantly scaled back.

Apparently, with McCarthyism only a dim memory for most moviegoers, the film-makers could only hype the film's 'alarming topicality'[43] with references to religious fundamentalism, child abuse scandals, and heavy-handed instances of political correctness. For some critics, the film's loss of any immediate political reference, like the play's McCarthyism, merely strengthens the 'universal' nature of Miller's story. However, others suggest that the play's sombre concern with

McCarthyism is replaced by the sensational sexual hysteria of the girls. Richard Corliss, for example, is barely able to contain himself as he describes the importance of 'Ryder's blood-slurping hysteria': 'Her cheeks flush, her winsome beauty seared with erotic rage, Ryder exposes the real roots of the piece. Forget McCarthyism; *The Crucible* is a colonial *Fatal Attraction*'.[44]

If Miller's revision replaces the play's politics with the sexual politics of *Fatal Attraction*, then a feminist reading of the film should be able to criticise this shift. The film-makers themselves are not shy about acknowledging the role the girls' sexuality has in their understanding of the historical event. Hytner says that their interpretation is based on '"the premise that the source of the girls' destructive energy is their emergent sexuality"'.[45] Costume designer Bob Crowley describes his part in this interpretation:

> And by not using buttons, by lacing everything, the clothes began to form around their little pubescent bodies. One is very aware of these bodies slightly bursting out of these tight little dresses. It's quite a sexy story, it's all about repressed sexuality, so when you cover things up, it's much sexier than when you reveal.[46]

Crowley's concept of sexual (female) bodies in restrictive clothing as a metaphor for sexual repression is part of a larger motif described by set designer Lilly Kilvert:

> It was fascinating to make a nice round, soft fertile world and stick all these geometric shapes on it. In many ways, what the play is about, when it's not being about McCarthyism, is sex, and people's fear of fertility. All that life – keep it stamped down.[47]

Crowley's costuming and Kilvert's set design are part of the 'opening out' of the play that has won Hytner much praise. Reading about the careful selection of a location, the painstaking recreation of houses, clothes, crops and animals, one cannot help but be impressed. It reminds one of André Bazin's famous distinction between theatre as a drama of human beings and film as a drama of nature. According to Crowley and Kilvert, apparently, the 'aesthetic catalyst', using Bazan's term, that allows *The Crucible* to 'take on the reality of nature'[48], is the female body.

If the drama of historical human beings is subsumed by a cinematic drama of 'nature' or 'repressed sexuality', one can also wonder about the film's 'realism' on another level. Kilvert explains that in recreating seventeenth-century Salem she decided against complete fidelity to history. In particular, there would have been no trees, since by the time of the Salem witch trials the colonists had deforested the land. 'But we decided that didn't happen,' she says, 'because it's too ugly.'[49] One has to wonder, did the Puritans see the deforested land as 'ugly'? If anything, they probably saw it as an attractive if not beautiful sign of their industry and God's having given them dominion over the plants and animals. No doubt most moviegoers would agree with Kilvert's view of what makes a landscape 'ugly' as well as its ability to suggest 'repressed sexuality' – just as most agreed with the casting of Ryder whose distinctive beauty, with its ability to evoke the past, makes her a 'natural' and 'realistic' choice. But under the guise of 'realism', *The Crucible*'s artistry encourages the moviegoer to confuse past and present, suggesting that the film tells us more about ourselves than the history it uses.

The film's reliance on 'repressed sexuality' emphasises a point that is crucial to the play's success as well. Stanley Kauffmann points out that when Miller was working on the play he 'saw his way into the historical material' when he read about a 'gesture of tenderness'[50] the historical Abigail Williams made towards John Proctor. Based on this 'evidence', Miller saw sexual jealousy as the motive for Abigail's charges. More concerned with how close Miller's play comes to 'naked, ancient drama'[51] Kauffmann ignores the sexual politics involved and concludes, 'No one can quarrel with the possible truth of Miller's interpretation.'[52]

However, Edmund S. Morgan one of the leading historians of Puritan life, directly questions Miller and Hytner's dramatic licence which bases the Salem tragedy on the 'emergent sexuality'[53] of the accusers. In his opinion, most of the girls would have been too young, and he points out that Abigail's age, which was twelve at the time of the trial, was advanced by Miller, who freely acknowledges this, for the purposes of the sexual drama.[54] This means that at the time of their supposed affair she would have been months or possibly even years younger.[55] Besides questioning the sexual maturity of the girls, Morgan also questions the popular view of Puritan prudery and sexual repression that has been current ever since Hawthorne's *The Scarlet Letter* and which *The Crucible* continues.

Given these reservations, it is somewhat odd to hear Morgan answer his own question: 'Does it matter that she [Abigail] could not have played in life the role that Miller assigns her? On the whole, I think it does not matter.'[56] For Morgan, whatever the play lacks in historical accuracy is made up for by its 'universal' theme or its 'artistry'.[57] However, for those interested in the sexual politics of history and of turning history into art, the fact that Abigail 'could not have played in life the role Miller assigns her' certainly does matter. Morgan goes on to finally concede that sexual repression is 'at least as plausible an explanation for [the girls'] behavior as any that historians have been able to offer'.[58] Another way of saying this, though, is that sexual repression is no more plausible than any other explanation. Miller and Hytner are entitled to their interpretation, but what Morgan's comparison of the play and film with the historical record shows is that their interpretation is as much a sexual fantasy as any enacted by Abigail and the other girls.

Furthermore, shorn of a specific political target, the play's sexual fantasy becomes the prevailing political message of the film. In terms of dramatic action this means the play's extensive courtroom argument is cut back so that the girls' hysteria takes centre stage.[59] On the formal level, this preference for action over dialogue is a wise move. But Miller's belief that the '"more wordless the film [is] the better"'[60] also means that the words which remain have a new force. Take, for example, the words Proctor uses in beginning his personal redemption before the judges by sacrificing his 'good name' in order to expose Abigail's true motives, which he tells the judges are those of a 'whore'. What passes by in the play as part of Miller's evocation of Puritan speech becomes part of a cathartic cleansing in the film as Proctor finally gives a name to the evil which he thought he could dismiss or ignore. At moments like this one, we can see that a far more radical revision is necessary for the film to transcend the play's reliance on the virgin–whore dichotomy represented by Proctor's wife Elizabeth, and ex-mistress Abigail. Ultimately, Proctor cannot live with either of these fantasy women, and in the film as in the play, his heroic standing requires that he reject the feminine in favour of death and his 'good name'.

Miller and Hytner did try to revise or at least soften the play's depiction of Abigail. For example, the film's postscript gives no mention of Abigail, unlike the play's postscript, 'Echoes Down the Corridor', which tells the reader that according to legend, 'Abigail turned up later as a prostitute in Boston'.[61] Instead, the film turns Abigail into a feminine outlaw as she runs away with her employer's savings and boards a ship sailing for Barbados. The destination is significant because it is the homeland of Tituba, the black servant of Abigail's uncle, Reverend Parris. Abigail's flight to Barbados then recalls her earlier partnership and betrayal of Tituba, whose 'difference' was the necessary first illusion to those other illusions that gave Abigail her perverse power over the community.

However, their most apparent effort to revise Abigail's 'whoreish' character is through the casting of Ryder. Ryder's 'good girl' persona precedes her,[62] and although some critics were unimpressed with her performance, most thought she made a credible Abigail. But being able just to play Abigail is, in this analysis, an achievement of little distinction if she is unable to significantly revise her character in the process. Two critics recognised Ryder's efforts in this regard. Peter Travers says, 'Ryder finds the lost child in Abigail, who is usually played as a calculating Lolita.'[63] J. Hoberman says much the same thing; he sees Ryder's Abigail as 'less vengeful vixen than stubborn child'.[64] But Hoberman takes this acknowledgement a significant step further in his analysis of the film's commitment to the play's 'reflexively liberal (and patriarchal) worldview'.[65] Committed as the play and Miller are to Proctor's innocence, or his 'good name', Ryder's performance can only get us to question Proctor's responsibility for turning

Abigail into a 'whore'. Any fuller dramatisation of his and society's responsibility would require dramatic changes far beyond anything Ryder's identification and virtuosity could bring to the role of Abigail.

So, for a brief moment in the mid-1990s, the careers of Moore and Ryder despite their differences reach a similar impasse. Both actresses, while drawn to the radical renunciation of patriarchy implicit in the feminine hysteria of Hester and Abigail, are unable to give adequate voice to their female complaints. For Moore, the obstacles are the heavy-handed direction and scriptwriting that interfere with her attempts to revise Hawthorne's character through feminine display and romance. For Ryder, on the other hand, the artistic restraint and realism of Miller and the film-makers prevent her from transcending their sexualisation of Abigail. Simultaneously artless and artful, Hollywood's late twentieth-century attempts to narrate a feminine resistance to its patriarchal (post)modernity are more noteworthy for their need to do so than their success in doing so.

Notes

1. Nathaniel Hawthorne, *The Scarlet Letter*, ed. Seymour Gross, 3rd edn (New York: W.W. Norton and Company, 1988).
2. Arthur Miller, *The Crucible* in *The Heath Anthology of American Literature*, ed. Paul Lauter, 2nd edn (Lexington, Massachusetts: D.C. Heath and Company, 1994), pp. 1980–2053.
3. Jerry Adler, 'Hester Prynncesse', *Newsweek*, 4 April 1994, p. 58. The impression that Hollywood benefits at the expense of classic literature may be too simplistic. See Joanne Kaufman's 'Big Screen Bonanzas', *People Weekly*, 11 December 1994, p. 44. She reports on the increased sales classic books often enjoy after being adapted by commercial films. *The Scarlet Letter*, for example, sold at 'five times the rate it did before Hollywood's high-concept treatment' (p. 44).
4. The recognition of a monetary incentive, on its own, shouldn't exclude the possibility of artistic merit. See Leo

Braudy, 'Acting: Stage vs. Screen' in Leo Braudy and Marshall Cohen (eds), *Film Theory and Criticism* (Oxford: Oxford University Press, 1999), pp. 419–25. Braudy points out how money, as a constitutive element of the production process, influences the discontinuity of film production which in turn requires actors with strong 'personality' (p. 421).

5. Dudley Andrew, 'Adaptation' in Leo Braudy and Marshall Cohen (ed.), *Film Theory and Criticism* (Oxford: Oxford University Press, 1999), pp. 452–60.

6. Jonathan Coe, '*The Crucible*', *New Statesman and Society*, 28 February 1997, p. 43.

7. For more about the historical Abigail which Miller uses, see Robert A. Martin, 'Arthur Miller's *The Crucible*: Background and Sources' in James J. Martine (ed.), *Critical Essays on Arthur Miller* (Boston: G.K. Hall and Company, 1979), pp. 93–104. For more on the historical sources of Hawthorne's Hester Prynne, see Michael J. Colacurcio, '"The Woman's Own Choice": Sex, Metaphor, and the Puritan "Sources" of *The Scarlet Letter*' in Michael J. Colacurcio (ed.), *New Essays on The Scarlet Letter* (Cambridge: Cambridge University Press, 1985), pp. 101–35.

8. Gregory Cerio, Carolyn Ramsay, Jeff Shnauffer, Liz McNeil and Greg Aunapu, 'Eye of the Tiger', *People Weekly*, 24 June 1996, pp. 88–96.

9. 'Winona Ryder', *People Weekly*, 12 May 1997, p. 133.

10. Ibid., p. 133.

11. Braudy, 'Stage and Screen', p. 419–25.

12. Ibid., p. 423.

13. Cerio *et al.*, 'Eye of the Tiger', p. 88.

14. Ibid., p. 91.

15. David Handelman, 'Winona Ryder' in Peter Travers (ed.), *The Rolling Stone Film Reader* (New York: Pocket Books, 1996), pp. 284–90.

16. Handelman, 'Winona Ryder', p. 288.

17. On her third day at a new junior high school, mistaken as an effeminate boy, Ryder was beaten up for being a 'faggot' (Handelman, p. 288) – learning in no uncertain

terms society's intolerance of gender confusion and 'disguise'.

18. Cerio, 'Eye of the Tiger', p. 91.
19. Ibid., p. 91.
20. Ibid., p. 91.
21. Handelman, 'Winona Ryder', p. 284.
22. Cerio, 'Eye of the Tiger', p. 91.
23. Handelman, 'Winona Ryder', p. 284.
24. Cerio, 'Eye of the Tiger', p. 90.
25. Handelman, 'Winona Ryder', p. 287.
26. Cerio, 'Eye of the Tiger', p. 91.
27. For a discussion of this split and its representation in popular film, see Michael Ryan and Douglas Kellner, 'The Politics of Sexuality', *Camera Politica: The Politics and Ideology of Contemporary Hollywood in Film* (Bloomington and Indianapolis: Indiana University Press, 1990), pp. 136–67.
28. Adler, 'Hester Prynncesse', p. 58.
29. See Richard Alleva, '"A" is for Appalling', *Commonweal*, 17 November 1995, pp. 20–1, and Richard Corliss, 'A "Scarlet" for the Unlettered', *Time*, 23 October 1995, p. 94.
30. See Stanley Kauffmann, '*Striptease*', *New Republic*, 29 July 1996, p. 25. Unlike most reviewers, Kauffmann praises Moore for attempting to act in a movie that is so different from her usual films: 'Unlike many top female stars, especially those specializing in sex bombing, she wants to vary her pictures, to do lots of different things.' But he dismisses the notion of the film's importance to Moore as a career move – 'it was simply a switch', he says.
31. See Tom Gunning, 'Narrative Discourse and the Narrator System' in Leo Braudy and Marshall Cohen (eds), *Film Theory and Criticism* (Oxford: Oxford University Press, 1999), pp. 461–72.
32. The term is André Bazin's. See 'Theater and Cinema' in Braudy and Cohen, *Film Theory and Criticism*, pp. 408–18.
33. How well he succeeded in this is a matter of some scholarly debate. See Nina Baym,'The Romantic Malgré Lui: Hawthorne in "The Custom-House"' in Seymour

Gross (ed.), *The Scarlet Letter*, 3rd edn (New York: W.W. Norton and Company, 1988), pp. 265–72.

34. In contrast to my reading, see Roger Bromley's insightful 'Imagining the Puritan Body: The 1995 Cinematic Version of Nathaniel Hawthorne's *The Scarlet Letter*' in Deborah Cartmell and Imelda Whelehan (eds), *Adaptations* (London: Routledge, 1999), pp. 63–80. Bromley sees the film's romantic revision of the novel's ending as the culmination of an asocial individualism which dehistoricises Hawthorne's dialectical under-standing of Hester and her relationship to the Puritan community. While I agree, I would still maintain that the film's move from history to romance provides a sense of feminine 'empowerment' (even if it is only in the con-servative sense of that word) typified by the popular romance genre, which would be hard for many readers, male and female, to extract from the novel's ending.

35. Corliss, 'A "Scarlet" for the Unlettered', p. 94.

36. Brian D. Johnson, '*The Scarlet Letter* Directed by Roland Joffé', *Maclean's*, 23 October 1995, p. 68.

37. Some of these historical figures are briefly mentioned in Hawthorne's novel (Ann Hutchinson and Ann Hibbens) and the film expands and combines them through the character of Harriet Hibbens. Others are historical figures or events imported into the story (Tituba/'Mituba', the Salem witch trial, Metacom, and King Philip's War). For more on Ann Hutchinson, see Michael J. Colacurcio, 'Footsteps of Ann Hutchinson: The Context of *The Scarlet Letter*' in Gross (ed.), *The Scarlet Letter*, pp. 213–30. For Ann Hibbens, see Charles Ryskamp, 'The New England Sources of *The Scarlet Letter*' in Gross (ed.), *The Scarlet Letter*, pp. 191–204. Mituba is based on the historical Tituba, an African American servant caught up in the Salem witch trials, who has reappeared in important works of fiction. Bromley in 'Imagining the Puritan Body' suggests that the sources for the film's incorporation of Tituba and the Salem witch trial conflates parts of Arthur Miller's *The Crucible* and Maryse Condé's *I, Tituba, Black Witch of Salem* (Charlottesville: University Press of Virginia, 1992). The historical Metacom or Metacomet,

renamed Philip and known to the Puritans as King Philip, led the Wampanoags and other Native American tribes in a military campaign, King Philip's War (1675–76), that severely threatened the Puritan settlements of Massachusetts.

38. Jill Lepore, 'The Scarlet Letter/Pocahontas', *American Historical Review*, Vol. 101, No. 4 (October 1996), pp. 1166–1168.

39. Lepore, 'The Scarlet Letter', p. 1168.

40. Midge Decter, 'The Witches of Arthur Miller', *Commentary*, Vol. 103, No. 3 (March 1997), pp. 54–6.

41. Jonathan Coe, 'The Crucible', *New Statesman and Society*, 28 February 1997, p. 43.

42. Martin, 'Arthur Miller's *The Crucible*: Background and Sources', p. 102.

43. Decter, 'The Witches of Arthur Miller', p. 56.

44. Richard Corliss, 'Going All the Way', *Time*, 2 December 1996, p. 81.

45. Quoted in Edmund S. Morgan, 'Bewitched', *New York Review of Books*, 9 January 1997, pp. 4–6.

46. Quoted in John Calhoun, '*The Crucible*', *TCI*, Vol. 31, No. 1 (January 1997), pp. 22–5

47. Quoted in Calhoun, '*The Crucible*', p. 23.

48. Bazin, 'Theater and Cinema', *Film Theory and Criticism*, p. 418.

49. Quoted in Calhoun, '*The Crucible*', p. 24.

50. Stanley Kauffmann, 'Later-day Look', *New Republic*, 16 December 1996, pp. 30–2.

51. Ibid., p. 32.

52. Ibid., p. 31.

53. Morgan, 'Bewitched', p. 6.

54. In this regard, costume designer Bob Crowley's revelation that as the movie progresses they change Ryder's look so that 'she ends up looking more like the village elders [while] the rest of the girls stay as they were' is significant. Calhoun, '*The Crucible*', p. 25.

55. Quoted in Morgan, 'Bewitched', p. 6.

56. Ibid., p. 6.

57. Morgan is following in a long line of critics who have defended Miller on this score. See E. Miller Budick,

'History and Other Spectres in *The Crucible*' in Harold Bloom (ed.), *Modern Critical Views: Arthur Miller* (New York: Chelsea House Publishers, 1987), pp. 127–44. While Budick acknowledges that Miller's revision of Abigail is a 'major historical fabrication' he defends it on the grounds that it helps to delineate 'that field of ambiguous moral constitution in which both the individual and his community must define and measure moral "goodness"' (p. 132). The point that Budick and others miss, however, is that the individual and her community may have a different understanding of one's 'moral constitution' based on sexual difference.

58. Morgan, 'Bewitched', p. 6.
59. J. Hoberman, 'The Witching Hour', *Village Voice*, 3 December 1996, p. 61.
60. Morgan, 'Bewitched', p. 4.
61. Miller, *The Crucible*, p. 2052.
62. See John Simon, 'Play Rach 3 for Me', *National Review*, 27 January 1997, pp. 56–7. Simon complains that before her role as Abigail, Ryder had been 'veering from sweet to sickening in ... good-girl roles' (p. 57).
63. Peter Travers, 'The Devil Made Them Do It', *Rolling Stone*, 12 December 1996, pp. 89–90.
64. Hoberman, 'The Witching Hour', p. 61.
65. Ibid., p. 61.

6

Mrs Dalloway and *Orlando*: The Subject of Time and Generic Transactions

Lesley Higgins and Marie-Christine Leps

> The problem's not the hero, but the struggle. Can you make a film about a struggle without going through the traditional process of creating heroes? It's a new form of an old problem.
>
> Michel Foucault, 'Film and Popular Memory'[1]

Virginia Woolf knew that powerful biographies never tell the story of a personal journey, but rather analyse the discursive practices which shape subjectivities and delimit their itineraries. She also knew that the plots we read and the plots we live by are inextricably linked; that the same cultural, political and economic pressures apply to both kinds of fiction. *Mrs Dalloway* (1925), for example, rewrites the day-in-the-life narrative, a modernist classic,[2] so that Clarissa Dalloway's preparations for a lavish party are made to make sense within the context of patriarchal, imperial England after the First World War. The text reveals that any private moment of civilised pleasure is suffused with the same power/knowledge relations which drive a shell-shocked veteran to suicide or compel an eminent physician to prescribe 'order' and 'proportion' for his patients. *Orlando: A Biography* (1928) inverts this strategy by allowing the eponymous character to experience being him- and her-self from the 1580s to the 1920s; as the undying subject of modernity changes and crosses sexes, the rarefaction produced by vectors of gender, class and race comes to light.

Woolf's various experiments in life-writing work to identify and at times redirect the forces and effects of present conditions of existence. These novels make visible the processes by which the past continues to impinge upon the present, and also how the common categories of common sense, which actualise past struggles, can be transformed to produce a different future. Through the distancing effects of irony, parody and personification, her texts inscribe the writer's intervention and summon the reader's participation in the politics of life forms.

Not surprisingly, both novels became films in the 1990s, when the nature and representation of identities saturated contemporary culture and warfare. The first segment of this chapter examines the problematic of identity and the subject of time in Woolf's biographical fictions. The second considers Marleen Gorris's *Mrs Dalloway* (1998) and Sally Potter's *Orlando* (1992) in order to explore the different interpretative possibilities afforded by the directors' present and by the cinematic medium. These analyses will allow us, finally, to trace how Woolf's past work continues to affect contemporary modes of knowing and being. But do such reverberations make these texts 'classics' of either literature or film? We will argue against such a claim because of Woolf's relentless efforts to demonstrate that mechanisms for controlling meaning and value (such as the label 'classic') are never timeless or universal but instead historical, normalising, conflictual, and sometimes deadly.

'I want to revolutionize biography in a night.' Virginia Woolf's jesting words actually foreground crucial issues regarding the politics of meaning and the production of identity in life and life-writing. Her innovative texts counter any notions that life is individual, substantial and knowable in its past and present. *Mrs Dalloway* and *Orlando* insist that subjectivity is social, relational and constructed; that identity is but an alibi that masks, with the semblance of coherence and closure, various and at times contradictory cultural investments. Furthermore, Woolf's revolutionary forms contrarily demonstrate that traditional biographies and realist novels are co-conspirators in the subjectivisation of individuals commonly identified as men and women, nobles and servants, soldiers and politicians. Meaning is not the integral, causal and developmental figure promoted by conventional texts (whether social-scientific, political or literary); put another way, biographies should not constitute history, but essay the present historically.

Mrs Dalloway deftly registers the extent to which regulatory mechanisms govern the one and the many. Characters' ostensibly random, independent meanderings along the streets of London are shown to follow prefigured political, economic, gender, ethnic and class lines. The novel purportedly tells the story of an ordinary June day in 1923 when an upper-class woman prepares to host a large party. But the privileged life of Clarissa Dalloway, seemingly undamaged by the recent war, is continually juxtaposed with that of Septimus Warren Smith, a shell-shocked veteran who can only reaffirm that 'life is good'[3] by ending it. Physicians have been prescribing liberal doses of the English way-of-life for his anguish (porridge, soccer, outings), insisting that he keep his sense of 'proportion, divine proportion'[4] as they prepare his isolation and confinement. But Warren Smith recognises his current enemies only too well: 'human nature, in short, was on him – the repulsive brute, with the blood-red nostrils'[5] – and this is what finally kills him. War, for Woolf, is not a temporary aberration, but the *reductio ad absurdum* of her culture's way of life.

Tied to this life–death tandem is a series of characters whose lives and positions instantiate the major institutional forces of governance: the judiciary, the army, the Empire, the industrial middle class, the church, health care services, and academia.[6] By moving from one strand of thought to another, from the present to the past, from quotidian observations to daydreams and hallucinations, the narrative demonstrates the extent to which '"the utmost happiness to be enjoyed in this life"'[7] serves only to strengthen the state.

The text carefully traces the ever-narrowing paths followed by all the characters: 'the wild, the daring, the romantic' Sally Seton becomes Lady Rosseter, wife of the cotton manufacturer, with the big house in Manchester and the 'five enormous boys';[8] Hugh Whitbread, the 'perfect specimen of the public school type' ('No country but England could have produced him'), becomes the food- and power-loving official

– the 'admirable Hugh';[9] Peter Walsh, the minor Anglo-Indian imperial bureaucrat, is so effectively subjectivised that the predictable string of failures which constitutes his life (as student, socialist, husband, civil servant, lover) does not prevent him from maintaining his admiration for 'the triumphs of civilisation', 'the splendid achievement [of] ... London; the season; civilisation';[10] and so on. Plot development relentlessly demonstrates how people's lives are rarefied and diminished until they become normal, ordinary, perfectly understandable for everyone, and yet strange and incomprehensible to themselves: 'But often now this body she wore ..., this body, with all its capacities, seemed nothing – nothing at all. She had the oddest sense of being herself invisible; unseen; unknown; there being no more marrying, no more having of children now, but only this astonishing and rather solemn progress with the rest of them, up Bond Street, this being Mrs Dalloway; not even Clarissa any more, this being Mrs Richard Dalloway.'[11]

The temporal compression of *Mrs Dalloway* is answered by the expansiveness of *Orlando*, which traces the various ways in which the possibilities of life have been governed and cir-cumscribed throughout modernity. Gender's enforcing hand is dramatised by placing the eponymous subject in a perpetual, playful state of becoming: a young English aristocrat (a favourite of Elizabeth I) becomes an official of Queen Anne's imperial government in Constantinople who becomes a woman who, returning to George II's London, needs to cross-dress to remain mobile, yet becomes a wife who becomes a Victorian mother who ends up a celebrated writer, at 'the twelfth stroke of midnight, Thursday, the eleventh of October, Nineteen hundred and Twenty Eight',[12] on a wild goose chase ... literally. In the final segment, Orlando the woman feels 'haunted':

[F]or though one may say, as Orlando said ... Orlando? still the Orlando she needs may not come; these selves of which we are built up, one on top of another, as plates are piled high on a waiter's hand, have attachments elsewhere, sympathies, little constitutions and rights of their own, call them what you will ... for everybody can multiply from his own experience the different terms which his different selves have made with him.[13]

Subjectivity (displayed and displaced in this passage's pronominal shifts from 'she' to 'their' to 'him') is enacted as a series of overlaying selves in a text which questions the meaning and limits of gender in the spaces of social and narrative representation. Yet the number of selves that are allowed to come out always depends upon actual contingencies.

Never, in either book, is the reader presented with an unobstructed view of the characters or their situations; a narrative presence mediates the reader's apprehension and calls attention to the constructedness of life forms – biological, social and biographical. In *Mrs Dalloway* the narrator functions as a conductor, orchestrating the reader's perception of disparate streams of consciousness, all the while subtly keeping time ('Big Ben was beginning to strike, first the warning, musical; then the hour, irrevocable'[14]). This narrative procedure of knowledge production (mapping the relational character of identity) is thematised in the novel when Peter Walsh remembers Clarissa Dalloway's theory 'to explain the feeling they had of dissatisfaction; not knowing people; not being known'.

> For how could they know each other? You met every day; then not for six months, or years ... But she said, sitting on the bus going up Shaftesbury Avenue, she felt herself everywhere; not 'here, here, here'; and she tapped the back of the seat; but everywhere ... So that to know her, or any one, one must seek out the people who completed them; even the places. Odd affinities she had with people she had never spoken to ... [T]he unseen part of us, which spreads wide, the unseen might survive, be recovered somehow attached to this person or that, or even haunting certain places, after death. Perhaps – perhaps'.[15]

Completion is the novel's project, shared by narrator and reader: a specific articulation of presences that makes possible new meanings by differently articulating intersections of the epistemological and ontological.

In *Orlando*, the narrator's identifying presence functions more like that of an overbearing, loud-speaking, self-obsessed tour guide repeatedly bemoaning the difficulties of his task. This playful, ironic device not only parodies Woolf's other writings, but life-writing in general. While purportedly tracing the becoming of Orlando, the narrator stubbornly remains at the surface, constantly insisting that nothing of interest ever takes place, evacuating meaning until the only recourse is to 'leave a great blank here', on page 242. Discontinuous historical tableaux stage social conventions of being and doing: gender roles and political offices are rendered through a flurry of fashion statements, tea parties, banquets of state, wax seals and legal parchments. Yet the serious work of the fictional parody is to reiterate inescapable forces of governance which limit the possibilities of life through gender, class, race and sexual orientation. Orlando can only survive through submission to monarchical whims, Augustan misogyny, Victorian crinolines, property entailments, marital estate, and bodily 'twangings and tinglings'.[16]

But how to translate such critical fictions into film? In her 1926 essay 'The Cinema' Woolf hypothesises that,

> if so much of our thinking and feeling is connected with seeing there must be some residue of visual emotion not seized by artist or painter-poet which may await the cinema ... Something abstract, something moving, something calling only for the very slightest help from words or from music to make itself intelligible – of such movements, of such abstractions, the films may in time to come be composed.[17]

Marleen Gorris's *Mrs Dalloway* (1997) and Sally Potter's *Orlando* (1992) realise this potential in several ways. Both films emphatically stage the pastness of the past: Gorris uses different film stocks (Kodak for richly coloured memories; Fuji for a bloodless postwar present);[18] Potter chromatically coordinates and keys each historical set design, allowing the colours and the lighting to 'brin[g] it all to life'.[19] Lavish costuming in both films is accentuated by camerawork that focuses on embroidery, jewels, hat design, a frayed cuff, the sound and smoke of a locomotive,[20] thus foregrounding the metonymic ruse which allows small details to signify entire social modes of production. '"A lot of those images"', Potter explains, '"represent what for a lot of my life I have been struggling against, whether it be inheritance or symbolic inheritance and all that it hides. But then whatever a camera looks at, it glamorises, and there is a beauty in all those shapes and textures ... [I] tried to subvert what is being set up – that seemed to me a useful way of looking at English history. In each scene, each frame even, there is an element of contra-diction which makes it not, I really hope, just a glorification of the English heritage."'[21] On the contrary, the film provides a powerful visual substantiation of Woolf's acerbic ironies and 'mock style'.[22]

Soundtracks intensify differently. Gorris uses the sounds of combat in the midst of a pastoral park scene or Bond Street to manifest the war's continuing, invasive presence in Warren Smith's afflicted life – a physical connection also imposed upon the listening audience. The plangent notes of strings, piano and exploding mortars connect his daily hallucinations with the moment of pause preceding his suicide, thereby con-cretising the functional equivalence between the way of life promulgated by his physicians and the way of death necessi-tated by economic and political imperatives. Intermixing the sounds of combat with those of classical music, using opera as the aural correlative of mortal anguish, forcefully signifies the inextricable relation between civilisation and war. Potter's carefully crafted soundtrack (she co-wrote the score with David Motion) includes the enhanced presence of heartbeats, bird song, scratching skate blades, wind and rain, thereby registering the sounds (and, synaesthetically, the feeling) of everyday life as the audience knows them in the midst of the 'irreality' of her cinematic narrative.[23]

Complementary visual and auditory textures thus bring the past to life with a keen immediacy of sensation. These cinematic pleasures come at a cost, however: the price of substantiation. In both films, the past *is* the past (singular, shared, linear, unalterable), and it leads to the present. In the film *Mrs Dalloway*, the consistent and progressive character of the flashbacks – so different from the temporally unsettling and tunnel-like intrusions of Woolf's novel[24] – concretise the past as a *real* set of events with a commonly available meaning.[25] The film concludes nostalgically with a freeze-frame of Clarissa, Sally and Peter enjoying the leisure of a privileged youth, before marriage. Such an ending confirms Gorris's film as the story of lost opportunities, missed love affairs and wasted potential. Even the rich and powerful, we are told, have their unhappy moments. Woolf's *Mrs Dalloway* conveys the infinite multiplicity of the past, known only partially and always refracted through the voluntary and involuntary memories of troubled consciousnesses. Scenes from the past impinge on the present, impede perception and limit the future. Nonetheless, the novel ends, stubbornly, with the recognition and reaffirmation of Clarissa's presence ('For there she was'[26]) as 'gift' and potential for transformation through understanding. Only Clarissa instinctively accepts Septimus's suicide and recognises the soul-forcing, 'obscurely evil' strength of social order and proportion; only Clarissa is inflamed with an all-consuming anger; only she knows her parties to be a tribute to life and an offering to others. The film, on the other hand, both hystericises Clarissa and elevates Peter into a dashing, tanned, romantic hero untouched by political complications.

However parodically, Woolf's *Orlando* tightens the correlation between gendered subjectivities and social order. The opening sentences interlace the governmental strands of patriarchy, property and empire:

He – for there could be no doubt of his sex, though the fashion of the time did something to disguise it – was in the act of slicing at the head of a Moor which swung from the rafters ... Orlando's father, or perhaps his grandfather, had struck it from the shoulders of a vast Pagan who had started up under the moon in the barbarian fields of Africa; and now it swung, gently, perpetually, in the ... attic rooms of the gigantic house of the lord who had slain him.[27]

Potter's *Orlando* begins, as it ends, as a story of personal development and ultimate freedom.[28] Orlando is introduced as a sensitive young man, more at home in a pastoral setting, who simply craves another. The introductory female voiceover description is interrupted by the character himself at the moment of pronominal identification: 'But when he – "that is, I" [Tilda Swinton's Orlando interjects, looking straight at the camera] – came into the world [the voiceover continues], he was looking for something else. Though heir to a name that meant power, land and property, surely when Orlando was born, it wasn't privilege he sought, but company.' From the outset, subjective camera techniques inscribe the viewer as complicitous company with a shared horizon of understanding: comments addressed to the camera, simple understatements such as 'very interesting person' (Queen Elizabeth I), 'terrific play' (*Othello*), or 'it would never have worked; a man must follow his heart', do not explain an unfamiliar scene so much as suggest that the protagonist is already our contemporary, as distant from the past as we are. Eventually, so complicitous has the audience become that words are superfluous – Orlando's knowing gaze in the audience's direction suffices to punctuate key moments of the diegesis with shared irony.[29]

Thus Orlando's desires and future are always assured in Potter's film, and indeed will come to include literary success, a beautiful daughter, and a singing angel who proclaims, 'At last, I am free. At last, at last, to be free of the past. And of a future that beckons me. I am coming, I am coming. Neither a woman nor a man. We are joined, we are one, with a human face.' Granted, the angel (impersonated by Jimmy Somerville, who sings throughout the film) is a send-up of the *deus ex machina* trope.[30] Granted, this figure parodies the movie's teleological drive as signalled by the constant motivation for change: this Orlando never ages because Queen Elizabeth stipulates perpetual youth as the condition for granting him property; this Orlando becomes a woman because he will not take up arms and kill another; this Orlando eschews marriage; and so on. According to Potter, these alterations were necessary '"to strengthen some of the narrative muscle for cinematic purposes – to supply little bits of motivation for the story's premise, to make it psychologically convincing on film'".[31] Just so: to paraphrase Foucault, Potter's film is about the hero's personal journey, not about social, political and economic struggles as they affect individuals. Orlando is always Orlando, whatever the mirror may reveal. 'Same person. No difference at all,' says Orlando as she admires her new female body; then, turning to address the camera, she adds, 'Just a different sex.' Woolf's novel would have it otherwise. Change is unmotivated and unexplained in her biography. The narrator's initial stipulation of sameness at the moment of biological transformation is soon contradicted; gender colonises the body, inflects its desires, and directs its actions elsewhere. 'Thus', the narrator reluctantly acknowledges, 'there is much to support the view that it is clothes that wear us and not we them; we may make them take the mould of arm or breast, but they mould our hearts, our brains, our tongues to their liking.'[32]

Both films, but especially Potter's, ultimately reiterate the liberal humanist dream of personal freedom and individual identity. Potter's Orlando is finally liberated from the fetters of gender, property and privilege, and accompanied by a videocamera-wielding daughter. Completing the narrative framing device, the voiceover asserts, 'But she is changed. She is no longer trapped by destiny. And, ever since she let go of the past, she found her life was beginning.' Woolf's Orlando knows no such easy answers. Social pressures are maintained rather than denied: only her son's birth entitles her position at the family estate; her compulsory husband, 'now grown a fine sea captain', returns home in an airplane. But this 'classic' happy ending is immediately subverted by the final figure of the wild goose '[springing] up over his head',[33] which confirms the fictional satire.

Why would Potter do such a thing – affirm an essential identity for all human beings? Perhaps because of her present: an era of multiplying genocides euphemistically known as ethnic cleansings, when the recognition of difference, in terms of race, religion, or sexual orientation, justifies war on the European and African continents, the fire-bomb deaths of three boys in Northern Ireland, or the lethal beating (yet another) of a gay man in a US college town. Declaring sameness could be more strategic, politically.

Yet there is a moment in Woolf's novel, judiciously translated to the screen by Potter, which inscribes the reader/viewer in the implied author's attempt to alter the balance of power relations, dislodge acceptable truths, and thus foreshadow the possibility of amending conditions of existence. Orlando's life-writer pauses briefly to mention the following curiosity:

> Near London Bridge, where the river had frozen to a depth of some twenty fathoms, a wrecked wherry boat was plainly visible, lying on the bed of the river ... The old bumboat woman, who was carrying her fruit to market on the Surrey side, sat there in her plaids and farthingales with her lap full of apples, for all the world as if she were to serve a customer, though a certain blueness about the lips hinted the truth.[34]

Having noted the presence of the frozen corpse, however, the biographer quickly moves on to describe enthusiastically the 'brilliancy' of the Great Frost, when aristocrats could dine and dance on the frozen Thames. Yet this act of narrative enfolding makes manifest the ethical responsiveness of the writing subject – marks its outrage, and summons the reader. With vivid directness, Potter's modified point-of-view shot forces the viewer into the woman's place under the ice's snowy surface. The scene begins with the sovereign's laughing face staring directly down, into the camera; on either side, two male courtiers replicate his gaze and gaiety, while a third witness looks sideways towards them, embodying a critical yet silent objection. Next, positioned behind the observers, the camera reveals the object of mirth: the peasant woman's frozen body. Then immediately, a larger shot features the king's attendants clumsily manoeuvring a cloth to prevent his feet from ever touching the ice. The royal progress is subsequently framed by subjects either labouring to survive or enjoying their leisurely ice-skating (including Orlando and his current love interest, Sasha). Rather than dismissing or obviating the constraints of gender, class privilege and governance, this particular episode compellingly transmits their deadly effects.

Asked about the differences between Virginia Woolf's *Orlando* and her own, Potter explains, '"So I made various changes with my heart in my mouth, as one does when dealing with a great classic of literature. I hope we're being true to the spirit of the book if not to the letter of it."'[35] Not according to critic Jane Marcus: 'I can't believe anyone who helped with the making of this mockery of genius has ever read the book ... They were not familiar with the contested meanings critics have seen in *Orlando*, because it is not even a minor "classic" in England, or they would not have dared to desecrate it.'[36] Ironically enough, both invoke the same, common understanding of 'the classic' to legitimate radically opposed interpretations of the novel (and the film). Thus 'the classic' functions as the discursive equivalent of Alice's 'tiny golden key' in Wonderland, opening doors marked 'authority', 'truth' and 'value'. The key serves to lock works of art, differentiate between essential and peripheral cultural moments, establish hierarchies, and govern meanings – so pervasive do such meanings and regulatory mechanisms become that the truth regime which produces 'classics', which maintains essentialist and totalising categories, must inevitably keep women in their places and send men off to wars. In *Mrs Dalloway*, for example, 'Shakespeare' is invoked by those who would dispatch large segments of the population: Warren Smith enlisted 'to save an England which consisted almost entirely of Shakespeare's plays and Miss Isabel Pole [who gave him 'a taste' of *Antony and Cleopatra*] in a green dress walking in a square';[37] Lady Bruton, loving 'this isle of men, this dear, dear land' in terms reminiscent of *Richard II*,[38] wants to resolve England's problem of the newly unemployed – demobilised soldiers and women forced to surrender wartime jobs – with 'a project for emigrating young people' to Canada.[39]

Accusations that Gorris's film fails the novel by recycling 'emotional set-pieces' and 'commonplace[s] of country-house cinema'[40] seem off the mark because Woolf's text repeatedly cites accepted categories of common sense to demonstrate the governing forces of normalisation in the experience of every day. Interpretative problems arise, however, concerning Clarissa Dalloway's crucial 'moment of being'. Woolf's novel brings the aesthetic and ethical project of completion to its climax when Mrs Dalloway walks away from the Bradshaws, enters a small room, and comprehends not only Warren Smith's death (it is through her thoughts alone that the event is described in the text), but its necessary relation to her life. When she goes to the window the sight of an old woman 'in the room opposite' doing the same, staring 'straight at her', reminds Clarissa that 'she must go back. She must assemble' and resume her normal duties[41] – which she does. In Gorris's film, on the other hand, Clarissa is rescued from near-collapse by her husband, who shepherds her away from the Bradshaws' discussion of shell-shock and suicide (her over-reaction is signalled by POV close-ups of their mouths). Dalloway's moment is further demeaned by displacing it to the window: unwittingly or not, the effect is to reiterate a cliché of the classic Hollywood 'woman's film', in which images of hysterical or paranoid women 'looking through windows or waiting at windows abound'.[42] Given that Septimus killed himself by 'plunging' out of a window, Clarissa's heightened awareness is correlated to his mental illness. Moreover, her voiceover thoughts are interrupted, repeatedly, by interspliced exchanges between Peter and Sally that recall the past and belittle Clarissa. The climax is thus reduced to a well worn, sexist resolution into the already known; predictably, the 'classic' scene impedes any new thought and can only reiterate established relations of power-knowledge.[43]

The production companies, distributors and marketing managers involved with both films depended upon the cachet of the novelist's name to promote their adaptations, but were disappointed by sluggish market reception. Perhaps they over-estimated the general appeal of a feminist icon, positioned as hero of what is now known as first-wave feminism. *Orlando*'s art-house credentials were recognised, but filmgoers expecting either a 'faithful' translation of Woolf's text onto the screen, or a celebration of same-sex desire, were disappointed.[44] *Mrs*

Dalloway's lack of appeal, when compared with other 'heritage' films such as *Remains of the Day* (James Ivory, 1993) and *Howards End* (James Ivory, 1992), might have been connected to viewer fatigue with the genre or the lack of a compelling romantic plot. Both works overlapped, but did not quite coincide, with accepted categories giving shape either to war movies or heritage films, for although viewers could recognise the main female protagonists, they could not, finally, sympathise with them (as they could with Rezia and Septimus, or perhaps even Peter). The problem might well have derived from Woolf's plots themselves. Her aesthetics manage to depersonalise individual lives and use them as signs of broader conflicts, fought loudly on various military and imperial fronts, and at a low rumble in the everyday business of flowers and parties – usually leading to fear, anger, violence and madness. Her texts' ethical imperatives call upon the receiving subject to re-view her or his own position, its gender, racial and class distinctions, and acknowledge involvement in these wider political plottings. Such lines are not easy to follow: they disturb, and require much more than assent or recognition. In other words, Woolf's novels are not the stuff that blockbusters are made of.

Ultimately, both films work through identification: the viewer is made to sympathise with characters, to pity workers, and to consider war as an inhuman aberration. Woolf's reader is always led to understand that personal empathy must be tempered by social critique. Subjectivity is transacted daily, its potential only realised in constant struggle. Subjugation is decried in every guise: the coloniser's tyranny abroad is directly connected to the patriarch's tyranny at and in his home; war is revealed as the necessary cost of masculinist, militaristic society. Instead of aspiring to sameness, the reader is urged by Woolf's austere pragmatism to acknowledge, analyse, and negotiate with difference.

Notes

1. Michel Foucault, 'Film and Popular Memory' (1974) in Sylvère Lotringer (ed.), *Foucault Live: Collected Interviews, 1961–1984*, trans. Lysa Hochroth and John Johnston

(New York: Semiotext[e], 1989), p. 125. In his discussion of cinema (specifically, *The Sorrow and the Pity*, 1970, *Lacombe Lucien*, 1974, and *The Night Porter*, 1974), as it constructs and distorts the 'history' of twentieth-century warfare, Foucault observes that,

> There's a real fight going on. Over what? Over what we can roughly describe as popular memory ... [A] whole number of apparatuses have been set up ('popular literature', cheap books, and the stuff that's taught in school as well) to obstruct the flow of this popular memory. And it could be said that this attempt has been pretty successful ... Today, cheap books aren't enough. There are much more effective means like television and the cinema. And I believe this was one way of reprogramming popular memory, which existed but had no way of expressing itself. So people are shown not what they were, but what they must remember having been ... In my view, the politically important phenomenon is, rather than any one particular film, that of the series, the network established by all these films and the place – excuse the pun – they 'occupy'. (Foucault, 'Film', pp. 123–5)

2. Woolf's narrative thus engages with and answers James Joyce's *Ulysses* (1922), even then considered the 'classic' modernist text, by relating formal and stylistic experiments to the politics of meaning in everyday life.
3. Virginia Woolf, *Mrs Dalloway* (Harmondsworth: Penguin, 1992), p. 132.
4. Woolf, *Mrs Dalloway*, p. 109.
5. Ibid., p. 101.
6. The state (the Prime Minister; various lords; politicians such as Richard Dalloway, MP; bureaucrats like Hugh Whitbread); the judiciary (Sir John Buckhurst); the industrial middle class (Sally Seton, wife of the cotton manufacturer); the army (Septimus Warren Smith, Evans, Mrs Foxcroft's 'nice boy [who] was killed', the soldiers who continue to march in London); the empire (Peter Walsh, the administrator, and Lady Bruton, who

advocates emigration for the unemployed); immigration (Rezia Smith, the Italian war bride; the 'colonial' who 'insulted the House of Windsor'); the church (Miss Kilman); mental and physical health (Drs Bradshaw and Holmes); and academia (Prof. Brierly). It has been suggested in the *Times Literary Supplement* that Potter's adaptation of *Orlando* included 'adding some feminist hints and anti-imperial touches' (Lindsay Duguid, 'A sapphic fantasy', *TLS*, No. 4694 [19 March 1993], p. 19). In fact, Woolf's critique of imperialism dates back to *The Voyage Out* (1914) and is further developed in both *Mrs Dalloway* and *Orlando*.

7. Foucault is quoting Delamare's *Compendium*; in Foucault, *Omnes et Singulatim: Towards a Criticism of 'Political Reason'*, The Tanner Lectures on Human Value, ed. S.M. McMurrin (Cambridge: Cambridge University Press, 1980–1981), Vol. 2, p. 250. For further discussion of Foucault's theory of governmentality and its relation to the problematics of identity, see Higgins and Leps, '"Passport, please": legal, literary, and critical fictions of identity', *College Literature*, Vol. 25, No.1 (Winter 1998), pp. 94–138.

8. Ibid., pp. 79, 188.

9. Ibid., pp. 80, 5.

10. Ibid., pp. 165, 60.

11. Ibid., p. 11.

12. Woolf, *Orlando: A Biography* (Oxford: Oxford University Press, 1992), p. 314.

13. Ibid., p. 294.

14. Woolf, *Mrs Dalloway*, p. 128.

15. Ibid., p. 167.

16. Woolf, *Orlando*, p. 234.

17. Woolf, *Essays*, Vol. 4: 1925–1928, ed. Andrew McNeillie (London: Hogarth Press), p. 351. For further discussion of 'The Cinema', see Lia M. Hotchkiss, 'Writing the Jump Cut: *Mrs Dalloway* in the Context of Cinema' in Beth Dougherty and Eileen Barrett (eds), *Virginia Woolf: Texts and Contexts*, Selected Papers from the Fifth Annual Conference (New York: Pace University Press, 1996), pp. 134–9; and Nicola Shaughnessy, 'Is s/he or isn't s/he?:

Screening *Orlando*' in Deborah Cartmell, I.Q. Hunter, Heidi Kaye, Imelda Whelehan (eds), *Pulping Fictions: Consuming Culture Across the Literature/Media Divide* (London: Pluto Press, 1996), pp. 43–55. Sharon Ouditt offers an insightful, opposing analysis of 'The Cinema' in her essay, which also identifies the cinematic treatment of images, movement and time in *Orlando*. Ouditt, '*Orlando*: Coming Across the Divide', in Cartmell and Whelehan (eds), *Adaptations* (London: Routledge, 1999), pp. 146–56.

18. In her interview with Liam Lacey, Gorris explains, '"There was no way of working directly from the book, where you can go from the present to the past and back again in a sentence ... Originally I had wanted to shoot the past with a 16mm camera, shot off the shoulder, with the present much more static."' The idea, as Lacey notes, 'was to establish the higher energy levels of the characters in their youth. Instead, she simply used different film stocks.' Lacey, 'To the festival, Mrs Dalloway', Review of *Mrs Dalloway* by Marleen Gorris, *Toronto Globe and Mail*, (11 September 1997), p. C3. Such formal innovations can mystify certain critics: according to Lindsay Duguid, the 'film is scrappily made and jumpy; the colour harsh and odd'. In Duguid, 'The diva exclaims', *Times Literary Supplement*, 13 March 1998, p. 20.

19. In collaboration with Potter [production designers Ben van Os and Jan Roelfs], have devised a 'colour coding' for each of the narrative's many historical periods which are sharply delineated and fetishistically rendered in Woolf's prose. 'The England of Elizabeth is gold and red, that of James grey and silver, the eighteenth century is dominated by a powdery blue, and so on ... [F]or the moment when Orlando becomes a woman, we draped the room with white ... It is the lighting that brings it all to life.' (Verlina Glaessner, 'Fire and Ice', *Sight and Sound*, n.s. Vol. 2, No. 4 (August 1992), p. 14).

20. Just as Woolf's *Mrs Dalloway* answers Joyce's text, so Potter's work engages with that of Derek Jarman and Peter Greenaway (as many critics note). Additionally,

Cristina Degli-Esposti suggests a relation between Potter and Chaplin:

> In *Orlando*'s 1850 sequence the passing of time and the arrival of the future are introduced by the sound of a locomotive and by engine smoke that fills the screen in a play of lights. The scene recalls the train station scene in Charlie Chaplin's *A Woman of Paris* (1923) where smoke and chiaroscuro light effects were used to indicate the passing both of a train and of time.' (Degli-Esposti, 'Sally Potter's *Orlando* and the Neo-Baroque Scopic Regime', *Cinema Journal,* Vol. 36, No. 1 (Fall 1996), p. 80)

21. Quoted in Lizzie Francke, 'A director comes in from the cold', *Guardian,* 11 March 1993, p. 5.
22. Woolf, *A Writer's Diary*, ed. Leonard Woolf (London: Triad Panther, 1978), p. 119. For a discussion of the film's 'irreality' and satire, see Julianne Pidduck, 'Travels with Sally Potter's *Orlando*: gender, narrative, movement', *Screen,* Vol. 38, No. 2 (Summer 1997), pp. 172–89.
23. Potter, who was '"searching for a musical identity for the film for months"', produced a moving soundtrack, as several critics admiringly note. See Gary Indiana, 'Spirits Either Sex Assume: Gary Indiana Talks with Sally Potter', *Artforum*, Vol. 31 (Summer 1993), p. 91; see also Gary Sinyor, 'Glimpse of Aspiration', review of *Orlando* by Sally Potter, *The Sunday Times,* 14 March 1993, p. 21. Woolf's description of the cinema's potential to produce emotion is recognisable in Amy Taubin's praise: 'It's the music – an impossible combination of parodic and heartfelt – as much as the meticulous cinematography, decisive editing, sumptuous art direction, and witty costuming – that accounts for *Orlando*'s emotional rush.' Taubin, 'About Time', *Village Voice,* 22 June 1993, p. 62.
24. 'It took me a year's groping', Woolf writes in her diary, 'to discover what I call my tunnelling process, by which I tell the past by instalments, as I have need of it. This is my prime discovery so far.' Woolf, *A Writer's Diary*, p. 66.

25. Flashbacks have emerged as a signature of Gorris's screen-writing and film-making, as in *A Question of Silence* (1982) and *Antonia's Line* (1995). Eileen Atkins wrote the screenplay for *Mrs Dalloway*.

26. Woolf, *Mrs Dalloway*, p. 213. The novel concludes:

    > [Peter] sat on for a moment. What is this terror? what is this ecstasy? he thought to himself. What is it that fills me with extraordinary excitement?
    >
    > It is Clarissa, he said.
    >
    > For there she was.

    The final statement of being could be attributed either to Walsh or the narrator. The screenplay distributes (and thereby diminishes) the declarative. Richard Dalloway, happy to see his wife rejoin the party, exclaims, 'There you are!'; Clarissa Dalloway apologetically says to Peter Walsh, 'Here I am at last' to excuse her long absence. Never is the gift of her presence fully acknowledged or articulated.

27. Woolf, *Orlando*, p. 13.

28. Potter's decision to cast well-known art-house film star Tilda Swinton in the role of Orlando informs the viewer, from the beginning, of his destiny as a woman. As Shaughnessy observes, 'the disjunction between eye and brain, as we see a male character, whilst knowing that it is a woman cross-dressed, establishes from the outset that gender identity is to be viewed sceptically, as a not altogether convincing masquerade'. Shaughnessy, 'Is s/he', pp. 43–4. Gender as performance is reiterated by the choice of Quentin Crisp to play Queen Elizabeth I. Antithetically, Woolf's novel argues that the social constructions of gender, for women and men, are destiny.

29. Critics have read Orlando's comments to the camera differently. Degli-Esposti considers them an 'interesting cinematic codification of Woolf's stream of consciousness'. Pidduck maintains that they 'usur[p] and commen[t] upon the constraints of narrative and social codes'. Shaughnessy suggests that they 'propel' the character 'out of the illusionist cinematic space' and

create 'a gesture of complicity'. Swinton herself describes these moments as '"a look of complicity, a look of safety; it's that moment when one really addresses oneself and comes to one's own defence. It's like looking into the mirror, only without judgment, but with love."' In Dennis and Joan West, 'Achieving a State of Limitlessness: An Interview with Tilda Swinton', *Cineaste*, Vol. 20, No. 1 (1993), p. 21. Degli-Esposti, 'Sally Potter's *Orlando*', p. 78; Pidduck, 'Travels', p. 183; Shaughnessy, 'Is s/he', pp. 46, 50.

30. In his analysis of 'classical Hollywood cinema', David Bordwell suggests that,

> There are two ways of regarding the classical ending. We can see it as the crowning of the structure, the logical conclusion of the string of events, the final effect of the initial cause ... [or] a more or less arbitrary readjustment of that world knocked awry in the previous eighty minutes ... We ought, then, to be prepared for either a skillful tying up of all loose ends or a more or less miraculous appearance of what Brecht called bourgeois literature's mounted messenger. 'The mounted messenger guarantees you a truly undisturbed appreciation of even the most intolerable conditions, so it is a sine qua non for a literature whose sine qua non is that it leads nowhere.' (Bordwell, 'Classical Hollywood Cinema: Narrational Principles and Procedures', in Philip Rosen (ed.), *Narrative, Apparatus, Ideology: A Film Theory Reader* (New York: Columbia University Press, 1986), p. 21)

31. In Indiana, 'Spirits', p. 90.
32. Woolf, *Orlando*, p. 180.
33. Ibid., p. 313.
34. Ibid., *Orlando*, p. 35.
35. In Indiana, 'Spirits', p. 90.
36. Marcus, 'A tale of two cultures. I', review of *Modern Fiction Studies*: *The Multiple Muses of Virginia Woolf, Women's Review of Books,* Vol. 11, No. 4 (January 1994), pp. 11–13. On-line.

37. Woolf, *Mrs Dalloway*, pp. 94, 93.
38. Ibid., p. 198.
39. Ibid., p. 119.
40. Duguid, 'The diva exclaims', p. 20.
41. Woolf, *Mrs Dalloway*, p. 204.
42. In Mary Ann Doane, 'The "Woman's Film": Possession and Address', in Doane, Patricia Mellencamp and Linda Williams (eds), *Revision: Essays in Feminist Film Criticism*, American Film Institute Monograph Series (Frederick: University Publications of America, 1984), pp. 72–3.
43. The films for which Gorris wrote the screenplay have had a very different, feminist emphasis. See for example Neil Sinyard, '"Even the Nice Ones Aren't Nice": Sisterhood and Feminist Theory in the Early Films of Marlene Gorris, with Particular Reference to *A Question of Silence*' in Cartmell, Hunter, Kaye and Whelehan (eds), *Sisterhoods: Across the Literature/Media Divide* (London: Pluto Press, 1998), pp. 101–18.
44. Regarding *Orlando*, Marcus contends that 'the film-makers didn't know of the novel's cult status in lesbian and gay culture'; many people, she argues, went to 'see a gay film. There is no sex but heterosex; Orlando does not make love to Sasha.' Marcus, 'A tale of two cultures. I', p. 11.

7

'Desire Projected Itself Visually': Watching *Death in Venice*

Stuart Burrows

> Yes, this was Venice, this the fair frailty that fawned and that betrayed, half fairy-tale, half-snare; the city in whose stagnating air the art of painting once put forth so lusty a growth, and where musicians were moved to accords so weirdly lulling and lascivious. Our adventurer felt his senses wooed by this voluptuousness of sight and sound, tasted his secret knowledge that the city sickened and hid its sickness for love of gain, and bent an ever more unbridled leer on the gondola that glided on before him.
>
> <div align="right">Thomas Mann, <i>Death in Venice</i> (pp. 55–6)</div>

With characteristic hubris, Luchino Visconti hoped that his 1971 film *Death in Venice* would be judged by the standards of the Thomas Mann novella from which it was adapted. His critics readily complied, charging Visconti with having 'emphasised homosexuality to a degree that actually changes the meaning of the story.'[1] Geoffrey Wagner thought that Dirk Bogarde, who played Aschenbach, looked 'like an absent-minded professor who is in reality a lecherous fag',[2] while Paul Zimmerman suggested that the film's 'sexual explicitness turns Aschenbach into a foolish dirty old man, and the boy into a pretty little tease'.[3] Thankfully, recent reactions to the film are free of such homophobia, although not of the vitriol: David Glassco, for example, pronounces that 'we must reject the kind of trite thoughts and obvious emotions provided by Visconti. There is a real condescension in the way he has travestied Mann.'[4]

The severity of these reactions to *Death in Venice* is a sign perhaps of critics' loyalty to Mann's purportedly 'classic' novella. Grounding their accusation that Visconti 'fail[ed] Thomas Mann'[5] is a belief in the existence of a necessarily single, authoritative reading of Mann's text. Joy Gould Boyum sums up the problem faced by directors intent on adapting literary 'classics' to the cinema:

> in the case of a classic literary work, an adaptation will be considered faithful to the extent that its interpretation remains consistent with those put forth by the interpretative community; with the interpretation (or possible interpretations) of that classic work, then, that made it a classic in the first place.[6]

According to Boyum, critical reaction to adaptations of literary classics has less to do with the 'classic' itself than with a belief in a certain interpretation of that 'classic' sanctioned by means of a retrospective appeal to the author. Much of the criticism of Visconti's film claims its authority through a tautological invocation of certain aesthetic qualities signified by the term 'classic' – timelessness, purity, truth – rather than through a reading of the text itself. In fact, the ironies and ambiguities of Mann's novella precisely guard against the sterility of these 'classic' virtues.

Frank Kermode, anxious to rescue the term 'classic' from its suggestion of the moribund, proposes that 'the books we call classics possess intrinsic qualities that endure, but possess also an openness to accommodation which keeps them alive under endlessly varying dispositions'.[7] For Kermode, imaginative re-readings, rather than intrinsic virtues, are necessary in order for a work to be deemed a 'classic'. Visconti's *Death in Venice* – attacked not only for its homoeroticism but for various crucial changes at the level of content – represents just such a re-reading. But following Kermode's definition of the 'classic' allows us to overturn the critical consensus on Visconti's film, to reveal how those critics who condemn Visconti for failing Mann's 'classic' text themselves fail to recognise how the film keeps alive the 'classic' nature of Mann's novella.

Visconti himself always insisted that his films were adoptions rather than adaptations of literary classics, and

Death in Venice succeeds precisely because it constitutes a reading of Mann's text rather than an exact transcription of novel into film. There are two crucial differences in the film: firstly, Visconti's emphasis on the sexual rather than aesthetic nature of Aschenbach's gaze; secondly, his decision to make Aschenbach a composer rather than a writer. A close examination of the novella, however, allows us to see that Visconti's film is indeed faithful to Mann – on a metaphorical if not a literal level. In order to perform a reading of the film, then, we must first offer a re-reading of the novella rather than trusting to the 'classic' reading established by the dominant interpretative community.

Both novella and film prepare the way for new readings through their shared concern with the nature of artistic reception; that is, both Mann and Visconti anticipate the ways in which their work will be read or watched. The different reactions produced by the novella and the film centre precisely on the difference between the experience of reading and the experience of watching. Whereas Mann's free indirect discourse offers almost direct access to Aschenbach's consciousness, leaving the reader to infer the form of his (the Master's) art, Visconti's adaptation provides direct access to Aschenbach's work – his music – while refusing the point-of-view of the artist except in the ambiguous form of the flashback. Visconti replaces the complex and often complicitous linguistic relationship between Aschenbach and the narrator of Mann's text with an equally fraught one between viewer, camera and Aschenbach, remaining true to the novella's ironic questioning of artistic reception by raising questions about how we watch and understand film.

The novella's anxieties about form – centring on the potential of vision to remake the world – are reworked by Visconti's film into an investigation of the cinematic gaze. *Death in Venice* challenges Laura Mulvey's famous model of scopophilia, whereby the (masculinised) spectator actively identifies with the power of the male protagonist's gaze, by offering a homoerotic gaze.[8] According to Freud, the scopophilic instinct is originally an autoerotic one.[9] Therefore, in priviliging the fact that Aschenbach's gaze is directed toward a subject of the same gender Visconti is in fact offering the viewer an allegory of the act of film viewing itself, which depends upon just the kind of autoerotic scopophilia we see Aschenbach display. The film underscores the autoerotic nature of the cinematic viewer's gaze through its representation of Aschenbach, whose own gaze both substitutes for and competes with the viewer's.

In emphasising the auto/homoerotic gaze Visconti is in fact being far more faithful to Mann than his critics would have us believe. Aschenbach's homoerotic gaze is precisely the agent of his corruption in the novella. And because Aschenbach's literal vision cannot be separated from the narrator's metaphorical insights, no place exists within the narrative from which to judge events safely – despite the narrator's increasing attempt to distance himself from the Master. Aschenbach's gaze reflects back the narrator's own, creating a series of ambivalences both on the level of content (the narrator seems as compromised by Aschenbach's gaze as is the protagonist) and on the level of form (the very figures used to represent Aschenbach's fall are themselves corrupted by representation). The hallucinatory images that prompt the writer to go to Venice, the 'primeval wilderness-world of islands, morasses, and alluvial channels'[10] are later mapped on by the narrator to Venice itself, whose corruption resembles the 'primeval-island jungle ... where life of every sort flourishes in rankest abundance' to depict the pestilence spreading through Venice.[11]

The novella opens with Aschenbach's attention being caught by a stranger's gaze. The two men stare at one another fiercely until Aschenbach finally lowers his eyes, almost immediately feeling an overwhelming desire to look upon other scenes. In a description that suggests a starting-point for Visconti, 'Desire projected itself visually' upon Aschenbach's consciousness.[12] Leaving duty behind him, Aschenbach boards a steamer first for an island in the Adriatic and then, after this disappoints, for Venice. What first catches his eye on arrival is not Venice, however, but a grotesquely over-made-up fop. Aschenbach stares at him until he realises that the apparent youth is no youth at all; what most distresses the Master, however, is that the fop's friends appear not to notice their companion's age. Perplexed by this failure of vision on the part of others, Aschenbach covers his own eyes 'as though the world were suffering a dreamlike distortion of perspective which he might arrest by shutting it all out for a few minutes and then looking at it afresh'.[13] He opens his eyes to find his vision troubled by a series of distorted but recognisable images. Aschenbach has entered into a completely visual world, one where moral questions are subsumed by his delight in being 'absorbed in looking'.[14]

What draws the full force of Aschenbach's gaze is, however, Tadzio's 'chaste perfection of form'.[15] Staring at the boy 'beneath the watchful eye of the functionaries',[16] Aschenbach is astonished at this singular vision of mortal beauty, forcing him to 'gather up his gaze and withdraw it from the illimitable'.[17] Disinterested spectatorship turns to consuming passion only at the moment Tadzio returns Aschenbach's gaze. Forcing himself away from this rapturous exchange of looks, Aschenbach attempts to flee Venice, but what forces him to stay – beyond the excuse of his missing luggage – is ultimately sight itself: 'The hardest part', he tells himself, 'the part that more than once it seemed he could not bear, was the thought that he should never see Venice again.'[18] Sight is no longer merely restorative, it is all-consuming; Aschenbach's life of service follows a new God – that of outward vision (scopophilia) rather than inner vision (creation). Returning to his hotel room, the worshipper of purity and beauty is moved to gesture outward, waving at the beach unseen by anyone except the narrator; it is almost as if he is waving at us, the readers. Having now given himself completely to the senses rather than the spirit, 'the delight of his eye was unending'.[19]

The narrator, however, suggests that Aschenbach's new-found gift of sight is related in complex and profound ways to his former artistic and inward vision. The narrator risks an explicit comparison between the pure strong will which had succeeded in bringing Tadzio, 'this godlike work of art', into being, and Aschenbach's cold fury which 'liberated from the marble mass of language the slender forms of his art which he saw with the eye of his mind'.[20] Aschenbach's novels are described in Apollonian terms as 'the mirror and image of spiritual beauty',[21] just as Tadzio's gaze is pictured as the mirror and image – 'the copy' – of his own. The echo is appropriate for Aschenbach's fall: abandoning his self-image as the Apollonian artist, who contemplates images aware that they are merely part of the 'beautiful illusion' of the world,[22] Aschenbach responds to the reflection of himself he sees in Tadzio's eyes, fusing with the image of his desires in a Dionysian self-forgetting. The pure (aesthetic) form Aschenbach has been in service to is ironically given to him 'in the language of pictures',[23] a (sexual) language both 'moral and immoral at once'.[24] Tadzio's return of his gaze, his recognition of Aschenbach's desire, affords the Master an insight into the poverty of the inner Apollonian vision that had produced his earlier novels; in a sense the writer falls in love with the knowledge about himself which he gains from the young boy's return of his gaze.

Tadzio is a contradictory image for both the pure form that Aschenbach has been searching for within himself and the writer's own desire, and to that end the novella refuses to specify whether Tadzio's gaze is a product of Aschenbach's 'mind's eye'.[25] Mann's ambiguity implicates the reader, who is forced to negotiate between opposed readings and therefore cannot distance her/himself from Aschenbach's corruption. The reader's fall is signalled by the novella's closing words, which ironically invoke the reaction of Aschenbach's audience to the news of his death – a reaction we can no longer share: 'Some minutes passed before anyone hastened to the aid of the elderly man sitting there collapsed in his chair. They bore him to his room. And before nightfall a shocked and respectful world received the news of his decease.'[26] The language shifts back into the neutral, objective register of the Apollonian – identifying Aschenbach coldly as 'the elderly man' – only to heighten still further the biting irony of the narrator's attitude toward the Master's literary achievements. This imposed division between the reader and Aschenbach's respectful audience causes us to reflect on the knowledge of the Master we have been granted, a knowledge that – as the narrator has previously told us – is the only thing capable of corrupting the experience of art.

The extent of the audience's complicity with Aschenbach's fate forms the principal question of Visconti's film adaptation, a question posed through a subtle manipulation of point-of-view. Visconti's camera positions and cuts constantly problematise the question of whose point-of-view the viewer is sharing in order to trouble the act of viewing itself. In contradistinction to the novella, Tadzio is certainly not seen from Aschenbach's point-of-view, the film being careful to establish that what we see is not a creation of Aschenbach's mind's eye.[27] Not a single shot of Tadzio fails to specify Aschenbach's position – which is never that of the camera; the viewer sees much more of Tadzio than Aschenbach, and often sees him when the composer cannot. Repeatedly, the viewer is given the illusion that s/he is being offered Aschenbach's point-of-view, only to experience the shock of recognition when the camera pans back to include the composer in the shot. The gaze that the viewer takes pleasure in and identifies with is revealed to be that of the camera, and thus by extension her/his own – rather than Aschenbach's. Watching the homoerotic gaze operate in *Death in Venice* thus becomes a curious form of autoeroticism, as the viewer is constantly made aware not just that s/he is watching a film, but that the film s/he is watching is precisely about the act of watching a film.[28]

The first shot of Aschenbach quickly establishes this rhythm of self-recognition. Huddled up against the cold on board the steamer carrying him to Venice, the famous composer looks out to sea, the camera cutting to a shot of the beach which, according to the syntactical logic of the cinema, the viewer reads as Aschenbach's own point-of-view. Yet a further cut to the prow of the ship, to which Aschenbach has his back turned, disproves this illusion, and this separation of what the viewer sees from what Aschenbach sees is compounded by the next shot, which shows the composer asleep. With our point of visual reference absent, we experience the steamer's silent entrance into Venice alone. The isolation which surrounds the composer, reflected in his near silence, extends to the viewer, who is subjected to long scenes of the quay, the hotel and allowed to draw any conclusion from what s/he sees. Indeed, the film throughout presents the world as not subject to Aschenbach's gaze: the camera constantly lingers on scenes after Aschenbach has left them, as if to emphasise that the scenes we see are shaped less by the composer's consciousness than presented for our benefit.

This sense that the scenes we witness are seen from a point-of-view other than Aschenbach's prepares us for the composer's death, when the world now emptied of his presence continues to be filmed. When Aschenbach makes his entrance into the film's crucial scene – the moment when he spies Tadzio – he does not occupy centre stage. Having dressed and prepared as if he were about to conduct an orchestra rather than eat dinner, Aschenbach enters the hotel lobby, where our view of him is obscured by a number of different objects in the foreground, most notably the blue vases which form the centrepiece of the room. We even lose sight of him altogether for a few seconds. The effect is to establish the viewer's gaze as partly independent of Aschenbach's, although subject for the most part to the same physical limitations. Once Aschenbach is seated, the camera traverses back across the crowded room, eavesdropping on a number of different conversations while the composer is absorbed in reading a newspaper. The composer only comes to share fully our interest in gazing at the world around him after he has sighted Tadzio. The viewer's scopophilic pleasure thus precedes Aschenbach's, as if the film is suggesting that corruption is as integral to the act of viewing as it is to the act of writing in Mann's novella.

The first shot of Tadzio is taken from the angle of Aschenbach's viewing position, before the camera moves backward to include the composer in the shot looking at the boy. Slowly the lobby empties of guests after the hotelier announces dinner, but neither Aschenbach nor Tadzio's family move. Soon they are the only people left in the room. Their isolation highlights their extraordinary closeness: Aschenbach sits mere feet away from Tadzio, evoking the viewer's own position in relation to the screen for, despite his proximity, the composer's gaze goes unnoticed. Finally, after the entrance of Tadzio's mother – which we again witness from behind a vase as if it is the viewer, rather than Aschenbach, who is anxious to remain unobserved – the Polish family file slowly past the composer's chair still seemingly oblivious of his presence. Only when Tadzio reaches the furthest point of the room does he turn and face his silent watcher, the breach of decorum further enhanced by the immobile figures of the functionaries behind him. And it is this moment of recognition that provokes a reaction beyond mere curiosity in Aschenbach: his expression changes to one of fascination. The composer's desire is provoked precisely by his being caught in the act of viewing.[29]

According to Nick Browne, point-of-view is as much a mental state as an ocular one: the viewer identifies with the object of the gaze as much as with its possessor. The spectator is thus 'in several places at once – with the fictional viewer, with the viewed, and at the same time in a position to evaluate and respond to the claims of each'.[30] The cumulative effect of this displacement of the spectator from moment to moment is the introduction of the viewer to 'the moral order of the text'.[31] The importance then of Visconti's problematising of point-of-view is precisely the way in which it foregrounds the moral status of Aschenbach's gaze. Critics such as Wagner and Zimmerman who accuse Visconti of betraying Mann's intentions not only ignore the ambiguities and complexities of Mann's 'classic' original, they also fail to examine their own reactions to Visconti's camera. Far from being degraded by the viewer's gaze, Tadzio is transformed into a work of art.

More importantly, this recognition of the viewer's complicity in the camera's gaze, echoing Mann's examination of narrative's moral failings, is evoked through formal structures that parallel those in the novella. The central visual element in the film, one repeated many times, is a close-up of Aschenbach, a cut to Tadzio's face looking just slightly to the left or right of the camera at the composer, and a pan back to include Aschenbach within the field of vision. The tripartite structure is similar to Dorrit Cohn's formulation of the narrator's rhetorical pattern in Mann's novella, where we are given 'an inside view of Aschenbach's mind, followed by a judgmental intervention cast in gnomic present tense, followed by a return to Aschenbach's now properly adjusted reactions'.[32] The difference, of course, is that in the film the adjustments are made by the viewer who, in the absence of access to Aschenbach's consciousness, becomes the potential victim of the corruption engendered by vision. Irving Singer makes the important point that Visconti's zooms 'implicate the camera as an erotic go-between',[33] but he fails to point out that the viewer's knowledge depends entirely upon the camera and that therefore s/he is implicated in this eroticism. The viewer experiences the composer's retreat into the silent world of the gaze, the camera moving from the excessively detailed representation of turn-of-the-century Venice to focus almost exclusively upon Tadzio. As our sight becomes gradually more obscured by a series of often foolish objects, such as the pineapple that hides Tadzio as he walks into breakfast, our position as viewer thus mirrors Aschenbach's own skulking behind pillars and within alcoves in search of Tadzio. In point of fact, we are often offered more seductive views of the boy than are available to his lover, as though it is we who are falling in love and not the composer.

The seven flashbacks that rhythmically punctuate the film offer the only moments when we appear to be seeing events from Aschenbach's point-of-view, although even these remain ambiguous. In the first flashback, for example, the composer is unconscious, having collapsed after a concert, and therefore unable to recall the worried conversation we hear. The beginning and ending of each flashback carefully mirror the action taking place in Venice: when the composer turns while out walking in Venice the cut introducing the second flashback is to a young Aschenbach completing the turn in Austria; when Aschenbach plays happily with his daughter on the grass the cut ending the fourth flashback is to Tadzio wrestling on the sand with a friend. The flashbacks are circular – the last one ends where the first one begins, at the final concert given by Aschenbach – and suggest that the past and the present are, if not the mirror and image of one another, at least complementary: the first flashback indeed ends with a cut to Aschenbach grooming his moustache in the mirror.

This suggestion of resonances between past and present reverses Mann's division between Aschenbach's strict and fastidious past and his joyful, forgetful present. The reason for insisting upon the circularity of Aschenbach's corruption is perhaps bound up with the different relation Mann's novella and Visconti's film have to Aschenbach's art. Mann and Aschenbach share one medium, language, producing a complex narrative voice uniting irony with mimicry. Mann's novella occupies the same textual ground as Aschenbach's prose, the prose it both produces and eclipses; the governing trope of Mann's text is therefore irony, which depends upon some (perhaps illusory) sense of temporal progression to be fully effective. Visconti's film, on the other hand, is necessarily distinct from the art *his* Aschenbach creates – music – although this distinction is somewhat elided by Visconti's ever-present soundtrack. The film enters into a new relation with Aschenbach's art, one that demands partly abandoning Mann's irony while yet retaining his focus on artistic reception. Unlike Mann's hero, Visconti's Aschenbach is already corrupted when he reaches Venice. The film therefore chooses to stress that this corruption is a necessary feature of all aesthetic production. Aschenbach's desire for Tadzio is no longer the moment he realises the futility of his earlier purity, as it is for Mann, but instead a recognition of the degradation at the centre of every experience of art.

Visconti's critics have pointed out that such departures from the novella transform the nature of Aschenbach's despair: the decisions to show him falling ill before he reaches Venice, and to make Aschenbach a composer, are particularly unpopular.[34] However, Visconti's decisions are in fact explicable according to the logic of Mann's text. Far from the early purity critics have claimed for the opening sections of the novella, Aschenbach's Apollonian prose depends for its power precisely on the 'unexpected contagion' of the imagination,[35] and visual metaphors of decay and decadence are present from the very opening of the story. Visconti transfers Mann's productive ambivalence about the morality of art to the screen through three complementary techniques:[36] the destabilising of the point-of-view; Aschenbach's gaze conceived of as mimetic of the viewer's own; the viewer's emotional and aesthetic response to the composer's music. The first two strategies have been discussed above; as regards this last, in suggesting that Aschenbach's corruption begins long before the composer's trip to Venice

the film complicates our enjoyment of Aschenbach's art –
represented by Mahler's Fifth and Third Symphonies which
accompany so many crucial scenes.[37] Yet, by revealing this
corruption in a series of flashbacks, the film ensures that this
knowledge is not exposed until the closing moments. Alfried
proclaims that man and music have touched bottom
moments before the composer collapses after his last concert,
but the words are not heard by the viewer until the morning
of Aschenbach's death. Thus the temporal sequence of the
flashbacks creates an interwoven parallel process of decadence
for artist, man and viewer.

The film shares the same rhythm of disclosure as the
novella, where the failure of the narrator's art to distance itself
from Aschenbach's fall becomes evident only in the last few
pages. What *is* radically different is the viewer's relationship
to Aschenbach's art. This relationship is highly complicated
in the novella, where the narrative style ironically echoes
Aschenbach's own without exactly reproducing it, and no less
so in the film. Aschenbach's – that is, Mahler's – music is
heard six times and its beauty complicates any moral
judgement of the composer's visual enjoyment of Tadzio. The
fact that we experience Aschenbach's work at the very
moments that we both witness and share his gaze unites
music and vision in the objectification of Tadzio, making it
harder for the viewer to separate her/himself from Visconti's
camera. Rather than forming a contrast to his work, then,
Aschenbach's love for Tadzio is seen as the inevitable
culmination of that work. Tadzio's foreignness, Mann's
Aschenbach reflects, 'raised his speech to music',[38] and it is
this music, this song ringing within him, which inspires the
'page and a half of choicest prose' that the Master writes on
the beach.[39] The seeds of Visconti's conflation of music and
language are therefore already present in Mann's novella, and
the Italian director's substitution of music for writing seems
perfectly in keeping with Mann's own concerns.[40]

In *Audio-Vision: Sound on Screen*, Michel Chion argues that
film works through synchresis, 'the forging of an immediate
and necessary relationship between something one sees and
something one hears'; one perception influences and
transforms the other.[41] Aschenbach's music is thus both

transformed by and transformative of his fall. When Glassco asks 'What is Visconti doing?' by offering us 'the emotional surge of Mahler's lush, romantic music [which] is the very antithesis of Aschenbach's Apollonian art',[42] he is missing the point. He fails to see that the film presents Aschenbach's fall as a product of rather than an ironic contrast to his art.[43] In fact, Visconti's reworking of the opposition between Apollonian and Dionysian is far less radical than his critics suggest. For Mann's narrative of the fall of the Apollonian artist into Dionysian self-forgetfulness is already profoundly ironic. Aschenbach 'taste[s] the bestial degradation of his fall'[44] in a dream, identified by Nietzsche in *The Birth of Tragedy* as the vehicle of Apollonian vision,[45] and the narrative in which this fall is denounced is marked by Dionysian excess.[46] Ambiguities such as these make Visconti's transformation of Aschenbach into a writer of music – identified by Nietzsche as the essence of the Dionysian – seem far less controversial.

Siegfried Kracauer remarks in *Theory of Film* that 'no sooner does music intervene than we perceive structured patterns where there were none before',[47] a perception taken advantage of by Visconti's fifth flashback, which recounts Aschenbach's trip to the prostitute. The scene is introduced and accompanied by diegetic music which appears to be continuous – first Tadzio and then Esmerelda play Beethoven's 'Für Elise' on the piano. The cut from the present to the past against the background of the same music – even when played in a noticeably different style – folds the two events into one almost continuous narrative. The seamlessness with which the narrative moves first into the past and then back again to the present suggests that Aschenbach's fall is already inscribed within the events that unfold. As the viewer perceives Aschenbach's fall sequentially – in the form of the flashbacks – the present is understood to be as much transformative of as constituted by the past. What is at stake is less Aschenbach's degradation, which has already taken place at the brothel, than our own relationship to this knowledge and the lateness of its revelation.

The repetition of the Adagio from Mahler's Fifth Symphony also encourages the viewer to collapse different narrative moments into a unifying pattern. The Adagio is first heard against the black background of the credits, which fades imperceptibly into the fierce blue of the sea. A steamer belching black smoke appears, forming a distinct contrast to the Romantic music. This pattern of – to borrow Chion's terms – anempathy and empathy will be often repeated, transforming the viewer's relationship to the music s/he hears and in turn leading to a re-examination of the images upon the screen. The Adagio swells up again at the moment Aschenbach realises that the mix-up over his trunk at the train station allows him to return to Venice absolved of responsibility for events. But once again the music is immediately linked to images of corruption – in this case by a cut to a beggar dying of cholera, the first visual indication of the disease sweeping Venice.

The Adagio is heard for the final time as an accompaniment to Aschenbach's death, which is at once moving and bathetic, surprising and inevitable. The viewer hears the beginning of the music as necessarily preparatory to the composer's death, for the scene is emptied of everyone except Aschenbach, who sits in vast acres of space gazing at Tadzio walking slowly out to sea. Aschenbach slumps back in his chair, his body is summarily removed, and we are left with nothing but the empty beach and the sound of his music, the only thing left to testify to his life. The sustained long shot of an almost empty scene focuses attention on what is happening offscreen, which in the final shots of *Death in Venice* is not so much the rest of the beach or the hotel but the imaginary space evoked by the music we hear.[48] And it is within this imaginary personal space that the final conflation of art and corruption takes place.

The Adagio, overtly linked with images of both beauty and corruption, imposes a unity on the entire narrative because it is independent of the notion of real time and space. Chion suggests that nondiegetic music 'communicates with all times and spaces of a film',[49] and the repetition of Mahler's music eventually becomes – along with the gaze shared by Aschenbach and Tadzio – an organising narrative force. The Adagio compensates us for the scarcity of shots of Venice itself, and it feels as if it is Mahler's music rather than Mann's city that spreads the disease which kills Aschenbach. Venice has of course a rich connection to music; Mann himself praised the city for being a place where 'the musical magic of ambiguity still lives'.[50] Visconti substitutes music for Venice itself, eschewing clichéd shots of the city for long shots of the crowded hotel lobby and beach, which are almost always accompanied by music. Here again Visconti remains faithful to Mann on a metaphorical rather than literal level. If the contagion spreading through Venice corrupts Mann's language, then it makes sense that Visconti, working in a different medium from his Aschenbach, should eschew shots of Venice in order to stress the corrupt elements within the music we hear. The fact that we can experience Aschenbach's creation, rather than merely having it described to us as that 'page and a half of choicest prose',[51] profoundly alters our relationship to his corruption. The viewer, rather than Aschenbach, becomes the central consciousness of the film; it is in her/his reaction to Aschenbach's music that the link between art and ideas of decadence and decay is forged.

    That Aschenbach's music has been recognised as the carrier of corruption by the end of the film is in keeping with the composer's transformation into Tadzio's rival for the viewer's scopophilic gaze. No longer avoiding men's eyes in his lust for Tadzio, Aschenbach gives in to his barber's flattery and is transformed into the same distorted parody of youth he decried in the old fop on the boat. He becomes an image of the very corruption – both moral and physical – raging within him; even his lips are turned the colour of ripe strawberries, reproducing the infected fruit he eats.[52] Aschenbach is not only the object of our gaze, but also by now the object of Tadzio's, a reversal Mann's novella insists upon in the Master's death scene. Aschenbach's last act is to lift his head 'as it were in answer to Tadzio's gaze. ... It seemed to him the pale and lovely Summoner out there smiled at him and beckoned; ... And, as so often before, he rose to follow.'[53] Visconti's film, unable to show Aschenbach's spiritual elevation, lingers instead on the composer's dead body. This final close-up on the dead Aschenbach makes us uneasy. We become aware firstly that our gaze ignores the bounds of propriety and secondly of a connection between our looking at Aschenbach's dead body and Tadzio's young one.

The long shot of Tadzio in silhouette pointing toward the sky at the end of the film includes a camera at the far right of the screen, just as Aschenbach's death in the novella is watched over by an apparently abandoned camera. Visconti's self-referentiality is thus in keeping with Kermode's definition of 'the classic': the shot represents both an adaptation of something already present in Mann's text and an adoption of a new point-of-view, for the camera obviously signifies quite differently in the context of a film. In Visconti's film, as in Mann's novella, desire projects itself visually, the difference being precisely to do with the medium of the camera first introduced by Mann himself. Visconti's critics, busy producing an anodyne 'classic' original, fail to see that Visconti's adaptation fits perfectly within an economy of the gaze first articulated by Mann's novella. The auto/homoerotic nature of this gaze must necessarily be stressed by Visconti's camera precisely because it represents the nature of the cinematic gaze itself.

Notes

1. Hans Rudolph Vaget, 'Film and Literature. The Case of *Death in Venice*: Luchino Visconti and Thomas Mann', *The German Quarterly*, LIV No. 2 (March 1980), p. 165.
2. Geoffrey Wagner, *The Novel and the Cinema* (Madison: Farleigh Dickinson University Press, 1975), p. 343.
3. Quoted in Wagner, *The Novel*, p. 343.
4. David Glassco, 'Films Out of Books: Bergman, Visconti, Mann', *Mosaic* 16:1–2 (Winter–Spring 1983), p. 172.
5. Joan Mellen, *Women and Their Sexuality in the New Film* (New York: Horizon Press, 1973), p. 211.
6. Joy Gould Boyum, *Double Exposure: Fiction into Film* (New York: New American Library, 1985), p. 77.
7. Frank Kermode, *The Classic: Literary Images of Permanence and Change*, 2nd edn (Cambridge, MA: Harvard University Press, 1983), p. 44.
8. Laura Mulvey, *Visual and Other Pleasures* (Bloomington: Indiana University Press, 1989), p. 20.

9. See Paul Willemen, 'Voyeurism, The Look, and Dwoskin' in Philip Rosen (ed.), *Narrative, Apparatus, Ideology: A Film Theory Reader* (New York: Columbia University Press, 1986), pp. 212–13.

10. Thomas Mann, *Death in Venice and Seven Other Stories*, trans. H.T. Lowe-Porter (New York: Vintage Books, 1954), p. 5.

11. Ibid., p. 63.

12. Ibid., p. 5. It is worth recalling here Mulvey's formulation that film is 'an illusion cut to the measure of desire' (Mulvey, *Visual*, p. 25).

13. Ibid., pp. 17–18.

14. Ibid., p. 27.

15. Ibid., p. 28.

16. Ibid., p. 29.

17. Ibid., p. 31.

18. Ibid., p. 38.

19. Ibid., p. 43.

20. Ibid., p. 44.

21. Ibid., p. 44.

22. Friedrich Nietzsche, *The Birth of Tragedy: Out of the Spirit of Music* in Nietzsche, *Basic Writings of Nietzsche* , trans. Walter Kaufman (New York: The Modern Library, 1992), p. 34.

23. Mann, *Death*, p. 51.

24. Ibid., p. 13.

25. Ibid., p. 54.

26. Ibid., p. 62.

27. Wagner complains that the glances Aschenbach and Tadzio exchange are all the more explicit – and therefore morally reprehensible – because they have not been filtered through the composer's consciousness. That Wagner should be made uncomfortable by the objectification of Tadzio is of course precisely the point; the morally reprehensible position here certainly does not seem to be Visconti's.

28. Neil Sinyard in *Filming Literature: The Art of Screen Adaptation* (New York: St. Martin's Press, 1986) sums up Visconti's method: 'The objectivity/subjectivity of the shots is at times left ambiguous, so that the point-of-view

of the spectator and Aschenbach coalesce and separate seamlessly. This ambiguity extends to the level of overall narration' (p. 169).

29. Tadzio's response to Aschenbach's gaze stages a diegetic breakdown of the central component of watching a film – what Christian Metz labels the cinema's 'double denial', where the scene must ignore that it is seen. Identifying with Aschenbach's physical location, if not (at this point) his aesthetic rapture, the viewer is forced to recognise her/himself as voyeur. In keeping with Metz's psychoanalytic paradigm, Aschenbach's response is paradigmatic of desire itself, which is always the desire for the other (the desire to be desired, to be recognised). See Slavoj Zizek (ed.), *Everything You Always Wanted to Know About Lacan, But Were Afraid to Ask Hitchcock* (London: Verso, 1992), p. 228.

30. Nick Browne, 'The Spectator-in-the-Text: The Rhetoric of *Stagecoach*' in Rosen, *Narrative*, p. 115.

31. Browne, 'Spectator', p. 117.

32. Dorrit Cohn, 'The Second Author of *Der Tod in Venedig*' in Inta M. Ezergelis (ed.), *Critical Essays on Thomas Mann* (Boston: G.K. Hall & Co., 1988), pp. 128–9.

33. Irving Singer, '*Death in Venice*: Visconti and Mann', *Modern Language Notes*, 91 (1976), p. 1350.

34. Angus Fletcher in 'Music, Visconti, Mann, Nietzsche: *Death in Venice*' (*Stanford Italian Review*, VI, 1–2 [1986] pp. 301–12) wittily suggests that due to Aschenbach's earlier sickness we cannot even be sure that the composer dies of the cholera sweeping Venice.

35. Mann, *Death*, p. 6.

36. An ambiguity insisted upon by the narrator:

> has not form two aspects? Is it not moral and immoral at once: moral in so far as it is the expression and result of discipline, immoral – yes, actually hostile to morality – in that of its very essence it is indifferent to good and evil, and deliberately concerned to make the moral world stoop beneath its proud and undivided sceptre? (Mann, *Death*, p. 13)

37. Glassco even suggests that the music we hear is not Aschenbach's at all: 'We hear a lot of Mahler's music. But there is no reason to think that this music is Aschenbach's'(Glassco, 'Films', p. 169). True, the crashing chord we hear at the end of Aschenbach's performance is not Mahler's, but such a reading goes against both logic and the fact that the music playing while Aschenbach writes on the beach – which we infer to be his – is also Mahler's. Alfried, after all, plays an extract from the Adagio to Aschenbach before saying, 'This is your music.'

38. Mann, *Death*, p. 43.

39. Ibid., p. 46.

40. Visconti's choice of the Adagio from Mahler's Fifth seems particularly appropriate in the light of Leonard Bernstein's championing of the piece as a triumph of ambiguity. See John Francis Fetzer, 'Visconti's Cinematic Version of *Death in Venice*' in Jeffrey B. Berlin (ed.), *Approaches to Teaching Mann's 'Death in Venice' and Other Short Fiction* (New York: MLA, 1992).

41. Michel Chion, *Audio-Vision: Sound on Screen*, trans. Claudia Gorbam (New York: Columbia University Press, 1994).

42. Glassco, 'Films', p. 169.

43. Glassco's question presupposes a 'timeless' existence for Aschenbach outside of representative practices. It makes no sense to talk about the Mahler music forming a contrast with Aschenbach's Apollonian art within the film, for there the music *is* Aschenbach's art.

44. Mann, *Death*, p. 63.

45. Nietzsche, *Birth*, p. 36.

46. Many critics have pointed out the musical structure of Mann's novella, suggesting an affinity with the Dionysian.

47. Siegfried Kracauer, *Theory of Film: The Redemption of Physical Reality* (New York: Oxford University Press, 1960), p. 135.

48. See Noël Burch, *Theory of Film Practice*, trans. Helen R. Lane (Princeton: Princeton University Press, 1981), pp. 16–30.

49. Chion, *Audio-Vision*, p. 81.

50. Douglas Radcliff-Umstead, 'The Journey of Fatal Longing: Mann and Visconti', *Annali d'Italianistica*, 6 (1988), p. 204.
51. Mann, *Death*, p. 46.
52. Maurice Blanchot claims that the strangeness of the image bears a striking resemblance to the strangeness of a cadaver, and it seems appropriate that Aschenbach's death coincides with his transformation into an object for the gaze. See the essay 'Two Versions of the Imaginary' in Blanchot, *The Gaze of Orpheus*, trans. Lydia Davis (New York: Station Hill, 1981), pp. 79–90.
53. Mann, *Death*, pp. 74–5.

8

Leopold Bloom Walks and Jimmy Stewart Stares: On Motion, Genre and the Classic

Kay Young

Linking points of destination for the traveller who moves along its plane, the city street defines the distance between goals, placement in space, predetermined paths for departure and arrival. It allows for the motion of forward and back to be traced in its very linearity. Yet, in addition to constructing this map of passage through space, the city street functions as a place. Gathering around it buildings, people, vehicles, animals, street signs, noise, parks, garbage, open spaces, attached constructions, designated locations for the pedestrian and the driver, the city street works not just as the means to arrive elsewhere, but as its own setting or scene. The architect William Ellis, writing on the spatial structure of streets, asserts that the primary structural quality of the city street is its 'felt volume', which is created by the planes of vertical walls that surround it. The interaction of street to wall transforms the street to work as 'exterior rooms in the city'.[1] Street 'rooms' like the piazza, square, courtyard, porch, archway work with the continuity of the road to create a dialectic of stasis and motion, inside and outside, length and width, horizontal and vertical. The joint qualities of 'link' and 'place' make the city street capable then of at once creating a continuum of space and a whole, self-contained sphere of space.

When Leopold Bloom strolls along the streets of Dublin in Chapter 5 of *Ulysses* (1922), the 'Lotus-eaters' episode, and when Jimmy Stewart stares into the back courtyard from his apartment window in Hitchcock's *Rear Window* (1954), they experience the spaces available to them of horizontal linearity

157

and of vertically contained volume. Bloom is set in motion down the interconnecting paths of streets that project his body forward along their maze-like planes. Stewart rests statically, and gazes out at the private outside 'room' or other side of the street formed by the contiguity of the back walls of the apartment buildings built around a shared green and cement. He examines the confined motions of his neighbours whose small-scale movements are framed for Stewart by the very windows and building walls which both delimit the radius of their motions and allow Stewart visual access to them. Significantly, the narrative that literalises motion – film (as moving pictures) – confines Stewart to a position of near-inertia as a man immobilised from his waist down in a cast, whereas the novel (a narrative that can merely suggest motion in its choice of words) propels Bloom's body forward along an ongoing, open plane. While the imagination of the reader through internal visualisation can play out on some level the activity of the novel's characters, *actual* motion and the novel only intersect at the point of the reader's eyes moving across its pages. What primarily constitutes film's 'filmness', its ontology, is its ability to visualise motion as the product of hundreds of stilled photographs joined at a speed which plot an illusion that convinces the eyes of ongoing change. The name 'movie' aptly describes its being – a thing that displays movement. The earliest movies made as their subjects objects that move, such as railroads and horses, the display of which thrilled early film audiences because of their ability, according to Keith Cohen, to 'dynamize the still photographic image by conferring a deeper sense of corporeality on the objects filmed'. Or in Edgar Morin's words: 'Movement is the decisive power of reality: it is in and through movement that space and time are real.'[2] Film, therefore, in its display of moving pictures, accomplishes something like the reproduction of 'reality', that which the novel (in its absence of such movement) apparently cannot do. And yet, what is 'novel' about the novel is not that it moves objects but that it demands a mental movement of conceptualisation that stands in our minds as an 'as if' reality which we cannot actually see (or see move) but which we can imagine. How we receive movies and novels meets, therefore, at the idea of motion, or at the nexus of seeing photographic motion and conceiving as mental motion. As motions, however, they are fundamentally different: one displays visual pictures of objects moving 'like reality': the other invites us to motivate into some imaginary being 'a world' from the prompt of written language. While joined around the idea of the street, the 'classic' modern novel *Ulysses* and the 'classic' Hollywood film *Rear Window* convey a curiosity in their seeming reversal of street function/location and the kind of motions which each allows. The medium of film lends itself to the openness of motion made possible by the street, whereas the novel more naturally makes as a site for its gaze the static inner room of the courtyard.[3] I would suggest that the presence of these street functions problematises not just the expectation of setting, but the narrative identities of the 'Lotus-eaters' episode of *Ulysses* and *Rear Window* by questioning their very beings as 'novel' and 'film' – not what we expect from 'classics'.

The *Oxford English Dictionary*'s definitions of the term 'classic' emphasise three ideas: the notion of the classic as the best and/or most famous instance of a form, as representative of a form, as of or belonging in style to Greek and Roman antiquity. Novels and movies are by their nature non-classics. Products of middle-class print and media culture, reflective of the tastes and concerns of popular culture, bound to the desire to 'imitate' the particularities of modern life, fiction and film 'unclassic' themselves in their resistance to the classic forms, conventions, themes and rhetorical rhythms defined by Aristotle's classifying *Poetics*. And yet, we do understand some novels and movies to be 'classics' – not because they function as lyrics, tragedies or epics, but because we allow these 'modern' forms of narrative to have representative forms and to have 'best' instances of themselves. A 'modern classic' is a paradox: it achieves classic status in its 'model/great' versions of what it is born out of, namely what it is not – the classical. We tend to grant the status of classic to the model/great nineteenth-century novels of realism and Hollywood films following the coming of sound in the 1920s and ending with the breakdown of the studio system in the

1950s. The BBC, for instance, codified and acted on this assessment of the modern classic in its decision to broadcast 'classic novels' on the even more modern radio as part of its responsibility to 'educate and inform' (more words on what a classic performs). Works chosen for the classic serial division were by Dickens, Trollope, Eliot, the Brontës, Austen, Hardy – the nineteenth-century British 'masters'.[4] Radio and film adaptations of their novels granted a legitimacy to the newer productions of media culture in the act of borrowing. To consider why the novels of the nineteenth century and why the movies of Hollywood from about 1927 to 1959 come to be thought 'classic material' has everything to do with their forms, that is with their drive to represent Life and to understand Life as whole, linear, and understandable.

Judith Mayne claims that we look to the nineteenth-century novel of realism to fill this role of modern classic through the way that those novels embrace middle-class ideals and focus their representation on the characters, motivations, and details of everyday middle-class experience.[5] What underlies Mayne's claim is the assertion that the classic suppresses any forms of contradiction to the governing ideology or set of social practices of its day, and beyond, if 'society' continues essentially to uphold that ideology and those practices. Mayne's view coheres with David Bordwell, Janet Staiger and Kristin Thompson's assessment in *The Classical Hollywood Cinema* of why we understand the films of Hollywood from the talkie through the 1950s to be the site of movie classics. Films of this time and place constitute a homogeneous style, a style, they assert, that produced no subversive films, only subversive moments. Christian Metz concludes that the classical film has come to take the place of the 'grand-epoch, nineteenth-century novel' in how it fills the same social function – that which represents middle-class culture to itself (the twentieth-century novel abandons this task in its resistance to representation).[6]

If we accept the notion of the classic as that which resists subversion or acts as the representative standard, then what are we to make of the classic that acts as model and is subversive? *Ulysses* seems to stand outside the realm of classic novel because of its modernist, anti-nineteenth-century-novel-of-realism state of being. And yet its status as 'the great novel' from the modernist period of 1895–1925 has made *Ulysses* the 'classic modern' text – call that a representative/subversive act. It stands as the model for how the modern novel writes by 'un-writing' the novel of realism, in Arnold Hauser's words, in its 'discontinuity of the plot and ... scenic development ... sudden emersion of the thoughts and moods ... relativity and the inconsistency of the time standards'.[7] Finally, *Ulysses*, in its playful and profound relation to the *Odyssey*, resuscitates the classic's relation to Greek antiquity, and yet, the classic novel removes itself from this influence or debt. *Ulysses*'s modernism, 'greatness', and sense of 'belonging' to the *Odyssey* complicate its status as a classic novel. However, *Ulysses* enacts its classic-non-classicness in an act peculiar to it. I want to say that it 'declassifies' itself as a novel, let alone a classic novel, in its exploration of motion.

Leopold Bloom's odyssey takes him onto the streets of Dublin at roughly 8.00 a.m., 16 June 1904 in quest of a pork kidney and perhaps a son, until he returns home to Eccles Street and Molly at about 1 a.m. on 17 June. That Bloom's activities can be plotted in space and time on a Dublin street map transforms the street from misty background to particularised foreground, bringing into focus what I take to be the primary motif of *Ulysses*: call it 'a Man Walks along a City's Streets Alone'. The actual map of Dublin of 1904 suggests a wheel of winding, concentric and intersecting streets. The river Liffey moves across its circular grid, and Dublin Castle marks its centre from which the city extends in any direction roughly at a four-mile radius. The streets would have been a mix of crowded broad boulevards and smaller streets in varying levels of decay, and would have displayed buildings of grey stone and red brick and dark soot, set in dialogue with a series of canal banks, bridges, squares and gardens – reminders of the British Empire's wealth and punishing departure. However, nothing of the quality of the streets is described by Joyce. Walking from Sir John Rogerson's quay to Westland Row, Leopold Bloom traces a trajectory of motion. Bloom, like his reference to falling matter, 'thirtytwo feet per second per second', moves as does falling matter, continuously.[8] Pausing only when he stops in the Post Office to receive his letter from Martha, speaks with M'Coy, looks at the billboard on Brunswick Street, sits to watch communion at All Hallows, and observes Bantom Lyons, Bloom and his constancy of thought transform any breaks in stride to become 'footfalls' of the eyes or imagination.

The implied map of Bloom's Dublin in Chapter 5 suppresses the first-time viewing, tourist markers of Dublin in its lack of references to Dublin Castle or the river Liffey. The naming of the streets on which Bloom moves, his arrival at the Post Office, chemist's, church, and baths, the traces he observes on those streets of hands which pinned up posters, dropped wrappers, and tore up a letter, and the motions of the street's inhabitants work as the markers of Bloom's map. Always in relation to Bloom, the street works as ground to his figure; in essence, while Bloom holds Molly and Stephen in his mind, the streets of Dublin hold him. The streets are Bloom's true companion, the other major 'character' of *Ulysses*.

Edmund Husserl, writing contemporaneously to Joyce, gives an account in the *General Introduction to Pure Phenomenology* of the 'Natural Standpoint' or ground from which the self operates in living, a position he will come to refer to as that of the 'Man in the Street'. His phenomenological depiction of the modern, urban self defines philosophically the position Joyce defines in narrative to be Bloom's:

> I am aware of a world, spread out in space endlessly, and in time becoming and become, without end. I am aware of it, that means, first of all, I discover it immediately, intuitively, I experience it. Through sight, touch, hearing, etc., in the different ways of sensory perception, corporeal things somehow spatially distributed are *for me simply there*, in verbal or figurative sense 'present', whether or not I pay them special attention by busying myself with them, considering, thinking, feeling, willing.[9]

The world for Husserl is a given: it is 'present' as the senses reveal it, whether or not one attends to it by acts of cognition like consideration, thought, volition, or by acts of affect.

Bloom assumes that 'natural standpoint' when he walks from Sir John Rogerson's quay, past Windmill Lane, through Lime Street, across Townsend Street to Westland Row. Being able to walk to Westland Row makes it 'present' for Bloom; it is so present for him that he never considers doubting its reality. He moves something like a camera – proceeding through space, confident in the presence of that space, and yet forgetful of it. The space taken in by Bloom's walk, the world printed by the camera, is just there, until the consciousness of Bloom (call that the 'camera' or 'audience' to the world) chooses to consider what it actually sees.

Because Westland Row is for Bloom a background to thought, it is the narrative voice of the text which defines the movement of Bloom in relation to that background space. We read: 'Mr Bloom walked soberly past Windmill Lane'; 'He strolled out of the post office and turned to the right'; 'Mr Bloom went round the corner and passed the drooping nags of the hazard.' This is a narrative voice of directions not description, a voice which also works, in addition to Bloom, like a camera pointing its lens to the right and straight ahead so that the motion of the figure it watches can be followed. Joyce's words as camera follow the path of Bloom's movement, as opposed to narrating its quality. And while film conveys the quality of motion as the motion occurs, it does not comment on or analyse that motion. While Bloom's sense of the street as the material presence which links his movement from one locale to another 'just simply is there', the objects which define the streets as places do prompt Bloom's consideration. This act of consideration will work to measure the distance Bloom travels along the streets.

Reading the legends of the leadpapered packets of tea in the window of the Belfast and Oriental Tea Company, observing as a stranger to the ritual of communion the movements of priest and parishoners in All Hallows, experiencing chance encounters with strangers that he observes for whom he has no names (the 'squatted child at marbles' on Cumberland Street, the 'chemist' – 'sandy shrivelled smell he seems to have') and with acquaintances with whom he speaks and addresses or recognises by name (M'Coy, Bantom Lyons), Bloom marks off his progress down the streets. With each new encounter, Bloom has moved further. No interaction is repeated. Each interaction displays a new point of arrival and a measure of the distance beyond where the last intersection occurred. With nothing and no one re-encountered, space is travelled and a film-like display made of distance. Bloom does not gather people around him; by not growing 'thick' with attachment to any one place and its people/objects, Bloom is at liberty to move on. Whereas the packets of tea in the windows remain stationary, as do the chemist and post office, the people on the streets with whom Bloom intersects presumably continue to move, though always differently from Bloom. We only walk with Bloom and experience a sense of forward motion in part because of his departure from those he bumps into and then bumps away from. So that while Bloom is a 'reader', in the sense that he observes objects and interprets them, he does not assume the passive stance of the reader. Unlike Molly, Bloom is out of bed and in motion.

When Bloom does bring pause to his motion in order to consider, he uses the film technique of voiceover. Because Joyce's words never act to reveal what's on Bloom's mind (what camera would?), it is Bloom's voice that we hear as the words of the text which 'speak' silently. He voices over the direction-giving voice of Joyce, but he voices 'under' in the sense that this is the utterance of thought, a language of non-utterance. Bloom, in Husserl's words, 'turn[s] temporally forwards and back' (p. 92) from a perception of what stands before him to its suggestion always of his experiences of the past, a stream of experience which ceaselessly haunts his present. Even in the small gesture of looking back toward the choir of All Hallows, Bloom faces the past: 'Who has the organ here I wonder? Old Glynn he knew how to make that instrument talk, the *vibrato*: fifty pounds a year they say he had in Gardiner Street. Molly was in fine voice that day, the *Stabat Mater* of Rossini' (p. 67). The 'flashback' is named for a film process – a flash of light reveals a changed visual landscape, a time of film from 'before'. Bloom's walk forward carries his mind backwards as he associates the knowledge of his life stored in memory to the images in the present he passes. His motion forwards, therefore, brings Bloom both to his past and to the film quality of flashback.

When Bloom meets up with M'Coy and then abandons reflecting on the actual presence of M'Coy so as to attend to the woman across the street who enters the carriage, he 'moved a little to the side of M'Coy's talking head', he brackets M'Coy to attend instead to another image. Husserl defines bracketing as placing an object in suspension so that the mind can reflect on itself;[10] for Bloom, bracketing works like focusing. Bloom focuses the lens of his attention on one object as opposed to another, as if his vision and the activity of selection make a zoom lens. Bracketing what stands before him in order to look past it and beyond to a distant image, an image about which the mind can fantasise and have no mutually acknowledged contact, is an experience which the city street affords. The range of the street's distances, its restriction on lengthy, intense conversations because of the presence of strangers and noise, the position of moving as a single figure down its passage crowded with an array of objects on which to gaze, make sense of, and use as features to which the ongoing play of mind responds, define Bloom's meeting *with* M'Coy as an encounter not *about* M'Coy as a city street experience. Film brings to life 'street experience' in its ability to connect simultaneously the sounds and random acts of commotion which define street life. The motion and commotion of being on the street, therefore, lend themselves to film that can capture the simultaneity of causes which create its vibrant life. Yet capturing the randomness of the street is precisely what this episode in the novel sets out to do.

Joyce concludes the chapter with a near-arrival at the baths and a falling into description. Motion has been arrested. With the pause of anticipation, the narrative pauses for Joyce to describe the anticipated future experience for Bloom of being in the bath:

> He foresaw his pale body reclined in it at full, in a womb of warmth, oiled by scented melting soap, softly laved. He saw his trunk and limbs riprippled over and sustained, buoyed lightly upward, lemonyellow: his navel, bud of flesh: and saw the dark tangled curls of his bush floating, floating hair

of the stream around the limp father of thousands, a languid floating flower. (p. 71)

The progressive motion of Bloom has been replaced by the descriptive pause of arrival at a destination. No longer a man walking down the street, Bloom is no longer a man of film-like motion. Instead, he is observed, fixed to a description, stationary as an object gazed upon. What this break concretises is a gap in or disconnection from what is the fundamental form of Chapter 5 – that of the flow of morning and thought unfolding, made concrete in the flow of Bloom's walk down Dublin's streets.[11] All descriptive pause is cancelled in order to continue the narrative flow of motion down the street names. According to Gérard Genette in *Narrative Discourse*, descriptive pause makes narrative time infinitely larger than story time because the motion of the story is stopped, paused to allow for a portrait in words to paint the quality of the scene or to render an analysis of the perceptual activity of the character.[12] Joyce fundamentally removes pause from his narrative of 'The Lotus Eaters' chapter and in so doing removes both a defining technique of the novel (why else are novels so long?) and an interruption to the flow of story time – the very flow which defines film. Uninterrupted, non-elliptical storytime is never stilled for a working through in narrative time of what it means to have arrived, which means to have stopped for description of an imagined future, until Bloom arrives at the story's end – at the 'lotus eaters'.

Alfred Hitchcock's *Rear Window* is a film that comes out of the Hollywood studio system of the 1950s, or the era of classic Hollywood film. Hitchcock performs the feat of the classic Hollywood director: master of the psychological thriller, Hitchcock above all else 'tells' a great story. *Rear Window*, like his other films, calls on the most plot-dependent of narrative forms – the detective story – to be the structural container for the psychological mystery that it holds. Both plots as good plots require 'solving'. *Rear Window* earns its classic status in part then because of the conventionality of Hitchcock's plot – we anticipate the linear structure of the detective plot's beginning, middle and end; we know that there will be a crime, something like its re-enactment, and its solution by a detective or detective-substitute figure. However, the definition of the classic as the best instance of the conventional becomes undone in the psychological 'working through' of the crime. While we grow comfortable in relation to the plotting structure or skeleton of the film, Hitchcock never allows us such ease in relation to the witnessing we must do, from whatever distance or angle filmed, of the motivations/interiorities of the players of the plot. To be a character, any character, in a Hitchcock film means to be a criminal, guilty in small or grand ways, at least in thought, if not action. A classic detective narrative wants to divide the world between those who commit crimes, those upon whom crimes are committed, and those who solve crimes. Hitchcock blurs these positions through the underlying assertion in *Rear Window* that every figure is capable of holding all three places: those who, along with the seated Jimmy Stewart, gaze out of his window upon the framed courtyard and its stories find themselves caught up in the desire to solve the mystery, experience at least moments of being a victim, but most of all, know in their conflicted, hidden hearts what it means to be criminal-like. Without clearly bounded roles to act the parts of the detective plot and with the playing out of multiple, complex internal dramas, the conventional, classic detective story undergoes subversion. However, it is not *Rear Window*'s complicated navigation between its 'classic-ness' and plot that I wish to pursue. *Ulysses* allies itself with classical antiquity in its ongoing reworking of the *Odyssey*, and so plays with its classic nature in its relation to classical literary origins, as it plays with its own genre in its peculiar writing of motion. *Rear Window*, in its ongoing engagement with photography – photographic equipment, photographs, Stewart as photographer – plays with something like the classic photographic origins of movies. However, the movie, while like a photo, is not a photo in that it is not still. And yet the movie *Rear Window* is about the still, or rather the desire to arrest motion so as to 'read' a series of photographs contained in an almost still city street space.

Unlike the forward-stepping Bloom, immobile, lounging in a wheelchair/bed, Jimmy Stewart gazes out from his window to scan the courtyard before him. The courtyard, as a contained, externally defined room with its joining together of back walls around an open space, interrupts the flow of the city street. This backside of the streets asserts a sense of enclosure, creates contained-volume, as does a room within a house. In *Rear Window* layered spaces of enclosure intersect with one another through the juxtaposition of their walls. The back exterior walls of the apartment buildings create this internal/external room of the city. Their back windows work as entrances to their apartments within, of which Stewart's is the model, from which we perch with him to observe the spaces before us. The alley way which breaks into the space of the courtyard allows the streets to peek through with their sense of motion, like a movie running before the eyes which reveals a stream of ongoing, differentiated motion.

The passive stance of Stewart propped up in bed joined to the examination of the 'text' before him framed by the window suggests the interaction of reader with novel. Significantly, when Hitchcock opens the film, he pans from right to left around the back facades of the buildings and then pans lower to film the people of the courtyard. The act of panning, where the camera scans in one continuous motion without itself moving, works like eyes across and down a page (though backwards to the reading of English). That there are no tracking shots in this film – lateral continuous shots which require the camera to move to take in the objects of the shots – reveals that everything can be read from this window. The space that is confined within the courtyard will carry with it the whole story, like the narrative that is contained by the book's bindings. The camera as eye studies the text before it. It is no coincidence that Stewart plays J.B. Jeffries the photo-journalist. Throughout the film Stewart moves from surveying with his own eyes to using binoculars, a slide viewer, a camera with long-range lens. Each piece of apparatus affords him closer study of the text before him; to study the individual motions of Raymond Burr requires the use of a zoom lens to enable him to be in the same room with Burr, much like Hitchcock's camera brings us next to Stewart. Stewart is

Hitchcock's double, and yet Hitchcock films the ongoing narrative *Rear Window*, while Stewart only photographs from his rear window. When we look through the equipment with Stewart, the point of focus is captured in a white light with black shading circling it as the outline of the circular lens. Imprinted/inscribed onto the text then is an 'eye': collectively, we are reading the scene from the passive reader's stance of one immobilised in bed through the eyes of the camera – Stewart's camera's eye, inside of Hitchcock's, inside of our own.

Hitchcock introduces us first to the building walls and then to the figures that inhabit them who will be the primary players of the film. Stewart assigns them names or roles: Miss Torso, Miss Lonelyhearts, the failed composer, the newlyweds, the eccentric sculptress. No new inhabitants of the courtyard appear once the film has begun; no progress, therefore, is marked off by a departure from or arrival of a character, as it is for Bloom. Likewise, we continually return to the same physical scene and study the minute adjustments of what has changed behind the windows. This continuity of ground, this return to what is the same through-circling with the camera and watching the clock questions any notion of progress or change. Like Stewart, stuck six weeks in a cast with nothing to do but look out the window at the same scene, the film makes as its topic a stilling of life in a contained space, with a contained set of players, experiencing a contained range of motion. If film has the capacity to take us through an ongoing range of experiences and change, *Rear Window* resists that capability to keep the same text always before our eyes. And what we see is always from the single point-of-view of Stewart, that which the panoramic view-making possibilities of film would seem always to resist

Stewart takes pictures. His room is filled with them – framed, action stills. When he looks out, he sees as a photographer, and sees even more by looking through the camera lens. However, now he takes pictures as he watches, not on film, but in his head. The actions of those before him are confined by the size of the courtyard and what part of land is allotted to each; inside the tenants' apartments, their motions are confined by walls. While the range of action is limited, the boundaries that confine it work to frame or define it, or, in essence, still it into shots. The windows and walls are the edges of the photos. Stewart sees individuated, though simply moving, shots – a dog digging in the garden, an invalid wife in bed, a man wrapping up a butcher knife and saw in newspaper, a man washing down a bathroom's walls, a man holding his wife's handbag and the wedding ring it contains. Hitchcock cuts from Stewart, to what Stewart sees, back and forth, to delineate what are the edges of the picture and who is its audience. These cuts also act like the eye blinking or like the turning of a page: with each momentary departure from picture to Stewart, the cut indicates the end of the examination of the object before the eye; the eye has moved on. Stewart marks the pictures of Raymond Burr with his watch. With each departure by Burr out into the rain, Stewart clocks him, which is a way of stilling the moment by saying 'this event happened at this instant'. Between each take of the clock, an ellipse occurs so that darkness falls between Burr's ventures in or out. Unlike film, which can create a seamless motion of time passing through the production of scenes linked one to the next, novels can tell time through the disjointing practice of ellipse.[13] Hitchcock uses the dissolve (or long cut) to insist on creating a frame in oncoming blackness around each shot until the shot disappears into the blackness: we are to remember these photos. Each picture works for Stewart as a piece of evidence to corroborate that an action that he could not see occurred. He has no shot of the actual murder; he has no access to the motion that such an event implies. Murder requires movement – where is the moment of murder in just one picture? How can the action of killing be seen in one shot?

A picture or photo works as description or pause in that it stops the time of action to define visually the study of an object. Like the novel that arrests time to bring forward the words to conjure up images, the photo works as the novel's visual counterpart in its desire to arrest the motion of life in order to say 'look at this moment'. It is this pausing through description which Joyce resists in his display of Bloom's continuous motion down the street. Yet, with only the murmurings of voices and music, and the walls and windows to interrupt the form and size of the motion of what is seen, *Rear Window* exhibits its narrative almost wholly through descriptive pause in that it collects the story like a photo album that Jimmy Stewart works to decipher, as if the images work as clues to an ongoing narrative occurring out of view. The pictures need filling in, therefore: they require a film to tell their story. That film is the narrative of Stewart, Grace Kelly and Thelma Ritter who 'take' the shots and tell the story they construct around them to the unbelieving audience of Lieutenant Doyle. The film is told wholly in the present tense: we see with Stewart at the moment he sees. The narrative which hovers around the photos, the Stewart/Kelly love story, is given little by way of a past or future. The topic of their future – marriage – is silenced even for Kelly who comes to find the pictures before her to be more interesting.[14] As 'readers' or the audience of *Rear Window*, we too suppress concern about the Stewart/Kelly relationship in order to lose ourselves in the suspense generated by the observation of the photos/story before us.

The seemingly stable positions of what is the ongoing, mobile narrative (the story of Stewart, Kelly and Ritter watching and narrating) and what is the stilled photograph (the pictures of Burr) become undone when Raymond Burr enters Stewart's apartment and throws Stewart out of the rear window and into the courtyard. This is the only motion of Stewart that the film can allow: for Stewart to leave his apartment through the front door and onto the street would take the film out of its world of the rear window/'rear room street' and into a world of the frontal, linear city street, like Bloom's. For Stewart to enter the courtyard as one of the objects to be read requires violence to shake him out of his immobility and to force him into the position of the one before the camera, as opposed to the one behind it who controls the shots. Using his only defence, Stewart fires flashes at Burr to blind him in hopes of upsetting his balance out the window, yet the active capabilities of the one photographed enable him to throw the passive photographer out instead. Stewart breaks his other leg after having spied on, photographed, read the scene before him. Reading is a dangerous activity: it necessitates the giving over of oneself to the text read; it makes one passive; it immobilises. For these roles to be swapped so that the photographed becomes the photographer and the photographer becomes the photographed, the film ends itself in order to begin again. Stewart will lie prone for a new seven weeks looking out at the same text, with one variation: new tenants will fill the freshly painted walls of Raymond Burr's former apartment, which will enable the next story.

The motions that each space allows define Stewart's courtyard to be inside and contained, and Bloom's city street to be horizontal and continuous. If writing writes the interior in that it imagines in language consciousness and film films the exterior in that it visualises in motion the objective world, then these narratives transpose the structures of their forms in response to the spatial setting which defines them. While it is the camera in *Rear Window* that takes what are almost photographs from varying angles of a repetition of small motions contained in a small, recurring space, it is the flow of language in *Ulysses* which moves the 'mind's eye' to see a continuous stream of movement embodied in a figure progressing down a city's streets. *Rear Window*, in its containment of space and stilling of motion, transforms the medium of film into something like the words of a 'photonovel', which must be read and decoded. And *Ulysses*, in its propelling of Bloom along the seemingly endless expanse of Dublin's streets without the presence of descriptive pause to stop that motion or contain that space, translates language to act like film. These two street narratives represent as part of film's ontology the capacity to make almost word-like pauses in stilled photographs, and make as part of the ontology of the novel the capacity to create the ongoing quality of a film-like motion in words. When viewed side by side, *Ulysses* and *Rear Window* instruct us to reconsider how the interrelations of space and motion work to define what we take the 'classic' novel and film to be in their very subversion of our expectations.

Notes

1. William Ellis, 'The Spatial Structure of Streets' in *On Streets*, ed. Stanford Anderson (Cambridge: M.I.T. Press, 1986), p. 118. Anderson's collection of essays offers a remarkable array of vantage points from which to view 'the street' as an historical, structural and social entity. Ellis's depiction of how the street's structure creates different felt qualities of space helped me to differentiate more precisely (because visually) Bloom's street experience from Stewart's. My argument is indebted to his vision.

2. See Keith Cohen, *Film and Fiction* (New Haven: Yale University Press, 1979), p. 42.

3. The picaresque novel is of course the great exception to this claim. However, one reason I would suggest the novel lends itself more readily and even successfully to fewer and more static settings has to do with the novel's inability finally to make moving pictures in a medium other than words – words suggest the ideas of pictures but are not themselves pictures. Words do make possible approaches toward internal states (this is how we know ideas, in words), whereas we know places by sight and then by the words that name them. While film can limit the range of its represented settings, those that do restrict themselves to one or just a few sites tend to create what feels like an obsessive, even claustrophobic relation to *that* space, as if they are filming 'plays' that imprison us as their viewers, enclosed just in *this* filmed room. In essence, this essay is a response against the claims of this note. I make a case in what follows for how *Ulysses* and *Rear Window* know themselves as themselves in their very 'adoption' of the other's medium.

4. See Robert Giddings, Keith Selby and Chris Wensley, *Screening the Novel* (New York: St. Martin's Press, 1990), p. 90.

5. Judith Mayne, *Private Novels, Public Films* (Athens: The University of Georgia Press, 1988), pp. 12–13.

6. See Christian Metz, *The Imaginary Signifier* (Bloomington: Indiana University Press, 1982), p. 7.

7. Arnold Hauser, *The Social History of Art*, Vol. 4 (New York: Vintage Books, 1985), p. 244.

8. James Joyce, *Ulysses* (New York: Vintage Books of Random House, 1968), p. 51. All subsequent citations refer to this edition.

9. Whereas Bloom never thinks his experience out loud in the sense that he defines what it means to walk down the urban street, one could say that Husserl's 'Man on the Street', as the philosophical embodiment of Bloom's position, speaks that meaning for him. See Edmund Husserl *Ideas*, trans. W.R. Boyce Gibson (New York: Collier Books of Macmillan Publishing, 1962), p. 91.

10. Husserl, *Ideas*, pp. 98–101.

11. It is important to note that the primary claim I am making about *Ulysses*, that it works like a film because (not exclusively but most particularly) of how it writes motion down a city street, is a claim about the 'Lotus Eaters' episode, Chapter 5. While Keith Cohen in *Film and Fiction* takes up the whole of *Ulysses* and other modernist texts as novels deeply indebted to film's montage technique and so regards them as a body of film-like fiction, I am more local in my assertion.

12. Genette's fundamental topic in *Narrative Discourse*, trans. Jane E. Lewin (Ithaca: Cornell University Press, 1985) is narrative as 'signifier, statement, discourse or narrative text itself', p. 27. He differentiates the *telling* of the story, therefore, from the *story* in part according to what the relation of narrative time is to story time. The progression of a story must stop, for example, to allow for description, a fundamental characteristic of the Victorian novel. Joyce resists that disjunction by eliminating descriptive pause from the 'Lotus Eaters' chapter. This positions his text somewhere closer to film than to the novel in that film has the capacity to make simultaneous description and advancement of story through the display of moving images.

13. See Genette's depiction of how narratives create or deny the passing/presence of time in his discussion of 'summary', 'ellipse', 'pause' and 'scene' in the chapter 'Duration', *Narrative Discourse*, pp. 86–113.

14.   I am indebted to Benjamin Strong's not only thoughtful but inventive response to this essay. Thinking about how the street structure of a narrative impacts on its plot, Benjamin pointed out to me that Bloom's progress down the linear street takes him away from the marriage (but eventually back to it as well). Jimmy Stewart, however, cannot escape the 'threat' of marriage to Grace Kelly, contained as he is in the room and window seat with her. However, the very position of the immobile invalid with a camera enables him to replace his own marriage with the activity of being a voyeur of the marriages which parade themselves before him in the courtyard and in the courtyard's windows. Another inversion, I would assert, therefore, occurs: Bloom's freedom to move away from the marriage plot moves him home to it; and Stewart's contained stasis leads him not to inhabit his own marriage but to resist it in order to observe/fantasise about the marriages of others.

9

Trial and Error: Combinatory Fidelity in Two Versions of Franz Kafka's *The Trial*

Paul M. Malone

On 6 November 1913 Franz Kafka wrote from Prague to his fiancée in Berlin, Felice Bauer: 'I keep no diary at all; I don't know why I should keep one, nothing happens to me that moves me deep inside. This is true even when I cry, as I did yesterday in a cinema in Verona. I am capable of enjoying human relationships, but not of experiencing them.'[1] Kafka had hardly seen her since their unofficial engagement in June; but then he had hardly seen her in the entire period of their acquaintance, since mid-August 1912. During this time Kafka used the conveniently distant Felice as a muse, and kept her distant for this very purpose. As Hanns Zischler writes, 'Kafka makes her into the great screen upon which he projects his mainly nocturnal letters in ever more rapid succession.'[2]

It was the light reflected from this screen that illuminated Kafka's breakthrough as a writer, producing his first noteworthy story, 'The Judgement'; the first of his unfinished novels, *America* (1927); and his short masterpiece, 'The Metamorphosis' (1916). Throughout, Kafka kept Bauer posted on his writing, confessed to her his infidelities, and told her regularly of his visits to the cinema – for Kafka was, according to his best friend Max Brod, an enthusiastic moviegoer.[3]

By the end of 1913, however, the relationship with Felice Bauer was stretched to breaking point. Kafka had most recently been unfaithful, less physically than emotionally, with Bauer's close friend Grete Bloch, who had been acting as go-between. In mid-July 1914 Kafka visited Berlin and was confronted by Bauer, her sister and Bloch in an unpleasant scene at his hotel. In the course of this informal tribunal, a

176

more telling betrayal – he had written disparagingly of Bauer in a letter to Bloch – finally led to the dissolution of the bizarre engagement.

Within three weeks of this traumatic experience, Kafka had begun work on his second novel, apparently writing the first and last chapters before he went on to compose the intervening sections. By this time, the First World War had broken out. Germany's declaration of war on Russia was noted only cursorily in Kafka's diary, given equal importance with his afternoon swimming lesson;[4] but the impending collapse of the Austro-Hungarian empire, as much as the coming collapse of Kafka's physical health and the recent debacle of the engagement to Bauer, permeates the atmosphere of Kafka's fictional world, introduced in the now famous words: 'Someone must have traduced Joseph K., for without having done anything wrong he was arrested one fine morning.'[5]

The plot of this novel, known to posterity as *The Trial* (1925), is simple: the bank clerk Joseph K. finds himself arrested although he has committed no crime. Oddly, the arrest hardly disrupts K.'s life. Over the course of the following year, he attempts to enlist the support of various women in pursuing his case – though his motives are often sexual as well. K. is introduced by his uncle to the lawyer Huld, who takes on K.'s case while Huld's nurse, Leni, seduces K. K's case makes little progress; increasingly preoccupied, he falls behind in his work. At last, the court painter informs K. that acquittal is practically impossible, and deferral of proceedings merely temporary. K. dismisses Huld. A priest at the cathedral criticises K. for seeking help from women and describes the workings of the law in a lengthy parable. Finally, a year after his arrest, K. encounters two strangers. He goes with them to a deserted spot where they lay him down and kill him with a kitchen knife.

The Trial in its present form unfolds in ten chapters, some of them further divided into titled sections. The novel's German title, *Der Prozess*, means either 'trial' or 'process'; it both draws attention to the fact that K.'s *trial* never actually arrives, and describes the *process* of mental and social breakdown which K. endures before resigning himself to death. This latter aspect of the narrative is reflected in the episodic form of the plot: each chapter leaves K. no further ahead than before, and just as there is no actual trial, so also there is no conventional climax to the action.

Kafka struggled with writing *The Trial* through the final quarter of 1914 and into the following year, but his usual difficulty in sustaining momentum when a piece could not be composed in a single burst of creativity finally dragged work on the novel to a halt by May 1915. The parable 'Before the Law' appeared as a short story in 1916; the rest of the novel was put aside. Other stories, some finished, some unfinished, issued from his pen; as the empire, defeated already in the first stages of the war, tottered towards disintegration, Kafka took up the relationship with Felice Bauer again. A new engagement, this time official, lasted only a few weeks in July 1917: the couple's attempt to spend time together only proved their incompatibility. By September of that year a haemorrhaging from Kafka's lungs revealed his tuberculosis. He took early retirement from his job as an insurance official and spent the next seven years shuttling between passionate but unsuitable women and sanitoria.

In 1920 he began a third novel, *The Castle* (1926), which also remained unfinished after two years' work. A move to Berlin away from the suffocating atmosphere of Prague and a promising new relationship seemed on the verge of allowing Kafka some semblance of a normal domestic life when the final crisis and decline began in 1923. Within a year he was on his deathbed, unable to communicate except by writing. He elicited a promise from his friend Max Brod: all the unfinished or unpublished writings were to be destroyed, and the already published stories never to be reissued.

Brod, famously, did not keep his promise, and for the rest of his life ingenuously maintained that if Kafka had really wanted his work destroyed, he would have asked someone else to do it. In prewar Prague, Brod had been the famous writer, with a string of novels and plays to his credit while Kafka struggled to produce a single story; yet it was Brod who idolised Kafka, and now Brod outdid his friend's attempt at self-effacement by devoting his life to promoting Kafka's work rather than his own.

Collecting Kafka's papers, Brod edited the unfinished novels and published them at terrific speed: *The Trial* appeared in 1925, the year after Kafka's death; *The Castle* in 1926; *America* in 1927. Successive editions integrated or appended alternate drafts, passages deleted by Kafka, editorial apparatus. A selection of shorter stories and aphorisms were published in 1931. Brod also wrote a biography of his friend (1937), as well as volumes of critical exegesis. Brod constructed Kafka as a 'classic' author in two ways: on the one hand, the works were interpreted as a universal philosophical dispensation, to be decoded by the expert; on the other, Franz Kafka himself was reborn in Brod's writings, both biographical and critical, as an author worthy of producing classic literature – a saintly, almost messianic thinker whose very life is to be interpreted spiritually, outside of all historical or literary context. In aid of reading Kafka's life, his diaries and volumes of his correspondence with friends, publishers, his sisters, and finally with the women in his life (eventually including Felice Bauer) began appearing after the Second World War, likewise pre-edited and pre-interpreted by Brod. Such unaesthetic details as Kafka's visits to prostitutes were excised from the posthumous publications along with grammatical infelicities and orthographic errors. Over the decades, an increasing number of critics took up Brod's mission, reinforcing the image of Kafka that Brod had created and labelling the atmosphere of his works, as perceived in accordance with this image, as 'Kafkaesque'.

The very existence of such a word indicates the degree of recognition afforded this well established image of Kafka. The validity of this image, however, is no longer uncontested: Milan Kundera, for one, has eloquently argued that Brod's posthumous pseudo-Kafka, and the self-propagating system of exegesis of his image which Kundera condemns as 'Kafkology', serve as a 'castrating shadow' obscuring the real novelist, Franz Kafka of Prague, and his achievements.[6] David Zane Mairowitz and Robert Crumb, in their *Kafka for Beginners* (1993), agree with Kundera that Kafka's being 'widely over-interpreted' has 'allowed the pork-butchers of modern culture to turn him into an ADJECTIVE';[7] as does George Steiner in his introduction to an English edition of *The Trial* (1992).[8]

Though Kundera and Mairowitz exaggerate their case for polemic purposes, they accurately describe the success of Brod and the first generations of Kafka criticism in disseminating a popular image of Kafka as a largely esoteric writer. Befitting the view of Kafka's work as a form of spiritual dispensation, 'Kafkology' is both personal – seeing Kafka's novels as allegories, whether religious or 'atheistic, psychoanalytic, existentialist, Marxist[,] ... sociological, political'[9] – and sectarian; critics from each of these persuasions seldom appreciate the approaches of critics from any other school. Despite this multiplicity of competing interpretations, which Steiner decries as 'cancerous',[10] the adjective 'Kafkaesque' has filtered down to general usage, 'irrevocably tied to fantasies of doom and gloom, ignoring the intricate Jewish joke that weaves itself through the bulk of Kafka's work'.[11]

The allure of such 'fantasies of doom and gloom' has been considerable in this century, however; Martin Esslin defines the Kafkaesque atmosphere thus: 'Kafka's novels [describe] the perplexity of man confronted with a soulless, over-mechanized, over-organized world ... more accurately and more truthfully than any purely naturalistic novel could have done.'[12] And further: 'The images of Kafka's own sense of loss of contact with reality, and his feelings of guilt at being unable to regain it ... have become the supreme expression of the situation of modern man.'[13] Indeed, Frederick Karl's massive 1991 biography proclaims in its very title that Kafka is the *Representative Man* of Modernism and of the twentieth century;[14] even Kundera's most cogent objections to Brod's legend-making cannot prevent our century from being labelled 'the Age of Kafka'.

Nonetheless, the first recorded adaptation of a Kafka work, Jean-Louis Barrault and André Gide's 1947 Paris dramatisation of *The Trial* as *Le Procès*, was taken by many critics as a bad omen. *Le Procès* prompted Theodor W. Adorno to remark: 'amid the rising tide of illiteracy, [Gide], at least, ought not to have forgotten that for works of art which deserve the name, the medium is not a matter of indifference. Adaptations should be reserved for the culture industry.'[15] Adorno's objections notwithstanding, theatrical adaptations of Kafka's works and particularly of *The Trial* have continued to be produced; film versions, however, have been rarer, whether due to the theatre's capacity to provide the appropriate atmosphere, or because film-makers have doubted that Kafka's name can provide the box-office numbers necessary to make a film profitable. In any case, except for an amateur 16mm version filmed in Argentina in 1956,[16] *The Trial* has been made into a motion picture only twice, 30 years apart and in very different contexts. A detailed examination of these two films in relation to their source would fill an entire book; but a few points can be made more briefly.

Orson Welles's 1963 production is dominated by Welles's own personality: a flamboyant neo-expressionist style portrays the 'soulless, over-mechanized, over-organized world' of which Esslin writes, in which Joseph K. (played by Anthony Perkins) nervously flits from arrest to crisis after crisis until the moment of his death – by explosion rather than knife – finally prompts him to resist. This final act of resistance, however futile, embodies Welles's critique of Kafka; or, more precisely, expresses Welles's hope that 'Kafka wouldn't have put that after the death of six million Jews ... I don't mean that my ending was a particularly good one, but it was the only possible solution.'[17]

David Jones's 1993 British version of the novel, by contrast, takes no such issue with Kafka. With a screenplay by Harold Pinter, who has often acknowledged his debt to Kafka, Jones's film is marked by its ostensible fidelity: both the director and the screenwriter, in this case, make the claim to have submerged their personalities in an attempt to communicate Kafka's vision virtually as if unmediated. Given the prior existence of Welles's version, however, the second film also involves a critique of Welles's interpretation; this critique is both implicit in the 1993 film's style, and explicit in Pinter's and Jones's statements both before and after the fact. Pinter, for example, has said both, 'I don't regard *The Trial* as a particularly political work';[18] and, 'I think Orson Welles was a genius but I think his film was quite wrong because he made it into an incoherent nightmare of spasmodic half-adjusted lines, images, effects in fact.'[19]

It is important to keep in mind that both these films are generally (though certainly not universally) considered failures – the ever-present danger when a classic is adapted, and particularly a classic with the marked emotional and cultural associations with which *The Trial* has become loaded.[20] Discussion of the 1993 film, however, like the film itself, must take Welles's version into consideration as well as the original; as Pinter was forced to admit when the BBC showed the 1963 film on television the week the 1993 version (co-produced by the BBC) opened in British theatres: 'It was an extraordinary decision for someone to do this. Whatever anyone thinks about the Orson Welles film, it's an Orson Welles film, and to show it to millions of people on television the same week ....'[21] Pinter's remark demonstrates the power of Welles's reputation as *auteur*: even for Pinter, the 1963 *Trial*'s status as part of the Welles *oeuvre* bestows 'classic' stature upon it.

The two films' different approaches to the material are obvious from their respective opening moments. Welles's film begins with a black screen. The titles, in functional white lettering, are shown while Albinoni's 'Adagio' plays. The final title announces, 'The prologue scenes by Alexandre Alexieff and Claire Parker on the "pin-screen"'; then Welles himself narrates the parable 'Before the Law' to the accompaniment of the pin-screen images. As appropriate to a parable, the images have a mythic, ahistorical quality. Welles's voice concludes the parable by intoning, 'This tale is told during the story called 'The Trial'. It has been said that this story has the logic of a dream ... of a nightmare.'[22] The last pin-screen image fades to black; fade up on a close-up of Anthony Perkins as the sleeping K.

To this point, the film has given little sign of being grounded in a specific time or place: the black screen, the classical music which sets a mood but has few concrete associations to the modern listener, the fantastic pin-screen pictures. Even in the first frames of the film story, when we finally see K.'s room, the walls are blank and bare; only when a police inspector enters the room in recognisable modern dress do we begin to feel a sense of location in time or space.

The opening of the 1993 film, on the other hand, plunges us almost immediately into a specific and tangible world. A brief black screen allows the opening sentence of the book to be quickly presented in small print: 'Someone must have been spreading lies about Josef K., for without having done anything wrong he was arrested one morning.' Almost immediately, the screen fades up to present 'one morning' visually: tradesmen sweeping the street and waiters readying the tables, shopkeepers opening to the early customers, all bathed in muted golden light. The period costumes, the cobblestones and the signs in German and Czech display Habsburg Prague to us as an accordion melody provides local colour. Only after this is set up does the accordion build into the ominous waltz (composed by Carl Davis) which will become the film's *leitmotiv*; at the same time, the camera sweeps by means of a combined dolly and crane shot from a low angle on the street upwards around a corner into a side street, zooming in on a second-floor balcony. A cut to the balcony seen through an inside window is followed by a pan across the room, furnished with appropriate period clutter, to reveal Kyle MacLachlan as K. in bed. This is the point where the published version of Pinter's screenplay begins; but Jones's film has already thrown down the gauntlet to its 1963 precursor.

The carefully constructed naturalism that marks the 1993 film represents Pinter's and Jones's attempt 'to strip away the layers of interpretation and go back to first base'.[23] Pinter's answer to both Welles's programmatic opening statement about 'the logic of a dream' and his explosive finale is revealed in a letter to producer Louis Marks: 'The film does not go from dream to reality, as it were. It is *all* reality or *all* dream. But one must remember that the knife which is plunged into K.'s heart is real.'[24] In this spirit, carefully selected Prague locations are used to create a simulacrum of Kafka's Prague as 'a very strong solid world indeed, with a worm of anxiety in the very middle of it'.[25] Welles's original intention, by contrast, had been to have the sets gradually vanish: 'The number of realistic elements was to gradually diminish, and to be seen to diminish by the spectators, until only open space remained, as if everything had been dissolved away.'[26] Only the collapse of funding arrangements forced Welles to alter his vision: since no sets could be built in Zagreb (the original location), the production was moved back to Paris where the abandoned Gare d'Orsay with its massive interiors became freely available. The final effect, if not a gradual disappearance of reality, is nonetheless one of bizarre and disconnected spaces, laid out in no rational or realistic manner.

The manner in which exterior footage shot in Yugoslavia (or later in Italy) is integrated on a shot-by-shot basis with the Paris footage to create this impression is all the more impressive given the enforced suddenness of the move, and has been compared to Lev Kuleshov's pioneering experiments with montage in the 1920s,[27] as well as to Kafka's own 'narrative theme of spatial disorientation'.[28] Thus, for example, when Welles's K. is summoned to his first hearing, Welles has him receive a note while taking in an evening show at an ornate and crowded opera house. Excusing himself repeatedly, the embarrassed K. makes his way through the seats. In the next shot he exits into what must be the empty foyer (in fact part of the Gare d'Orsay) to meet the inspector, who leads him into a warren of increasingly cramped, ill-lit and dilapidated alleyways before giving him a map to the location of the hearing. K. then walks through a massive square where blankly functional modern buildings and a shrouded statue dwarf rows of gaunt and half-naked figures wearing numbered signs around their necks (elderly Yugoslavian extras whose drawn features are reminiscent both of photos from the Nazi death camps and of Goya's late drawings). Finally he enters a nondescript series of unfurnished industrial rooms – the Gare d'Orsay again – before gaining entry to the courtroom, which is as crowded as the opera house he left less than four minutes of screen time previously. This series of many brief shots links footage from several locations into a coherent narrative progression which nonetheless defeats any attempt by the viewer to visualise the geography of K.'s city, and thus mimics Kafka's own narrative gift for combining detailed verbal description with vague and malleable spatial relationships.

Even Welles's motive for selecting the original location runs counter to Jones's and Pinter's later intention: Welles chose Yugoslavia 'for its natural settings, which most audiences would find difficult to place'.[29] Under the conditions of the Cold War, when even the most open areas of Eastern Europe were little-known to West Europeans and Americans, Zagreb and environs offered Welles the perfect world. In the post-Soviet era, however, modern-day Prague became an obvious choice for Jones's film not only because of its naturalistic approach, but also because the penetration of Western media into the former Eastern bloc has made it increasingly easy for audiences to 'read' Eastern Europe.

As a result, when Jones's K. sets off to find the hearing, the audience sees him pass from his usual middle-class haunts into working-class streets of the period, both lovingly recreated in broad daylight. The terse description of these scenes in the published screenplay hardly does the filmed version justice.[30] Jones expands Pinter's description into a sequence which starts with the dapper K. apparently under surveillance by two of his colleagues in a passing tram. Respectable citizens of Prague file into church as K. passes a stand in the street selling books and engravings; with a quick cut K. moves from the Baroque architecture of bourgeois Prague into the crowded streets in a poorer neighbourhood, teeming with hawkers, food-sellers and livestock. He finds his destination and descends through a narrow passage before coming into an inner tenement courtyard. Pinter supplies some of his trademark uninformative dialogue when K. asks residents of the tenement for a fictitious plumber named Lanz (a non-existent carpenter in the novel, and unmentioned in Welles's film): as one resident tells him, 'No, I'll tell you what, there is a plumber upstairs, at least I think he's a plumber, I mean that's what he says he is, but I wouldn't swear his name was Lanz, I mean if I had to swear it on oath, I wouldn't swear it.'[31] Jones, for his part, foreshadows K.'s difficulties with the court by having children playing in the stairways trip K. up, and by K.'s stumbling over derelict furniture on the narrow tenement balconies.

If the shooting and editing of this sequence in Jones's film has a plainness and clarity compared to the surreal and dis-orienting effect of Welles's sequence – Jones's version uses fewer individual shots and is a full minute shorter – this clarity serves to make clear to the audience K.'s own increasing disorientation and dislocation as he moves from familiar territory into *terra incognita*. Indeed, this sequence puts into practice Pinter's statement that 'With Kafka the nightmare takes place in the day. It's certainly not abstract or fantastic; it is very plain and proceeds in a quite logical way. Although it ceases to be logical when you try to examine it, you don't know where the natural flow of events slips into something which is totally inexplicable.'[32]

The sincerity of Jones's and Pinter's belief in their method is demonstrated by the fact that they are overwhelmingly interested in Prague's atmosphere and not at all in its landmarks. The 1993 film thus resolutely refuses to furnish the postcard views which typify 'location shooting' – for shots of the Charles Bridge or the Hradschin, one must see Steven Soderbergh's fantasia *Kafka* (1991).

The fact that Pinter and Jones forgo the usual 'proofs' of location in this way also reflects a return to political 'normalcy' after the 50-year hiatus of the Cold War; Welles knew that Eastern Europe would be exotic to his audience, but Pinter and Jones know that it is no longer exotic, merely 'authentic' for their purpose – even if some of the shots have the stilted look that betokens avoiding views of television aerials and neon signs. This is appropriate for Jones's film, given that none of these recognisable features appear in the novel. In fact, the only toponym even mentioned in Kafka's text is the Juliusstrasse, the address of K.'s hearing; and there is no such street in Prague (though the name may be a play on Kafka's mother's name, Julie, symbolically alluding to his maternal city, which he once described as a 'little mother' – with claws).[33] Ironically, even as the 1993 film avoids the stereotypical features of Prague in the interests of naturalism, its makers' investment in a sort of 'authenticity' also motivates them to use the real city to depict a location that never existed.

The very naturalism of the 1993 film's style is, in a sense, a long set-up for the scene which Pinter regards as 'his most vivid memory from the book'.[34] This is the 'Flogger' scene, about one-third into both the novel and the film.[35] Pinter's intention is elucidated by Francis Gillen: 'Because Pinter, unlike Welles, has kept the screenplay on a matter-of-fact level, an audience is shocked, as is K., to find the two arresting warders being whipped savagely in a lumber room near K.'s office in the bank.'[36]

This is certainly a reasonable assertion, and Jones's film does have the required effect; though it is difficult to prove that Welles's version does *not* provide the same shock, particularly since Welles takes care to set up the room as an innocent storeroom in an earlier scene, rather like a conjurer – which Welles was – showing us an empty box from which a dove will later be produced.[37] Even viewers of Pinter's 'matter-of-fact' screenplay, however, may find the shock diminished, given that they have already seen the naturalistic façade crack when K.'s hearing takes place in an assembly room far too large to occupy the position at the top of the tenement where K. finds it; and when, from the beginning of the film, a senior bank clerk in a major city is addressed – and identifies himself – by his initial rather than his surname. In short, as Frederick Karl puts it: 'In his very candor about Kafka's supremacy, [Pinter] has overdetermined the novelist's realism.' Karl further suggests that Brod's determination to 'classicise' Kafka by minimising the ambiguity of his texts has misled Pinter into following this strategy.[38]

As for Welles's treatment of the same scene, given the already theatrically heightened world he has created for K., he has no choice but to turn up the intensity accordingly when K. opens the storeroom door. In Jones's film, MacLachlan as K. is presented with the Flogger and the two warders as in a set piece: they appear to have taken their positions waiting for an audience, and they are lit from below by an illuminated floor in what almost seems a parody of stock 'eerie' lighting. Perkins's K., however, opens the door into a confusion of voices and almost abstract shapes, as faces are picked out of the darkness by the single hanging lamp. Quick cuts and extreme close-ups give the scene a very different dynamic; and when the Flogger begins his work in the tiny space, the lamp is struck with a clang and begins swinging, throwing the patterns of light and dark into confusion.

David Thomson has observed that Welles's *Trial* 'is surely enriched by one other movie: I doubt it would be as good and unnerving without Perkins's extraordinary performance in [Alfred] Hitchcock's *Psycho* [1960]'.[39] Thomson refers specifically to the self-incriminating *double entendres* which Welles writes into Perkins's dialogue as K., echoing the wordplay in Perkins's scene with Janet Leigh in the Hitchcock classic; but in the storeroom in *The Trial*, the swinging lamp echoes the light bulb set swinging in *Psycho* when the corpse of Norman Bates's mother is discovered in the attic. Welles wanted Perkins for the part to capture K.'s 'aggressiveness',[40] but perhaps he also wanted to play on Perkins's fame as Bates – since Welles believed that K. was guilty, 'not guilty of what he's accused of, but he's guilty all the same'.[41] In any case, in this scene, the tables are turned: it is Perkins who is horrified as light and noise swirl all around him. The voices are even more disturbing because of their similarity: Welles dubbed the voices of most of the male characters himself in post-production, including the Flogger and the two warders (the synchronisation is technically very impressive, given that the swinging light submerges faces in darkness periodically). Perhaps this scene is the section that prompted Pinter to describe Welles's film as 'an incoherent nightmare';[42] but it is entirely appropriate in context. When K. attempts to leave the storeroom, unlike MacLachlan who leaves unhindered, Perkins must extricate himself from the grabbing hands of one of the warders; as the shot cuts to a view of outside the room, the angle from which the doorway is seen is so acute that it appears for a moment that K. is struggling to free himself from a mirror, like Alice in the looking glass. K.'s anxious dance of indecision outside the storeroom is a fitting response to his escape.

If such moments as these provoke some critics to regard Perkins's K. as 'an incompetent neurotic',[43] the fact is that Perkins, in Welles's more theatrical style, is merely playing openly what MacLachlan, in his best scenes in Jones's film (including the end of the 'Flogger' scene), is stolidly but visibly keeping bottled up. So too is the slightly narcissistic self-certainty of MacLachlan's K. foreshadowed in Welles's film, when Perkins's K. rejects being labelled by his lawyer as 'a victim of society' with the simple, muted – and Wellesian – response, 'I am a member of society.'[44] Given the seedy appearance of the police and law officials who uphold this society, and the prurient imaginations of his own landlady and bank manager, however, Welles's K. can hardly make this claim without damning himself further.

What the two K.s have most in common is a superficial resemblance to their creator. Joseph K. is never described in the novel – there is no reason why he might not be blond, portly, and mustachioed – and yet, perhaps as a legacy of Kundera's 'Kafkology', adaptations for both stage and screen have typically chosen to portray K. as an avatar of Kafka. Both Perkins and MacLachlan are tall, dark, slim, good-looking, not unlike Kafka himself. Of the two, only Perkins has Kafka's almost unnatural gangliness and, at least to some observers, the ambiguous sexuality that Kafka also projects in his writing.[45] By coincidence, Perkins was thirty during filming, exactly the same age as Joseph K., and Kafka's age in 1913.

The 33-year-old MacLachlan, by comparison, instead of Perkins's unflattering 1960s business suit and side-parted haircut, has the natty dress sense evident in many of Kafka's photographs, as well as the austere, thick, back-combed hair of the dying author's last dour portrait of 1923/24. K.'s elegant appearance in Jones's film clearly differentiates him from most of the denizens of the court: his fine clothes make him stand out against the usually crumpled and never stylish apparel of the court's warders, inspectors, and magistrates, while MacLachlan's wobbly mid-Atlantic accent (an approximation of Received Pronunciation) contrasts with the more working-class British dialects of, at least, the lower court officials and tenement dwellers. Curiously, while Kafka writes in the novel that most of the accused who frequent the shabby court waiting rooms belong to the upper classes,[46] Jones's *Trial* puts most of them in workingman's clothes (which Pinter's published screenplay does not demand). Indeed, the one accused man whom MacLachlan/K. addresses in the court offices is not only dressed as a labourer, but is also one of the few actors in the film with a Czech accent.

Moreover, Jones's K. is not burdened with the guilt of Norman Bates. Rather, in addition to his matinee-idol good looks, MacLachlan brings to the role associations from his frequent work with director David Lynch. In *Dune* (1984), *Blue Velvet* (1986), and the *Twin Peaks* television series (1990) and theatrical film (1992), MacLachlan's characters surmount equally bizarre circumstances to solve mysteries or otherwise emerge triumphant, raising the expectation that his K. may do the same. To his credit, MacLachlan does not trade on these associations, but enters wholly into the spirit of K.'s middle-class smugness and repression, covering any guilt feelings (which Welles and Perkins often telegraph by means of dialogue and body language) with the contained annoyance and condescension which K. frequently displays in the novel. To sum up the two films' adaptive strategies in their protagonists, one could easily say that Welles and Perkins have chosen to portray the *inner* Joseph K., in keeping with the 1963 version's expressionistic leanings, while Pinter, Jones and MacLachlan have elected to show the *outer* K.; not in a spirit of superficiality, but rather in a courageous attempt to avoid interpretation. Both Ks exist in the novel: it is pointless to try to prove that one film provides us with a 'truer' Joseph K. than the other.

Ultimately, there is just as little point in arguing which adaptation is more faithful to Kafka's original, totting up what one or the other cuts or retains, alters or keeps of the novel. Kafka's mastery, which has survived Brod's clumsy editing, hundreds of adaptations into other forms and countless critical interpretations, lies in his ability to use the pellucid clarity of his language in such a way that he seems to be describing a normal world. Only upon reflection does the reader realise that the detailed descriptions render no clear image, that there remains an unsettling void at the centre. In Kafka, the normalcy and the void coexist; but adaptations, like interpretations, are often reduced to choosing between the two. As David Jones says of the naturalist view: 'It seemed to me that was the way to go; there is another way which Welles ... took.'[47] Kafka, however, always takes the middle way – or both ways at once.

As a result of their contradictions in style and intent, these two very different films complement one another, combining into a sort of stereoscopic view of the novel, each choosing to illuminate different levels of the original text. Both Welles and the team of Pinter and Jones have every right to be proud of their achievements. Welles once remarked, 'Say what you like but *The Trial* is the best film I ever made;'[48] while Pinter has written of his screenplay, 'This is one of the most satisfying projects that I've ever been associated with.'[49]

Frederick Karl, in his detailed critique of Pinter's and Jones's film, found much to admire in it, but was forced in the end to judge that Pinter's adaptation 'cannot give us the Kafkaesque, which is, all in all, the essence of the novelist's significance'.[50] One of Welles's biographers, David Thomson, was much impressed by the earlier version, and yet ultimately came to the same conclusion – but he put it more positively, and his words, like Karl's, can be applied with equal justice to both films: 'And if the result isn't quite Kafka, and not entirely Kafkaesque, Kafka can live with that.'[51] Kafka's work will remain a classic on its own terms for as long as it can survive adaptation. Welles's film, if it is judged a classic, will survive Jones's film; and if, in another 30 years, Kafka is still being read, then perhaps another film will test all three of them.

Notes

1. Franz Kafka, *Briefe an Felice* (Tübingen: Fischer, 1967), p. 472. All translations from German sources are my own unless otherwise indicated.
2. Hanns Zischler, *Kafka geht ins Kino* (Reinbek bei Hamburg: Rowohlt, 1996), p. 93.
3. Zischler, *Kafka*, p. 51.
4. Franz Kafka, *Tagebücher 1910–1923* (Frankfurt: Fischer, 1983), p. 305.
5. Franz Kafka, *The Trial*, trans. Willa and Edwin Muir, revised with additional translation by E.M. Butler (New York: Vintage, 1969), p. 3.
6. Milan Kundera, 'In Saint Garta's shadow: Rescuing Kafka from the Kafkologists', trans. Barbara Wright, *Times Literary Supplement*, 24 May 1991, p. 5.
7. David Zane Mairowitz and Robert Crumb, *Kafka for Beginners* (Cambridge: Icon, 1993), p. 5; emphasis in the original.
8. George Steiner, 'Introduction' in Franz Kafka, *The Trial*, trans. Willa and Edwin Muir and revised with additional material translated by E.M. Butler (New York: Schocken, 1992), p. vii.

9. Kundera, 'Saint Garta', p. 3.

10. Steiner, 'Introduction', p. vii.

11. Mairowitz and Crumb, *Kafka*, p. 5.

12. Martin Esslin, *The Theatre of the Absurd* (Harmondsworth: Penguin, 1983), pp. 316–7.

13. Esslin, *Theatre*, p. 345.

14. Frederick R. Karl, *Franz Kafka: Representative Man* (New York: Ticknor & Fields, 1991).

15. Theodor W. Adorno, *Prisms*, trans. Samuel and Shierry Weber (London: Spearman, 1967), pp. 262–3.

16. José Agustín Mahieu, 'Kafka y el cine', *Cuadernos Hispanoamericanos* 401 (November 1983), p. 77.

17. Orson Welles, *The Trial* (London: Lorrimer, 1970), p. 9.

18. Mel Gussow, *Conversations with Pinter* (London: Nick Hern, 1994), p. 136.

19. Gussow, *Conversations*, pp. 88–9.

20. For negative appraisals of Welles's film, see Joseph McBride, *Orson Welles*, revised and expanded edn (New York: Da Capo, 1996), pp. 155–61; Geoffrey Wagner, *The Novel and the Cinema* (Rutherford: Farleigh Dickinson University Press, 1975) pp. 328–34. For unfavourable comparisons of Welles's film to Jones's, see Michael Billington, *The Life and Work of Harold Pinter* (London: Faber, 1996), pp. 348–51; Francis Gillen, 'From Novel to Film: Harold Pinter's Adaptation of *The Trial*' in Katherine H. Burkman and John L. Kundert-Gibbs (eds), *Pinter at Sixty* (Bloomington: Indiana University Press, 1993), pp. 137–48. For positive accounts of Welles's *Trial*, see 'Anonymous', 'All's Welles [*The Trial*]' in Morris Beja (ed.), *Perspectives on Orson Welles* (New York: G.K. Hall, 1995), pp. 31–2; Noël Carroll, 'Welles and Kafka' in *Interpreting the Moving Image* (Cambridge: Cambridge University Press, 1998), pp. 191–202; David Thomson, *Rosebud: The Story of Orson Welles* (New York: Knopf, 1996), pp. 366–71.

21. Gussow, *Conversations*, p. 117.

22. Welles, *Trial*, p. 17.

23. Billington, *The Life*, p. 349.

24. Louis Marks, 'Producing Pinter' in Burkman and Kundert-Gibbs, *Pinter*, p. 18.

25. Gussow, *Conversations*, p. 136.

26. Welles, *Trial*, p. 11.
27. Frank Brady, *Citizen Welles: A Biography of Orson Welles* (New York: Scribner's, 1989), p. 530.
28. Carroll, 'Welles', p. 192.
29. Brady, *Citizen*, p. 529.
30. Harold Pinter, *The Trial* (London: Faber and Faber, 1993), pp. 15–18.
31. Pinter, *Trial*, pp. 16–17.
32. Pinter, quoted in Billington, *The Life*, p. 348.
33. Elizabeth M. Rajec, *Namen und ihre Bedeutungen im Werke Franz Kafkas: Ein interpretatorischer Versuch* (Bern: Peter Lang, 1977), pp. 138–9.
34. Marks, 'Producing', p. 22.
35. Franz Kafka, *Der Prozess* (Frankfurt: Fischer, 1958), pp. 103–11; Pinter, *Trial*, pp. 31–2.
36. Gillen, 'Novel to Film', p. 141.
37. Welles, *Trial*, p. 45–6.
38. Frederick R. Karl, 'Comments on Harold Pinter's Adaptation of Franz Kafka's *The Trial*', *The Pinter Review: Annual Essays 1994* Tampa, FL: University of Tampa Press), pp. 81–2.
39. Thomson, *Rosebud*, p. 369.
40. Barbara Leaming, *Orson Welles* (New York: Viking, 1985), p. 460.
41. Welles, *Trial*, p. 9.
42. Gussow, *Conversations*, pp. 88–9.
43. Wagner, *Novel*, p. 331.
44. Welles, *Trial*, p. 168.
45. Thomson, *Rosebud*, p. 367. For a much earlier perception of Perkins/K. as sexually ambiguous, and a negative reaction to it, see Wagner, *Novel*, p. 331.
46. Kafka, *Prozess*, p. 80.
47. Billington, *The Life*, p. 350.
48. Welles, *Trial*, p. 10.
49. Francis Gillen, 'Harold Pinter on *The Trial*', *The Pinter Review: Annual Essays 1992–1993* (Tampa, FL: University of Tampa Press), p. 62.
50. Karl, 'Comments', p. 83.
51. Thomson, *Rosebud*, p. 366.

10

In Cold Blood: Yellow Birds, New Realism and Killer Culture

Paul Wells

Truman Capote's *In Cold Blood* (1966) was arguably the most complete formulation until then of the 'non-fiction' novel.[1] It told the true story of the apparently motiveless murder of Herbert, Bonnie, Nancy and Kenyon Clutter in Holcomb, Kansas in November 1959, and the subsequent capture and execution of their slayers, Perry Smith and Richard Hickok. Upon its publication and in the discussions that have since followed, a number of issues have been raised about the ethics of the project and the form in which it was constructed.[2] These issues were compounded by the filming of the book in 1967, and again, some thirty years later, with the publication of George Plympton's oral biography of Truman Capote, and a new television serialisation of the novel.

The purpose of this chapter is to address the underlying principles of the novel, the film and the television adaptation as shifting paradigms of the non-fiction docu-drama, and to explore the claims of the novel as a classic of American postwar fiction. Further, and perhaps more importantly, I will address *In Cold Blood* as a model of historical reportage, an engagement with the crises of mid-twentieth century masculinity, and a pertinent social analysis which anticipated the burgeoning serial killer culture of the 1980s and 1990s.

While researching *In Cold Blood*, initially an assignment for the *New Yorker* magazine, Truman Capote's effete, socialite and intellectual pretensions were initially greeted with understandable scepticism by the already troubled citizens of Holcomb, Kansas.[3] Capote eventually adapted himself to the environment, partly helped by the presence of his companion, Harper Lee, author of *To Kill a Mockingbird*

(1960), and partly, although unknowingly for those partici-
pating at the time, because he offered a mode of therapy for
those traumatised by the murder of one of the most respected
and model families in the community. It is Capote's approach
to the project and the aesthetic techniques he employed
which have come under most scrutiny, especially in the light
of the outcomes of the novel and its matters of emphasis and
concern. Capote perceived the case as an opportunity to reassess the role and function of 'the reporter' and the purpose
and effect of journalistic practice within the novel form. In
this he anticipated 'the New Journalism', later embraced by
Norman Mailer and Tom Wolfe, which would call into
question how social acts become historical events and in turn
texts with ideological, representational and aesthetic implications. Mailer defines the New Journalism as 'an enormously
personalised journalism where the character of the narrator
was one of the elements not only in the telling of the story
but in the way that the reader would assess the experience ...
[W]hat was wrong with journalism was that the reporter
pretended to be objective and that was one of the great lies of
all time,' adding 'What this really was, was an all-out assault
on *New Yorker* writing.'[4] In many ways, although Capote is
arguably more 'embedded' in the *In Cold Blood* narrative, he
effectively personalises the narrative, bringing to it a literary
styling drawn from an understanding of both the context and
the tradition he writes within.

Blurring the lines between fiction and documentary,
Capote raises issues about the status of both. Eager to create
material that would transcend the ephemeral nature of
journalism yet embrace the living 'history' it transiently
recorded, Capote sought a narrative with a complex and
enduring theme which would not date in significance. A
motiveless murder proved an appropriate topic because of
both the level of transgression it embodied and the aftermath
that could be explored with the various parties involved.

Tony Hilfer notes four key tendencies in postwar American
fiction which are relevant in this context. These four modes
– naturalistic social protest, poetic or modernist realism,
traditional realism, and postmodernism – all find purchase in
Capote's narrative, and in doing so position the novel as a

'classic' on which succeeding generations of readers find new perspectives. Hilfer suggests that naturalistic social protest 'usually centres on characters destroyed by psychological, social and economic factors beyond their control', while poetic or modernist realism has realist conventions but is informed by 'subtextual webs of symbolism that intimate interior states of the character and/or metaphysical concepts about the world'. Traditional realism deals with 'characters who seem recognisably like those of the reader's experience, and whose moral choices and their consequences are the focus of the novel', while postmodernism collapses narrational orthodoxies, adopts self-conscious and parodic 'literary' strategies, resists the notion of a consistent and consensual order, and, crucially, engages with the 'myth of an American society that allows for a relatively unimpeded social mobility [which] gives Americans a sense of identity as fluid and performative, a question of choice, rather than historical and determinate, a matter of destiny'.[5]

In Cold Blood controversially embraces 'naturalistic social protest' in its concentration on Perry Smith as a victim of his upbringing. His mother was a prostitute and alcoholic; his father, a brutal, almost schizophrenic, romantic; and his guardian nuns were cruel and patronising – all of which suggests that his demise was made inevitable by both his social and economic disempowerment and his predilection for introspection, which was prompted by his failure to realise his dreams of becoming a singer or an explorer. Capote also implies that Smith is a victim of the promise of the American Dream, an ideological and economic construct embodied in the achievements and status of the Clutter family.[6] The novel's 'poetic, modernist realist' credentials also lie in Capote's use of Perry Smith's romantic preoccupations as symbolic elements that complement his own literary style. Smith's recurring dream of a liberating and redemptive 'Yellow Bird' of death, along with his desire to emulate the masculine bravura of the adventurers in *Treasure of the Sierra Madre* (John Huston, 1948), serve as a transcendent rhetoric set against the perpetual reminder of his pain from a motorcycle accident and his constant need to motivate himself in the face of rejection by his family. Capote uses stated and assumed 'interiority' as the presiding text of his novel, deliberately foregrounding its status as a reported narrative. It is in this use of 'personal' motifs as the substantive aspects of 'plot' that Capote redetermines the use of 'stream of consciousness' writing and the self-conscious use of 'interior monologue', redefining it as journalistic story-telling.

This strategy contrasts with the 'traditional realism' under-pinning Capote's depiction of the Clutter family and the Holcomb community. In detailing the naturalised rhythms and relationships of these people, Capote creates a picture of stability and moral certainty only slightly ruffled by the subtle rebellion of Nancy and Kenyon Clutter. Nancy and Kenyon do not, however, represent the early stages of emerging youth culture in the United States. Rather, they epitomise the small-town machinations that Capote draws upon at a more symbolic level. Nancy, a Methodist, is advised by her father to break off her relationship with Bobby Rupp, who is Catholic, because it can have no future, while Kenyon suffers from feelings of inadequacy in the light of his father's success and status. These issues become part of an oedipal thematic which suggests that when Perry Smith murders Herb Clutter, he symbolically murders his own father and challenges the limits of postwar America's inhibiting and unstable patriarchal order.

It is here that Capote's work defines a key moment in American postmodernity and embraces the literary 'strategies' which signal a postmodern address. Capote plays out his self-conscious 'romantic' style within the narrational demands of quasi-picaresque reportage, defining Perry and Dick as embodiments of identity in crisis who 'perform' themselves in response to their mobility, their lack of social position, and the insistent 'oppression' of the mythic promise of the American Dream. As Capote himself suggested, after receiving a significant amount of correspondence following the publication of the novel: 'About 70 percent of the letters think of the book as a reflection on American life – this collision between the desperate, ruthless, wandering, savage part of American life, and the other, which is insular and safe, more or less', adding, 'Perry Smith wasn't an evil person ...

[B]ut every illusion he'd ever had, well, they all evaporated, so on that night he was so full of self-hatred and self-pity that I think he would have killed *some*body ... You can't go through life without getting anything you want, ever.'[7] Just as Capote constructs the Clutter family to epitomise the historically determined and somehow 'pre-ordained' achievement possible in American life, so he uses Perry to deny this middle-class ideology of an inevitable claim upon opportunity and fulfilment. Perry is the consequence of alienation from this paradigm. His exhaustive reclamation of refundable empty Coca-Cola bottles jettisoned alongside the desert highway for-tuitously parodies, for Capote, Smith's actual participation in the promise of America's myth-laden market economy. However, it is Capote's selection and prioritisation of such true events which raise questions about the way he privileges his 'literary' achievements over his moral responsibilities in representing the 'real life' events in which he participated.

Capote's research for the novel included interviewing relevant protagonists, direct observation, using available insti-tutional records, and embracing new theories in criminology. However, his interviews and those by Harper Lee were not recorded, but memorised. Without the evidence of conversa-tion, Capote may be accused of merely manipulating the material to his own ends – a charge substantiated by Capote's chosen technique of the absent but omniscient narrator and by the privileging of Perry Smith as the novel's main character. On the other hand, Capote's cross-checking and verification in regard to public records are equally in evidence, adding weight to the view that although Capote's work is provocative in its structural and aesthetic strategies, it is sound in its non-campaigning and almost amoral position. In short, it is Capote's transposition of the material through his own ideological and, arguably, sexual filters which raises questions about the ethical stance of the piece and the point of view that finally prevails. Perhaps most important is Capote's consistent claim that he embraced the material in a spirit directed always to creating a work of art and nothing else – social, psychoanalytic, political or otherwise. This raises key questions about the moral obligation of 'art'. As Graham Caveney remarks: 'To whom do tragedies belong? The innocent dead or their self-appointed poetic witness? At what point does empathy become exploitation? What are the consequences of one man's murder becoming another man's metaphor?'[8] The answer to these questions clearly lies in the repositioning of 'art' as an act of 'historicism', played out through the ability of the novelist to *inhabit* known scenarios and their implications rather than invent and extrapolate 'meaning' from them. In essence, what is left is only 'narrative', and nothing which remains easily distinguishable as fiction or non-fiction.

The novel is divided into four discrete sections: 'The Last to See Them Alive', the parallel and intersecting narrative of Hickok's and Smith's journey to Holcomb and the everyday practices of the Clutter family; 'Persons Unknown', the aftermath of the murders; 'Answer', the resolution of the murder in the capture and confession of Hickok and Smith; and 'The Corner', dealing with the prolonged prosecution and final execution of the murderers. Capote's clear imperative is to maintain the key engine of the 'detective story' by prolonging suspense and providing a satisfying but challenging explanation of events. Furthermore, he wishes to create some empathy and identification with characters who are not in principle sympathetic in order to address issues beyond the self-evident ease of an apparently self-evident resolution which merely endorses a self-evident notion of right and wrong. He wishes to create an 'openness' in the narrative that destabilises consensual certainties about not only the ethical and social issues raised in the novel, but also the act of storytelling itself. Of yet more importance is Capote's recognition in the structure of his work that 'notions of both rationality and system are undermined by the visible evidence that "History" is the concatenated and reified effect of incoherent motives and chance convergences'.[9] In refusing the distinctions of both literary and historical 'objects', Capote maps a terrain which, Hayden White suggests, redetermines an event as 'a hypothetical presupposition necessary to the constitution of a documentary record whose inconsistencies, contradictions, gaps and distortions ... presumed to be [its] common referent itself moves to the fore as the principal object of investigation'.[10]

The sense of inevitability and foreboding that Capote creates in the early part of the novel, as the tragic trajectories of murderers and murdered come together, is coupled with a detailed interrogation of the enigma at the heart of Perry Smith and Richard Hickok and a search for the reasons why the brutal murders occurred. Arguably, though Capote provides the evidence and partly mythologises the murderers, his conclusion remains that there are no conclusions: a model thereafter embraced by many 'serial killer' texts. This ambivalence speaks to the creation of what may be seen as an aesthetic of inevitability, which accepts that there is no explanation available and no lesson to be learned – even though these are often the underpinning *raisons d'être* for the construction of historical 'events'. Ironically, authorial intervention in this model uses the multiplicity of approaches to relinquish a model of authorship that insists upon accepting any one version of an event as 'truth', or any full determination of the 'facts' as the presiding fault-line by which morality and social justice may be understood.

It is doubly ironic, then, that the subsequent film and television adaptations of *In Cold Blood* have sought to return to the conventions of 'realism' in order to impart a high degree of authenticity to their depiction of 'events' and their apparently self-evident meanings. While Capote never abandoned 'historicity' but refracted it through the literary modifications of the New Journalism, Richard Brooks's 1967 film embraces neo-realism in order to recall historical events and 'fix' their moment. The 'events' are not merely the substantive elements of 'the plot', but do much to emphasise the relationship between the crime itself and its repercussions, a relationship which becomes increasingly distanciated in the novel when Capote becomes more interested in creating 'characters to whom he attributed inner lives of which they were tragically (blissfully) unaware'.[11] Brooks's film, somewhat paradoxically, attempts an 'objectification' of the Clutter murder, which Capote had narrativised, by focusing on the events themselves and not the discourses surrounding them. Although the film recognises Capote's presence in the narrative – acknowledged in the casting of a 'reporter' within the film – this very intervention alone signals Brooks's intention to return to the 'outside' of the story and not its more ambivalent interior.

Reviewing Brooks's film, Max Kozloff suggests that Brooks's apparently 'objective' approach is insufficiently interrogative and that, in failing to raise issues, is merely complicit rather than provocative. In short, Brooks 'lets everyone off the hook'.[12] Kozloff says, 'Dramatically static, by virtue of the fixed psychology of the protagonist [Perry Smith], *In Cold Blood* is, or pretends to be, morally neutral.'[13] Arguably, this fails to take into account how the 'events' as they are drawn from the novel actually foreground not only Perry Smith's psychological and emotional profile, but also the issue of capital punishment. The film makes no attempt to solicit pity for Smith, merely to advance an understanding of his possible motives and the societal context which has created him. Brooks's 'objectivity', however, is still predicated on Capote's structure, and does not, for example, foreground the Clutter family as the later television serialisation seeks to do. Brooks is more preoccupied with staging the events to authenticate their 'seriousness' and their significance to the 'actual' condition of law and order, masculinity, and the family in the 1960s – social factors seemingly trivialised in the representations available through the increasingly influential rise of television in the domestic sphere.

Interestingly, Capote recommended that Brooks should undertake the adaptation of the novel, judging his strength of character by his surviving an evening of vitriolic abuse from director John Huston.[14] Brooks, a pragmatist with a high degree of attention to detail, tried to ground the film in the very locations where the events had actually taken place. Drawing from the ethos of the burgeoning *vérité* work of Robert Drew and his associates, which sought to be non-interventionist in its recording of events, Brooks attempted to represent actuality in the fictional context by systematically re-creating contexts which allowed re-enactment of and direct empathy with the story. FBI agent Charles McAtee recalls that Brooks wanted to film in the penitentiary and at the gallows where Smith and Hickok were executed, or failing that ship them to Hollywood for filming; though this did not happen, McAtee remembers that 'we did sell him the latrine facilities that were in Smith and Hickok's cells during their five years plus on death row ... I think they were $150 a piece'.[15] This quest for environmental authenticity is best expressed in the film's use of the Clutter household as the set for the re-enactment of the murders. To echo Caveney once again, there are clearly issues here about intrusiveness and taste in the pursuit of representing 'the truth'. Perhaps surprisingly, it is Larry Cohen, the director of the horror films *It's Alive* (1973) and *It Lives Again* (1978), who questions the film's approach, suggesting,

> That is really gruesome! – to have those people killed all over again in the rooms where they were actually murdered ... It's just something weird. Being murdered is a very private thing, and it seems an invasion of privacy to me to have a movie company come in and exploit that for profit. I mean you died, and you're dead. If anything *belongs* to you, it's your death. They're taking something from you.[16]

If Capote could be accused of exploiting the murders for his own literary and financial ends, this seems even more graphically the case in the film version. This is largely because Brooks does not have the discursive detail and textual rhetoric of the novel to prevent the events from being anything but *literal*. Ironically, this proves reductive both in relation to the 'shock' intended by 'reproducing' events, but also in diverting attention from the purpose in actually inter-preting and imposing narrative structure on the events as Capote had done. Brooks had taken Capote too literally, and in doing so misrepresented the cinematic possibilities of addressing the subject.

Writing for *Cahiers du cinéma* at the same time as the film of *In Cold Blood* appeared, novelist Italo Calvino considered the relationship between cinema and the novel form, noting that the *essay-film* was in the ascendant in attempting to ally the distinctive language of film to the written word. He notes that

> the sociological-inquiry film and the historical-research film make sense only if they are not filmed explanations of the truth that sociology and historiography are saying ...

> For a true essay film I envisage an attitude not of pedagogy
> but of interrogation, with none of that inferiority complex
> toward the written word that has bedevilled relations
> between literature and cinema.[17]

Brooks's fidelity to Capote's 'story' not only misrepresents
both the capacity of 'the essay-film' – arguably the most
pertinent epithet for the kind of realist reportage Brooks was
attempting to illustrate – but also compromises the claims of
the dead to find representation in explanation rather than
exploitation. It is this which the much later television serialisation of Capote's novel seeks to address and, arguably, redress.

Jonathan Kaplan's Pacific Motion Pictures television
adaptation of *In Cold Blood* (1997), featuring Anthony
Edwards and Eric Roberts as Hickok and Smith, and Sam Neill
as Detective Alvin Dewey, plays out Capote's narrative in a
way that rejects the 'authenticity' of Brooks's environmental
integrity and enhancement of selected events. It prefers to use
more detail from Capote's novel in order more properly to
foreground the Clutter family and the Holcomb community.
Considerable attention is played to the small events and
behavioural patterns of the Kansas people – Nancy Clutter's
participation in a play; Kenyon Clutter's driving lesson; the
activities at Bess Hartman's cafe, etc. – in order to counter-
balance the increasingly *melodramatic* portrayals of Smith and
Hickok, which have more in common with American soap
opera than with the quasi-Method performances given in the
film version. This does much to heighten the sense of 'storytelling' and 'performance' in the television version, not only
leavening the darker aspects of the piece and making it more
suitable for television, but drawing attention to the narrative's
contemporary relevance.

Late millennial America is fully aware of its 'Killer Culture':
the quasi-mythic stature of its serial killers; the fictional
popularity of literary figures like Hannibal Lecter in Thomas
Harris's novels and the designer chic ambivalence of Bret
Easton Ellis's *American Psycho* (1991); the representation of
serial killers in a range of films from *Henry: Portrait of a Serial
Killer* (John McNaughton, 1990) to *Natural Born Killers* (Oliver

Stone, 1994); and the media spectacle of the O.J. Simpson trial and a number of 'schoolhouse' gun-sprees. Perry Smith is described in Capote's novel, the film and the television version as 'a natural born killer', but compared to the absolute motivelessness of many of the aforementioned killers, Perry Smith has very clear motives for what he did. The intervening years have shown an escalation in violent crime and social disorder. Increased social destabilisation has resulted in fewer and fewer clearly determined explanations for events. In this context, the story of Perry Smith as Capote tells it provides clarity. Furthermore, the TV serialisation's new emphasis on representing the Clutters and the community is not merely about redressing the balance; it is, rather, allied directly to the serialisation's overt emphasis on their Christian fundament-alism, an emphasis which offers solace to contemporary audiences in the face of secular determinism and the seeming collapse of old paradigms of law and order.

The television version of *In Cold Blood* offers comfort. Even in recording a deeply symptomatic moment of postwar change in American cultural life, it 'rehistoricises' Capote's text in order to reclaim the archetypal relationship between 'good' and 'evil' that is still in evidence in Capote's writing. His explanation of the banality of evil, the deep-rooted social and ideological malaise that produced it, and the US's nostalgia for the empty mythology of its past are ironically preferred to the 'meaningless' cultural conflict underpinning the arbitrary violence of contemporary American society.

The novel's 'classic' status is thus assured in that its prescience and literary innovation find ready purchase in negotiating a space betweeen the formulation of 'modernist' paradigms in a *popular* idiom – investigative reportage – and the realms of 'postmodernity' as a context in which the trustworthy authorities of the 'text' and its social implications are consistently questioned. The social importance of a 'text' may never be fully recovered, but its content and approach will still remain significant if appropriate to the codes and conventions of contemporary expression, and the broad pre-occupations of the 'social' as it has been redetermined by the multiplicity of common 'popular' voices embracing any one theme or cultural dynamic. *In Cold Blood* – novel, film, or television adaptation – becomes a symbolic version of one of the key narratives of American experience in the millennial era – the apparently motiveless murder as the epitome of the breakdown of traditional notions of social order and mythic history – and consequently, in offering explanation, process, and a rich resource of socio-personalised 'detail', operates as a shifting literary/cultural paradigm where 'classic' becomes synonymous with an appeasing 'apprehension' of events, which may never again be properly understood, either as 'text' or social norm.

Notes

1. Arguably, a number of fictional works have been underpinned by the recounting of factual material and real occurrences, but the overt attempt to facilitate texts through the full application and interpretation of multiple evidential sources in an aestheticised reportage is perhaps only most obviously recognisable in a novel like Lillian Ross's *Picture* (1952), which pre-dates Capote's novel, but works less consciously with the possible imperatives of the genre. Capote himself was aware of Ross's work, and further cited Rebecca West and Joseph Mitchell as pioneers in the area. See George Plympton, *Truman Capote* (New York and London: Doubleday, 1998).

2. The most notable of these criticisms was advanced by the *Observer* drama critic Kenneth Tynan who, in the words of Capote biographer John Brinnin, alleged that 'Truman had, for cold cash, exploited the young murderers about whom he wrote and not lifted a finger to save them from execution ... What disturbed me more were reports that – by some move equivalent to a class action suit – certain individuals were prepared to join together and go to court in an effort to see that British royalties accruing to *In Cold Blood* were confiscated.' John Malcolm Brinnin, *Truman Capote : A Memoir* (London: Sidgwick & Jackson, 1987), p. 136.

3. Duane West, a Kansas prosecutor, notes, 'He'd make a kind of deliberate effort to play the part of the kook. In the wintertime, when he came out here, he ran around in a huge coat and with a pillbox hat on his head. It

made him look extremely ... "funny" is the term that comes to mind' (Plympton, *Capote*, p. 169). Harold Nye, one of the KBI agents assigned to the Clutter killings, was less charitable: 'here he is in a kind of new pink negligee, silk with lace, and he's strutting across the floor with his hands on his hips telling us all about how he's going to write this book ... I did not get a very good impression.' Plympton, *Capote*, p. 170.

4. Hilary Mills, 'The Mad Butler', Interview with Norman Mailer (1981), in Michael Lennon (ed.), *Pontifications* (Boston and Toronto: Little, Brown & Company, 1982), pp. 145–6.

5. Tony Hilfer, *American Fiction Since 1940* (London and New York: Longman, 1992), pp. 10–12.

6. Norman Mailer is particularly critical of Capote's approach in this respect because he argues that Capote had made up his mind about Smith and Hickok, and that 'his killers were doomed and directed to act in this fashion; there was no other possible outcome'. Plympton, *Capote*, pp. 214–5.

7. Ibid., p. 211.

8. Graham Caveney, 'The Executioner's Throng', *Independent*, 5 June 1999.

9. Vivian Sobchack, 'History Happens' in Sobchack (ed.), *The Persistence of History* (London and New York: Routledge, 1996), p. 2.

10. Hayden White, 'The Modernist Event' in Sobchack (ed.), *Persistence*, p. 22.

11. Caveney, 'Executioner's', p. 12.

12. Max Kozloff, *'In Cold Blood'* in *Sight and Sound*, 37.3 (Summer 1968), p. 150.

13. Ibid.

14. P. McGilligan (ed.), *Backstory 2: Screenwriters of the 1940s and 1950s* (Los Angeles and Oxford: University of California Press, 1991), pp. 6–62.

15. Plympton, *Capote*, pp. 185–6.

16. 'Interview with Larry Cohen' in V. Vale and A. Juno (eds), *Incredibly Strange Films* (London: Plexus, 1986), p. 134.

17. Italo Calvino, *The Literature Machine* (London: Secker and Warburg, 1987), p. 79.

11

Home by Tea-time: Fear of Imagination in Disney's *Alice in Wonderland*

Deborah Ross

The 1994 video version of Disney's *Alice in Wonderland* begins with a commercial for the Disney Masterpieces video collection that plays shamelessly on a whole range of parental vulnerabilities. First, since these 'classic stories' are 'part of our heritage', parents must feel responsible for preserving an endangered sacred tradition. Second, since 'every child should have' these 'family keepsakes for every generation', we are also to feel responsible for providing our children with the same wholesome pleasures – and, it is hinted, the good old family values – that saved us from crack-smoking gangsterhood. The implied promise is that these movies will help keep children good, safe, and happy; happy, because these 'timeless gifts of imagination' will nourish their hungry imaginations.

I take this commercial as a challenge. How do these movies really affect children's imaginative development? My own close examination of the movies and of children as they watch them has led me to believe that these 'classics' – and more recent Disney movies as well – in some ways do the opposite of what their advertising promises. In fact, in a movie such as *Alice in Wonderland* the effect is more stereo-typically Victorian or repressive than the actual Victorian classic that inspired it.

This statement is not intended as fashionable Disney-bashing. I don't exactly share Marc Eliot's vision of the man as a Satanic 'prince' who, through the studio that he created, is still working to control our national fantasy life for his own 'dark' purposes.[1] I do believe, however, that for a number of complex causes Disney animated features contain conflicting discourses about the value of imagination that may harm young viewers – especially when they are viewed on video, over and over and over again. The movies *are* magic, just as they claim to be; but they also say a lot *against* magic, and therefore punish the audience for enjoying them. This confusion and the guilt it may produce are most pronounced in 'girls' movies' such as *Alice in Wonderland* (1951).

The primary cause of the guilt and confusion, I believe, is a problem Disney movies have in dealing with the implications of their own medium, the animated cartoon. To illustrate, let me take a brief look back at another Masterpiece from ten years before *Alice*: *Dumbo* (1941). Like *Alice*, this one ran for about three months nightly in our own home theatre, mainly because my three-year-old son was hooked on 'Pink Elephants on Parade', an alcoholic hallucination involving elephant-shaped bubbles that inflate and stretch themselves into camels, ice skaters, samba dancers, racing cars, and finally into pink clouds as Dumbo and his mouse manager awake to find themselves, miraculously, in a tree. This famous sequence, in which objects transform and combine into new, surprising things, is animation at its most imaginative – and at its most surreal.

Surrealism is the essence of animation, and animated cartoons may be the best medium for the expression of the surrealist impulse. As a 'nonphotographic application of a photographic medium', cartoons are free from the demands of realism. In fact, in cartoons 'representationality and realist conventions are persistently invoked, only to be defied'.[2] When the early Dada and surrealist artists engaged in this kind of aesthetic defiance, they consciously connected it with radical politics, declaring in early manifestos that rejecting linear, cause-and-effect narrative was a means of rebelling against society and a world at war.[3] Well into the 1930s and 1940s, the surrealistic, 'subversive' medium of cartoons[4] tended to attract artists whose interest in aesthetic and technical experimentation accompanied political leanings to the left (and the Disney staff was no exception).[5] Yet 'subversive' is surely not a word often associated with 'Disney' – either the man Walt, whose staff went on strike against his tyrannical management style during the production of

Dumbo, or the mega-corporation that some recent artists have nicknamed 'Mouschwitz'.[6] Nor is it a word American parents have ever much liked to see associated with their children's entertainments.

On the whole, *Dumbo's* story is so conservative one wonders how something as fresh and free as 'Pink Elephants' could have been included.[7] One can easily see it as a reactionary allegory – by Disney himself or his non-striking staff – about the Hollywood 'circus' of 1940, and especially about the crude, self-important, greedy 'clowns' who were Disney's own discontented writers, artists, and performers.[8] Yet clearly for the making of 'Pink Elephants' *someone* must have been allowed to run wild. The movie manages to exploit the creativity of the sequence – and of the artists who produced it – while presenting it in such a way that its terrifying moments are more memorable than its equally frequent moments of whimsy and beauty. The narrative context sets a negative tone by showing the cruel, heedless clowns letting their whiskey spill into Dumbo's drinking water as they plot how they can best cash in on the popularity the little elephant has brought to their sadistic comedy act. Then, while Dumbo blows the bubbles that grow ever weirder as he slips into a dream state, the scary score and lyrics – 'Chase them away, chase them away, I'm afraid, need your aid' – distract us from an important narrative fact: that as the imaginations of the artists are soaring so, literally, is the hero. As he dreams, Dumbo flies, thus finding the talent that will ultimately mean liberation from his tormentors. This sequence might have been designed to celebrate all kinds of freedom. Instead, despite the old drinking joke that forms its premise (a joke lost on most children anyway), 'Pink Elephants' conveys a little of the horror of the surrealistic *delirium tremens* nightmare in *The Lost Weekend* (1945).

From observing my son's reaction, I can attest that this movie's ambivalence about imagination does affect some children, even at a very young age. A year later, he still sometimes has nightmares about elephants. Sometimes his eagerness to see this section of film is cancelled out by fear; and when he does ask for it I am disconcerted by the almost masochistic quality of his fascination. I am even more concerned, however, about my daughter, who has been a close watcher of Disney videos since she was born two years ago, and who already seems in some sense to be following them as narratives. For I see the same tendency to encourage and then punish imagination in Disney movies, including *Alice in Wonderland*, that belong to what is now called in Disney stores the 'Princess Collection': a group of videos and paraphernalia especially marketed for little girls; and little girls in our society are especially sensitive to incitements to masochism from the media.

Without question girls have been and remain less confident than boys; they have received and still receive less encouragement to dream, and to pursue their dreams. They also have a long history of seeking guidance about the value of dreaming from fictional narratives – at least as far back, I have argued elsewhere, as the seventeenth century.[9] Lewis Carroll's *Alice in Wonderland* (1865) and *Through the Looking Glass* (1871) added a revolutionary chapter to this history, encouraging girls to fantasise in a way that was far from typical of girls' fiction either before or during the author's time.[10] Disney's *Alice in Wonderland*, on the other hand, was produced at a point when revolutionary style and reactionary politics at the Disney studios had become completely polarised; when Disney's artists were learning from Salvador Dali[11] while Disney himself raved about labour unions, Communists, and the League of Women Voters.[12] As a result, Disney shaped Carroll's surrealistic material into a cautionary tale worthy of the author's primmest Victorian contemporary. At the same time, he bequeathed to us a perfect example for the study of Disney's problem with imagination – especially female imagination.

Before we can understand Disney's personal problems with the more radical implications of his chosen art form, I would like to mention another root cause of the conflicting messages in Disney films, a cause residing in the history of narrative itself. The linear narrative rejected by the surrealists is the product of centuries of conflicting discourses about imagination. Those conflicts are especially pronounced during the period in the development of the romance or novel (historicist critics do not agree about when exactly each of these labels is applicable) in which the influence of female readers was most strongly felt.

Fictional narratives for centuries have been trying to have it both ways: that is, to include exciting, fantastic adventures while overtly expressing disapproval or ridicule of anything unnatural and improbable. Long before what is now called 'the novel' was born, romance writers criticised unbridled imagination by bragging about the superior realism of their own narratives compared to those of the previous generation – only to have the next generation point out how much wild fantasy still remained for themselves to excise. Cervantes's ambivalent treatment of Don Quixote's fantasies, or delusions, can be found in a less sophisticated form in the very romances that are supposed to have separated the hero from his sanity. In 1692, when William Congreve distinguished between the novel, a source of calm, rational 'delight', and the romance, which produced in the reader a hectic, overwrought 'wonder',[13] he was simply using new terminology to say what decades of romance writers had said before him, and what novelists after him would be sure to contradict as they claimed their own exclusive rights to reality. In fact, just as surrealism would be meaningless without a realism to react against, conversely, no novelist or *romancier* could truly get along without fantasy, or without the fiction of having outgrown it.

The most popular romances during Congreve's time were not the quest tales that inspired Don Quixote, but later French pastoral romances such as d'Urfé's and Scudery's. These works tended to be about women; they were sometimes written by women; most of the readers who admitted to reading them were women; and therefore, they were instrumental in earning women the right to dream. Granted, the heroines were passive rather than active, their plots zigzagging narrowly between abductions and digressions about other heroines' abductions, ending after thousands of pages in marriage for love; thus they are justly seen today as the source of an imprisoning rather than a liberating set of archetypes.[14] But these romances remind us that there was a time when even the idea that a woman could have her own preferences about marriage was new, bewildering and threatening to the social order. And that threat was real: after women had been reading romances and novels for about a century, Jane Austen could assume (at the end of *Northanger Abbey* (1818), for example) that a girl's marital decisions were generally granted to be her own business.

During the eighteenth century, when stories about and for women were self-consciously didactic, authors used the figure of the imaginative heroine, an archetype as ancient as Eve and Pandora,[15] to make either conservative or progressive statements about female imagination. But partly because of the realism paradox mentioned above, and partly because of social pressures on women writers, these novels also tended, like Disney movies, to try to have it both ways. Charlotte Lennox's 1752 variation on Cervantes's theme, *The Female Quixote*, is a perfect example. The opening chapters seem to establish a simple anti-romantic programme; unlike Don Quixote's favourite books, the romances Arabella reads – mainly Scudery's – are presented as neither morally nor aesthetically deserving of an intelligent woman's attention.[16]

The heroine's misspent leisure has given her an exaggerated idea of her own importance. Over the course of her novel she is to learn that nothing exciting is going to happen to her, that every man she meets is not in love with her or planning to carry her off, and that she ought to be gratefully in love with the one nice suitor who does present himself. In the end, her delusions of grandeur cured by close argument with a clergyman who sounds suspiciously like Samuel Johnson (pp. 410–21), she begs her suitor – whom she initially rejected on the grounds of her father's approval – to accept her as his wife (p. 423). The ostensible thesis is that reality is better than fantasy, and that a woman cannot be trusted to formulate her own desires.

Fortunately, there is much in this novel that contradicts that conservative, patriarchal thesis – much that makes this novel itself an example of the romance genre it satirises. First, Lennox lends credence to Arabella's delusion by giving her many of the romance heroine's attributes. She is by far the most intelligent and interesting character in her book, much superior to the fashionable young ladies of the 'real' world who don't read romances, or anything else. She is beautiful, and by sheer force of will she draws the attention to herself she feels is her due – for example, by wearing a centuries-old costume at a Bath assembly (p. 305). Second, even when 'cured', Arabella never quite admits that the world of her romances is inferior to the one in which she will have to live once she is safely married (p. 420). Third, the author makes clear through satirical chapter headings – 'A mistake, which produces no great consequences'; 'an extraordinary comment on a behaviour natural enough'(p. 14) – how much she relies on her heroine's delusions to give her novel a plot. Clearly Lennox has endowed Arabella with some of her own imagination, and the heroine has returned the favour by providing her author with a creative outlet.

The Female Quixote, with its double message about the value of female imagination, shows the paradox inherent in the themes and archetypes Disney had to work with in female-quixote movies such as *Alice*, *Cinderella* (1950), *The Little Mermaid* (1989), and *Beauty and the Beast* (1991). It also points up by contrast the revolutionary quality of Carroll's Alice stories, which eschew Lennox's conservative thesis in a time when actual young girls' behaviour was more constrained than ever. The word 'wonder' in the title of *Alice in Wonderland* recalls Congreve's distinction between novel and romance and clearly sets Carroll's tale on the side of romance's 'miraculous Contingencies and impossible Performances'.[17] By sending Alice to Wonderland, a place of open-ended possibility where her 'Why?' can be answered (by the dormouse) with 'Why not?',[18] Carroll frees his heroine from the limitations of realism while invoking the conventions of the form that, in Congreve's time, had come to be seen as feminine.[19]

The word 'adventures' in Carroll's title also brings to mind the tradition of the feminine romance. In *The Female Quixote*, when Arabella, following the only etiquette she knows, asks a countess she has just met to recite the story of her adventures, the embarrassed lady must forgive her for the 'offence to decorum' such a request implies (p. 365). Nice girls don't have adventures, in 1865 as in 1752. But Alice not only has adventures; she is more than happy to recite them on demand (pp. 137–8). In this sense her story could be called anti-anti-romantic, a reaction against more than a century of conservative narratives warning girls to be fearful and ashamed of their fantasies.

Carroll's Alice is not sought after, like a Scudery heroine; she is a seeker. 'Curiouser and curiouser' describes not only Alice's adventures but Alice herself – an incarnation of Eve or Pandora whose quest for knowledge and experience has no ill effects on either herself or mankind. She wants to find out about the white rabbit; she wants to get into the garden; she wants to get to the eighth square to be crowned queen. No matter how scary the adventures may be (and the creatures she encounters are sometimes menacing and often rude) she always pushes forward, never back. In fact, in *Looking-Glass* she has to work very hard *not* to go back, since until she gets the hang of this world's anti-logic, every time she tries to leave the house it appears again before her (p. 200). In this house are the only authorities who might punish her curiosity, as they scold her away from the fireplace (p. 185); these are the authorities Alice's author helps her to defy. In the end, he rewards her with adulthood and a sense of competence: she can control her size; she can tell the Queen and her armies that they are 'nothing but a pack of cards' (p. 161); in *Looking Glass* she can ask her royal examiners if *they* can do sums (they can't) (p. 322). When she awakens, she runs home to tea (p. 162), not relieved to be back, but 'thinking while she ran, as well she might, what a wonderful dream it had been' – to the envy of her older sister, who knows that 'dull reality' is always there for the unfortunately wakeful adult (p. 163).

Carroll empowered his young female audience (the real Alice Liddell and her sisters as well as the future generations of his readers) by telling them it was good to dream. He also encouraged their authorship of their own dreams by allowing them to participate in the creation of these stories, a participation chronicled in the stories themselves. When Alice muses about being the heroine of a book, her next thought is that she will write it herself when she gets home (p. 59). And write she does in her story, taking hold of the White King's pencil as he tries to make a memorandum (p. 190), and vehemently asserting that the Red King is a figure in *her* dream rather than the other way around (p. 293). Carroll also permits Alice, temporarily, to escape his own authorship in a section of plot with Lacanian overtones about a wood in which names are forgotten. Here, where signifiers float free from their signifieds, a fawn can lose all fear of humans by forgetting the difference imposed by Adam when he named God's creatures; and here Alice, too, is safe from all possibility of summons or command (p. 224).

It would be difficult for any narrative to sustain this kind of freedom for its heroine without falling apart. And certainly, in 1951, the now famously fascistic Walt Disney would not willingly have granted a mere piece of celluloid more autonomy than he would permit his workers. But, in a sense, Alice did get away from him. He had been attracted to Carroll's tale since his own early days as a cartoonist – *Alice in Cartoonland* was one of his first ventures[20] – and he had begun toying with an animated *Alice* back in 1931.[21] But 20 years later, Robin Allan reports, he had mixed feelings about the story and had trouble deciding how it ought to be used.[22] Looking back on the movie years after, Disney commented that he disliked the heroine, finding her (in Schickel's paraphrase) too 'prissy' and 'passive'[23] – an odd, probably anglophobic sentiment that leaves one baffled about why his cartoon Alice is so much more passive than the original. If there is a double message about imagination in Disney's *Alice in Wonderland*, then, the reason is partly to be found in Walt Disney's inner turmoil about this project. And that, in turn, can partly be understood in the context of the previous decade's developments in his already confused, and confusing, aesthetic principles, as well as in his increasingly tense relationship with his staff.

First of all, although Eliot has found evidence that Disney was actively involved in fighting Hollywood unions and informing for the FBI as far back as the late 1930s,[24] his political ideology was never simply conservative.[25] During most of his life, he claimed to have no politics[26] – a statement that may in itself have a reactionary ring to readers of Marxist criticism.[27] But Steven Watts describes the younger Disney as a 'sentimental populist', in the same category as Norman Rockwell or Woody Guthrie;[28] a Roosevelt supporter and son of a socialist; a man whose views would have seemed left of centre in the 1930s,[29] and who even into the next decade was producing cartoons sympathetically portraying the plight of the working man.[30] Disney's turn to the right, according to Watts, came about after the strike at his studios in 1941 and during the Second World War, as he became increasingly convinced that 'the people' and their freedoms were being threatened rather than protected by organised labour and big government.[31] Disney's recent biographers add psychological causes for this turn, describing a man whose difficult childhood and early experiences in the movie business made him desperate for control of every aspect of his surroundings, and especially liable to clamp down hard when faced with rebellion.

Disney's aesthetic principles, like his politics, also resist easy classification. Watts sees a parallel between Disney's complex political ideology and his relation to the modernist movement in the arts. In early cartoons, both shorts and features such as *Dumbo*, Watts sees the 'preoccupation with the dream state' and 'dark, nightmarish visions'[32] associated with surrealism. Certainly many of Mickey Mouse's adventures, and probably all of Donald Duck's, contain the kind of black humour that originated in the surrealist movement's interest in accidents that seem to reveal something scary about the way the universe is organised.[33] And certainly it was this imaginative freedom that attracted artists to Disney – only to find, during the 1940s, that he was moving in a different direction, and that both his politics and his artistic vision would make his studios an impossible place for many of them to work.[34]

During the 1940s as Disney's politics became more conservative and his management style more authoritarian, he began to emphasise realism over fantasy in his instructions to his artists. Of course, 'realism' is always a tricky term, and it's especially hard to see in what sense it can be applied to *Bambi* (1942) (or, as it has been applied more recently, to *Pocahontas* (1995)).[35] But apparently the idea was to make audiences believe that if deer could talk, this is what they would say. The effect was created by bringing in real deer for the artists to study, but not too closely; paradoxically, too much imitation of real details, Disney believed, would not create a realistic impression.[36] Clearly, Disney had come to feel – as Congreve had felt in 1692 – that fantasy isn't very effective unless kept in check by nature and probability. This development was completely in line with a principle he had outlined in a memo to the studio art instructor back in 1935, when *Bambi* was begun, explaining the importance of 'the actual', not for its own sake, but as 'a basis upon which to go into the fantastic, the unreal, the imaginative – and yet to let it have a foundation of fact'.[37]

There is nothing inherently conservative about combining realism with fantasy; after all, that is exactly what the original surrealists had done. The political implications are determined by what the end product looks like, and what purpose it is made to serve. Increasingly, for Disney, the combination was used to create 'cuteness'[38] or a conventional, sentimental ideal – something Watts calls, in a phrase borrowed from Northrop Frye, 'stupid realism'.[39] This aesthetic conservatism had political implications that were not lost on Disney's staff. Some of the more radical and imaginative – those who somehow had not quit or been fired during the time of the strike – disliked the way the focus on realism forced them to abandon one of the most important functions of cartoons: to provide social criticism.[40] When Disney finally stopped avoiding politics, as everyone had to when the United States entered the war, he went beyond obligatory anti-Nazi satire to propagandise for strategic bombing with his animated film of *Victory Through Air Power*[41] – thus taking a right-wing stand that angered the Navy brass for whom his studio had been making training films.[42] By 1945, he had also produced two 'good neighbour' films about South America that imperialistically recreate the Third World as an inferior 'other' by combining cartoons with live action – or fantasy with realism.[43]

This is certainly not the sort of politics envisioned by the founders of Dada and surrealism in the years following the First World War.[44] Yet surrealist art was very much alive at the Disney studios during the 1940s. Salvador Dali worked on a project there in 1946, and although it was never completed, Allan believes his influence was still to be seen in *Alice*,[45] which would have been completed at about the same time if Disney's strike-breaking attempts had not interrupted production.[46] The artists were freer than usual to pursue this free direction, despite the generally paternalistic atmosphere, partly because of Disney's reservations about the project, as mentioned earlier,[47] and partly because he was losing interest in the art of animation[48] and was increasingly exerting his control over story rather than drawing.[49] Therefore, as backgrounds artist Claude Coats commented, 'We let ourselves go with some wild designs.'[50] Surrealist images were created; but Disney the story man and Disney the boss could still ensure that they would be firmly kept in their place. Therefore Disney's *Alice in Wonderland* took material unequivocally supportive of female imagination and turned it into something both fascinating and yet painful to watch – and to watch children watch.

First, Disney made the story itself conservative. It begins faithfully enough, with an apparently sympathetic depiction of Alice's motives for fantasy: curiosity (inevitably), but also boredom at listening to history lessons from a book without pictures in it; and a will to power, a desire to make a 'world of my own' in which every book would be nothing but pictures. Since this Alice *is* a picture, and her 'history' is to be told in pictures, the viewer might expect that, in defiance of her sister's ridicule, her desires are to be supported and encouraged in what is to follow. Certainly the drawing simulates a camera and a point-of-view that move us quickly from sister and history to Alice and fantasy. And this 'camera' does follow Alice and encounter, as she does, an apparently random arrangement of Carrollian wonders such as singing flowers and strange, looking-glass insects. But Disney's liberal cutting and pasting of Carroll's plot soon give the story a sinister turn.

The changes are subtle at first. For example, Alice's first conversation with the Cheshire cat is largely preserved. Given a choice of visiting either the Mad Hatter or the March Hare, both of whom are mad, Alice protests in both the story and the movie, 'But I don't want to go among mad people'; to which the cat replies, 'Oh, you can't help that ... we're all mad here.' However, the movie omits the rest of his comment: 'I'm mad. You're mad' (p. 89). Instead, he merely remarks that he himself is 'not all there', prompting Alice to decide to be careful to avoid upsetting the people she meets. Her own sanity is never in question; she is already an alien in Wonderland, which will eventually become to her a terrifying snake pit. Her discomfort increases during the Mad Tea Party, and soon after she finds herself wandering through a dark wood and a new section of plot written especially for the movie, one that will completely reverse the message of Carroll's story.

This is the Tulgey Wood sequence – the name comes from Carroll's 'Jabberwocky', but there the indebtedness ends – in which Alice decides she's had quite enough 'nonsense' and it's time to go home. Here, like the original Alice, she says she'll write a book about her adventures; but where in the original that statement sounds bold and assertive, here, because it accompanies the decision to flee, it suggests that one should write *instead of* adventuring. Soon, the cartoon Alice is overjoyed to find what looks like a path – at last, some outside authority and direction – and she skips ahead of the camera, chattering gleefully about getting home in time for tea after all. But when the path is erased by a fanciful broom creature, she can do nothing but sit down and cry, a tiny, pathetic figure in the centre of a dark frame, and recite what she must often have been told a child should do when lost: stop acting independently, stay where you are, and wait to be rescued. As she waits, she sings a song: 'I give myself very good advice (but I very seldom follow it).' The line is taken from an earlier section in the book in which Carroll's Alice is trying to stop herself from crying – not because she wants to go home, but because she's frustrated at not being able to reach the key to the lovely garden (p. 32). In the movie, this kind of desire is exactly what the heroine berates herself for – for lacking patience, for getting curious, for wanting to see strange sights, and hence for always getting into trouble. Here, in effect, she undoes herself and her whole story.

Now and then before the end of the movie, Alice's spirits rally, but for the most part she's a defeated little girl. When the cat reappears to ask about the white rabbit, she no longer cares about him. And though she does talk back to the queen when, for a moment, she has grown large again, some force beyond her control immediately shrinks her and sends her running for her life, all the creatures from her dream in mad pursuit. She tries to get back through the garden door and is relieved when the doorknob tells her she is already on the other side, placidly asleep under a tree. Thus, the recommended response to the terrors of one's unconscious is flight. Instead of going forward into maturity, Disney's Alice retreats into perpetual childhood, learning to treasure 'dull reality' rather than the memory of the dream that alone, to Carroll, made reality tolerable.

This very conservative narrative is supported by the way images are used in the Disney version. Being a picture necessarily objectifies Alice to some extent; Carroll's Alice can be much more a mind than a body, since the Tenniel illustrations are occasional and secondary to the words. Yet movies can make even female on-screen characters into subjects. There are few close-ups (as Elizabeth Bell has remarked, in Disney movies these are usually reserved for *femmes fatales*[51]), and even in the first, viewer-orienting moments of the film, the cat, Dinah, has as many reaction shots as her owner. Alice's sudden changes in size are usually shown from outside as she shoots above the camera to grow or slides below it to shrink. Thus the viewer is momentarily left in the point-of-view of a normative minor character – the doorknob, or the Red Queen. We often see things that Alice cannot see: she has her eyes closed, or we are looking down from above at a scene she is seeing while crouched on the ground. When the camera does follow her, it is often from a far distance, above and behind her shoulder, a slowly walking or stationary adult watching a more energetic child. The overall effect is to make Alice less a subject than an excuse for presenting images to the audience. Nor does she enjoy what subjecthood she has; at the end she can't wait to become again the object she sees through the keyhole: inactive – asleep – and ready to be taught, commanded and fed once more.

The style of the drawings which carry this imitation of 'real' photography also helps to push Alice back to domestic passivity. Allan credits Disney with trying to 'introduce an anarchic zany element which critics found mixing uneasily with the decorum of the English original';[52] and certainly the movie does fill the eye in a way that can make a viewer dizzy. However, with all there is to look at here, one may not notice right away that the specific images are not in themselves very interesting. It is the supposedly decorous original that is 'anarchic', or surrealistic – in its substitution of dream logic for waking logic[53] – and therefore even a faithful or 'realistic' rendering of Carroll's prose will seem imaginative. In the fall down the rabbit hole, for instance, Alice encounters a series of funny and surprising objects, most of which had appeared in the story, but in an easy, linear fashion – nothing like 'Pink Elephants'. If the artists did, as Coats said, 'let [them]selves go', it seems to have been mainly in quantity. There are a few wonderful moments: the mad proliferation of crockery during the tea party, and the often-praised smoke puns puffed by the caterpillar (when he asks 'Why' we see a letter 'Y', and so forth). But surely smoke, like bubbles, is a medium capable of more radical surrealistic transformation than this.

The only extended sequence that shows real imaginative freedom is the Tulgey Wood section. Here Alice encounters unique creatures made from combinations of familiar objects: telephone ducks; drum and cymbal frogs; a bird with a bird-cage for a stomach, containing two smaller live birds (this one, like 'Pink Elephants', both attracts and scares my son). This is the essence of surrealism – and it occurs at exactly that point in the story when Alice has declared her allegiance to home and hearth, her cat and her tea. Far from being fascinated by these 'curious' animals, Alice only feels threatened by them – until, like the little squirrels and deer in *Snow White* (1937), they weep in sympathy as she sings her self-deprecating lament. The very moment in which the movie most indulges its creators' imaginations is the one in which the heroine is most severely punished for indulging hers. The viewer is entrapped, although a child viewer won't understand how it happened. I suspect she'll only know that the more interesting this movie gets, the more she feels frightened or even guilty about watching it.

The fear and guilt this movie engenders might even extend beyond itself to the movie-watching experience in general.

After all, Alice flees an attractive but dangerous world of pictures to return to a world of books without pictures – a world the viewer, by definition, can't see, but one which has been accorded superior value to the one we have been looking at. This implication also extends a negative charge to other female quixote stories, both in pictures and in words. Since Alice exists here only as a picture, in the world to which she returns she will cease to be – in fact, the last we see of her, she is getting smaller and smaller and fading into a shadow. This is indeed a worse fate than the 'dwindling into a wife' (to borrow yet another phrase from Congreve)[54] undergone by Lennox's heroine; it's Carroll's Alice's worst fear realised: that something she eats or drinks will shrink her so far that she will '[go] out altogether, like a candle'(p. 32).

If it was Walt himself who put the fear of imagination into Alice, it might seem that we have little to worry about now that he's no longer with us. Yet I have seen no lessening of this double message in the movies produced after his death. *The Little Mermaid, Aladdin* (1992), *The Hunchback of Notre Dame* (1996) and *Hercules* (1997) also simultaneously exploit and condemn the imaginative freedom of surrealist animation by making the idea of magical transformation seem immature, dangerous or evil. *The Lion King* (1993), *Pocahontas* and *Mulan* (1998) deliberately forego this style altogether in favour of the 'realism' of pseudo-ecology and pseudo-history. Not that these films aren't beautiful to watch: but the most stunning images – in *Hunchback* and *Mulan* at any rate, as in the earlier *Sleeping Beauty* (1959) – are imitations of paintings.

The problem seems to be bigger than Disney himself, bigger than Jeffrey Katzenberg (former chief of Disney Studios, who left in 1994), bigger than any one person. The problem is business. Over the last 60 years, the Disney Corporation has bought more and more children's classics, oversimplifying and packaging them for audiences much younger than those their authors had in mind. By the time our eight-year-olds have developed the vocabulary and syntactical sophistication to appreciate the humour and style of Milne or Grahame or Carroll (if in fact they ever do), they reject their works as 'baby stuff'. Since these stories will then be known to our children only in the Disney version, Disney has gained a monopoly on the next generation's fantasies in the same way the corporation is trying to get a monopoly on our sources of information by buying television networks.[55] Controlling the contents of our children's imaginations is the surest way to create a big market for Disney products.

But if the problem is business – if, without a paranoid Walt in charge, there is no longer any guiding idea behind the 'Mouschwitz' some still see as Disney, other than naked greed – then we are right back where we started, with the question of parental responsibility. For clearly, while the Disney Empire is no doubt trying to make as many of us as possible into the kind of people who will buy what they are selling,[56] they can also only sell us what we are willing to buy. The superficially PC quality of the recent movies – the wildlife conservation of *The Lion King*, the multiculturalism of *Pocahontas* and *Mulan*, the mainstreaming of the physically challenged in *The Hunchback of Notre Dame* – reflect a generation's political tastes. If these surface messages satisfy us – if we ignore the fact that the Lion King rules by divine right, or that Pocahontas was deliberately drawn to be 'a babe',[57] or that the best that Quasimodo can hope to achieve in life is cuteness – then these movies will have reflected the superficiality of our own political ideas and commitments. And if we buy Disney Masterpiece videos in order to populate our children's minds with the same, familiar, safe imaginary characters we once 'treasured', the sales figures will reflect something of our own fear of our children's imaginations – that wonderland beyond the reach of our voices, where we can't tell them how to behave or protect them from danger.[58] 'And the moral of *that* is', as the Duchess would say (p. 121): we should be careful what we wish for, lest, in the words of Disney Masterpiece heroine Cinderella, 'The dream that you wish will come true.'

Notes

1. Marc Eliot, *Walt Disney: Hollywood's Dark Prince* (New York: Birch Lane Press, 1993).

2. J. Burton-Carvajal, '"Surprise Package": Looking Southward with Disney' in Eric Smoodin (ed.), *Disney Discourse: Producing the Magic Kingdom* (New York: Routledge, 1994), p. 139.

3. I. Hedges, *Languages of Revolt: Dada and Surrealist Literature and Film* (Durham, NC: Duke University Press, 1983), pp. xii–xiv, xvi.

4. Burton-Carvajal, '"Surprise"', p. 139.

5. See Richard Schickel, *The Disney Version* (New York: Simon and Schuster, 1968), p. 58.

6. J. Lewis, 'Disney After Disney' in Smoodin, *Disney Discourse*, p. 88.

7. One factor may have been that Disney himself was out of the country during most of the creation of the film (Schickel, *The Disney Version*, pp. 264–5); however, one can be sure that it was not released without his complete scrutiny and approval, since to the end of his life Disney continued to fuss over the smallest details of every film project (p. 348).

8. H. Allen and M. Denning, 'The Cartoonists' Front' in *South Atlantic Quarterly*, Vol. 92, No. 1 (Winter 1993), p. 89. I am aware that it is often hopeless to try to extract political statements from cartoons; Richard Schickel discusses the problem with Disney cartoons at some length (*The Disney Version*, p. 166). In the case of *Dumbo*, however, references to the strike seem so blatant I find it hard to resist – as does Schickel himself (p. 265).

9. Deborah Ross, *The Excellence of Falsehood* (Lexington: University Press of Kentucky, 1991).

10. Teresa de Lauretis denies that Caroll's Alice is a feminist heroine in *Alice Doesn't: Feminism, Semiotics, Cinema* (Bloomington: Indiana University Press, 1984), p. 2; yet if she were not one I doubt that she would be such a useful symbol for women trying to forge an identity in a land of male discourse, both in de Lauretis's own work and in that of others such as Sheila Rowbotham (de Lauretis, *Alice*, p. 36). Jack Zipes does include Carroll in his list of authors who have used fairy tales in subversive ways. See 'Breaking the Disney Spell' in Elizabeth Bell *et*

al., (eds), *From Mouse to Mermaid* (Bloomington: Indiana University Press, 1995), pp. 26–7.

11. Robin Allan, 'Alice in Disneyland,' in *Sight and Sound* (Vol. 54, Spring 1985), p. 137.
12. Allen and Denning, 'Cartoonists', p. 98.
13. William Congreve, *Complete Works*, Vol. 1 (London: Nonesuch, 1923), p. 111.
14. J. Russ, *To Write Like a Woman: Essays in Feminism and Science Fiction* (Bloomington: Indiana University Press, 1995), pp. 83, 85.
15. Laura Mulvey, *Visual and Other Pleasures* (Bloomington: Indiana University Press, 1989), p. x.
16. Charlotte Lennox, *The Female Quixote* (Boston: Pandora, 1986), p. 7. Subsequent references are to this edition and are in the text.
17. Congreve, *Complete Works*, Vol. 1, p. 111.
18. Lewis Carroll, *The Annotated Alice: Alice's Adventures in Wonderland and Through the Looking Glass*, ed. Martin Gardner (New York: Bramhall House, 1960), p. 103. Subsequent references are to this edition and are in the text.
19. Evidence of this association may be found in Henry Fielding's Preface to *Joseph Andrews*, in which he painstakingly invents a classical tradition for his own novel in order to avoid association with either French romance or the popular scandal novels of his contemporary, Mary Delarivier Manley. See H. Fielding, *Joseph Andrews* (New York: Penguin, 1979), pp. 15, 30.
20. See Schickel, *The Disney Version*, pp. 87, 105–7; Eliot, *Walt Disney*, pp. 25–9.
21. Eliot, *Walt Disney*, p. 92.
22. Allan, 'Alice', p. 137.
23. Schickel, *The Disney Version*, p. 295.
24. Eliot, *Walt Disney*, pp. 120, 125.
25. Eric Smoodin, 'How to Read Walt Disney,' in Smoodin, *Disney Discourse*, pp. 2–3.
26. Schickel, *The Disney Version*, p. 157.
27. See Fredric Jameson, *The Political Unconscious: Narrative as a Socially Symbolic Act* (Ithaca: Cornell University Press, 1981), p. 58.

28. Steven Watts, 'Walt Disney: Art and Politics in the American Century', in *Journal of American History* (June 1995), pp. 96–8.
29. Ibid., p. 100.
30. Smoodin, 'How to Read', p. 17.
31. Watts, 'Walt Disney: Art and Politics', pp. 103–4.
32. Ibid., p. 88.
33. Hedges, *Languages*, pp. xvii–xviii.
34. Allen and Denning, 'Cartoonists', p. 104; Schickel, *The Disney Version*, p. 260; Eliot, *Walt Disney*, pp. 68, 83–4.
35. A. Kim, 'A Whole New World?' in *Entertainment Weekly* (28 June 1995), p. 25. Schickel reports that there were complaints about this realism from reviewers at the time, one asking, 'Why have cartoons at all' if this is all that is to be done with them? See *The Disney Version*, pp. 267–8. For a provocative discussion of the 'reality' *Bambi* does portray, see David Payne's very sensitive essay 'Bambi' in Bell (*et al.*), *From Mouse to Mermaid*, pp. 137–47.
36. Schickel, *The Disney Version*, p. 180.
37. Quoted in Watts, 'Walt Disney: Art and Politics', p. 94.
38. Schickel, *The Disney Version*, p. 174.
39. Watts, 'Walt Disney: Art and Politics', p. 90.
40. Allen and Denning, 'Cartoonists', p. 108.
41. W. Wanger, 'Film Phenomena' (1943), reprinted in Smoodin, *Disney Discourse*, p. 42; W. Wanger, 'Mickey Icarus' (1943), reprinted in Smoodin, *Disney Discourse*, p. 45.
42. Schickel, *The Disney Version*, pp. 273–4.
43. Burton-Carvajal, '"Surprise"', pp. 131, 133. See also Ariel Dorfman for an extended discussion of Disney's recreation of South America, *The Empire's Old Clothes* (New York: Pantheon, 1983).
44. Hedges, *Languages*, p. xi.
45. Allan, 'Alice', p. 137.
46. Eliot, *Walt Disney*, p. 200.
47. Allan, 'Alice', p. 137.
48. Eliot, *Walt Disney*, p. 200.
49. R. deRoos, 'The Magic Worlds of Walt Disney', *National Geographic* (August, 1963), reprinted in Smoodin, *Disney Discourse*, p. 51; Schickel, *The Disney Version*, pp. 136,

173–5. Eliot reports that Roy Disney scolded his brother for not more actively supervising *Alice*, which lost money at the box office (*Walt Disney*, p. 210).
50. Allan, 'Alice', p. 138.
51. Elizabeth Bell, 'Somatexts at the Disney Shop', in Bell *et al.* (eds), *From Mouse to Mermaid*, p. 116.
52. Allan, 'Alice', p. 137.
53. Hedges, *Languages*, p. xvi.
54. From Congreve, *The Way of the World*, IV, i.
55. M. Miller, 'A Disney World', in *Honolulu Weekly* (Vol. 6, No. 13, 27 March 1996), p. 6.
56. Smoodin, 'How to Read', p. 19.
57. Kim, 'A Whole New World', pp. 24–5. See Jacquelyn Kirkpatrick, 'Disney's "Politically Correct" *Pocahontas*', *Cineaste* (Vol. 21, No. 4), pp. 36, 37.
58. This is what Schickel was worried about over 30 years ago: that Disney wanted to 'force everyone to share the same formative dreams' (*The Disney Version*, p. 18).

Index

Compiled by Sue Carlton